Einstein famously posited, "Everything should be made as simple as possible, but not simpler." This modern corollary to Occam's Razor is often honored in the breach, especially the final three words, and especially in the IT industry. Distributed systems, like security and error handling, are inherently difficult, and no amount of layered abstraction will overcome that simple fact. A deep understanding of what makes distributed systems architecture different from monolithic systems architecture is critically important in a networked world of services such as that promised by Service Oriented Architecture, and Puder, Römer and Pilhofer deliver that deep understanding in a straightforward, step-by-step fashion, from the inside out—as simple as possible, but not simpler. Every application developer today is a distributed systems developer, and this book therefore belongs on the bookshelf of every developer, architect and development manager.

Richard Mark Soley, Ph.D.
Chairman and CEO
Object Management Group, Inc.

DISTRIBUTED SYSTEMS
ARCHITECTURE

DISTRIBUTED SYSTEMS ARCHITECTURE

A Middleware Approach

ARNO PUDER
San Francisco State University

KAY RÖMER
Swiss Federal Institute of Technology

FRANK PILHOFER
Mercury Computer Systems, Inc.

MORGAN KAUFMANN PUBLISHERS
An imprint of Elsevier

Distributed Systems Architecture
Puder, Römer and Pilhofer

Morgan Kaufmann Publishers
An imprint of Elsevier
500 Sansome Street, Suite 400,
San Francisco, CA 94111

Original ISBN: 978-1-55860-648-7

First Printed in India 2008

Reprinted 2008

Indian Reprint ISBN: 978-81-312-1665-1

Published by Elsevier, a division of Reed Elsevier India Private Limited,
Logix Park, Ist Floor, A-4 & 5, Sector-16, Noida-201301, UP (India)

Printed and bound in India by Sheel Print-N-Pack
D-132, Hosiery Complex, Phase II, NOIDA 201 305.

Dedication

"To everyone in the MICO developer community"

ABOUT THE AUTHORS

Arno Puder received his master's degree in computer science from the University of Kaiserslautern and his Ph.D. from the University of Frankfurt/Main, Germany. After working for Deutsche Telekom AG and AT&T Labs, he is currently a professor of computer science at San Francisco State University. His special interests include distributed systems and wireless sensor networks.

Kay Römer is currently a senior researcher and lecturer at ETH Zurich (Swiss Federal Institute of Technology), Switzerland. He received his Ph.D. in computer science from ETH with a thesis on sensor networks. Kay holds a master's degree in computer science from the University of Frankfurt/Main, Germany. His research interests encompass sensor networks, software infrastructures for ubiquitous computing, and middleware for distributed systems.

Frank Pilhofer received his masters in computer science from the University of Frankfurt/Main, Germany. After completing MICO's CORBA Components implementation, he joined Mercury Computer Systems, where he now works on component-based, real-time data streaming middleware for Software Radio.

PREFACE

The idea for this book came from our interest in producing a practical book about middleware for distributed systems. Our inspiration was Andrew S. Tanenbaum's legendary textbook on operating systems (see [35]). From a pedagogical standpoint, Tanenbaum developed an important bridge between theory and practice by first developing an operating system and then structuring a textbook based on its implementation. He therefore not only explains the concepts governing operating systems but also demonstrates how these concepts are converted into *lines of code*.

We have taken a similar approach in our own book, but focusing instead on middleware for distributed systems. Our first task in preparing to write this book was to develop an infrastructure for distributed systems. To avoid reinventing the wheel, we selected the freely available CORBA specification as the basis for our implementation. There are many different middleware standards available, and Web Services especially have gained momentum in recent years. But the concepts we explain in this book are universal and independent of a specific middleware technology.

The result of our implementation efforts is MICO. Originally the acronym MICO stood for *Mini CORBA*, based on Minix (Mini Unix) and developed by Tanenbaum. There were two things that were not available to Tanenbaum at the time: the World Wide Web and a strong Open Source community. Although it was not our initial intention, MICO evolved into a complete CORBA implementation. As a result of this development, we decided to change the interpretation of the acronym MICO into *Mico Is CORBA* as a tribute to the GNU project, which was the first to promote the idea of free software.

Because we ourselves have invested far more work in MICO than was our intention at the outset, we see this book as coming full circle in terms of our original ambitions. This book deals with the design and the architecture of middleware platforms. True to the approach taken by Tanenbaum, we use MICO as a concrete example. We hope that the experience we gained in the development of MICO and have documented in this book will be of benefit to the reader.

In a project of this scope, it is impossible to thank everyone who has supported us. Numerous people have helped us to make MICO what it is today. Those who assisted us with the implementation of MICO are noted in the change logs with their respective contributions. We thank all of them and express our deepest respect for their work.

We thank all of the reviewers, Andrew Forrest, Eric Ironside, Letha Etzkorn, Michi Henning, Dr. Priya Narasimhan, Karel Gardas, Gregor Hohpe and Twittie Senivonqse.

Arno Puder, Kay Römer, and Frank Pilhofer
San Francisco, Zurich, and Boston
January 2005

CONTENTS

CHAPTER 1

INTRODUCTION

The goal of this introduction is to present an overview of the content of this book. We will also use it as a vehicle for explaining our motivation behind writing the book and the objectives we set out to achieve. We identify the target group we want to reach with this book and then present a chapter-by-chapter breakdown of the topics discussed.

1.1 INFRASTRUCTURES FOR DISTRIBUTED APPLICATIONS

The pervasiveness of networking technology both locally (e.g., local area networks) and globally (e.g., the Internet) enables the proliferation of distributed applications. Since the parts of a distributed application execute in different physical locations, these applications offer a number of advantages: geographical constraints can be matched, applications become fault tolerant through replication, and performance can be improved by parallelizing a task—to name just a few. Taking a closer look at the execution environment reveals its heterogeneity: different hardware platforms, network technologies, operating systems, and programming languages can make the development of distributed applications a big challenge.

Middleware

What is needed for distributed systems, therefore, is an infrastructure that suitably supports the development and the execution of distributed applications. A *middleware platform* presents such an infrastructure because it provides a buffer between the applications and the network (see Figure 1.1). The network merely supplies a transport mechanism; access to it depends heavily on technological factors and differs between various physical platforms. Middle-

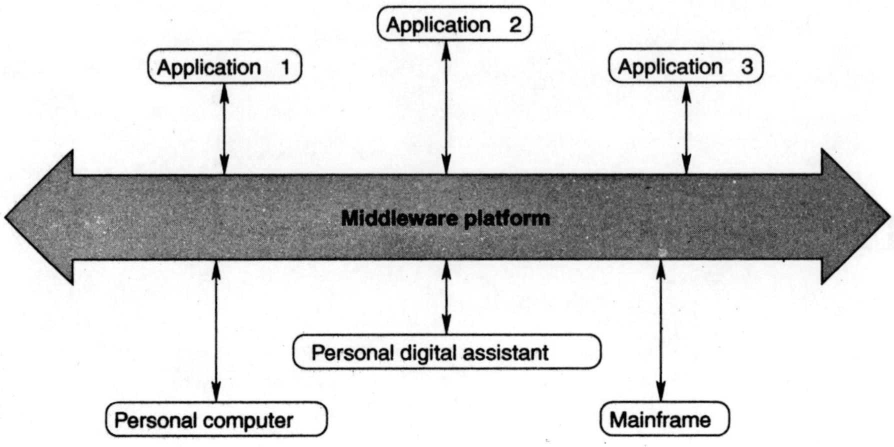

FIGURE 1.1 Middleware as an infrastructure for distributed systems.

ware homogenizes access to networks and offers generic services for applications. It also bridges technological domains and encapsulates the differences between different systems.

Two views of middleware

In this book we describe middleware from two different perspectives: from the view of applications programmers and from the view of systems programmers. Applications programmers regard middleware as a tool that helps them in the development of distributed applications. These programmers are not normally interested in how the middleware is implemented but only in how it is used. Applications programmers see the distribution platform as a *black box* with a well-defined interface and prescribed functionality.

Systems programmers take a complementary view. They regard the distribution platform as a *white box* and are interested primarily in its internal processes. The application running on a middleware is of minor importance. The common reference point for both types of programmer is the interface to the middleware that is used by applications programmers and provided by systems programmers.

Our approach is to look at middleware from both points of view and to use this information as the basis for honing the knowledge of systems and applications programmers. Systems programmers are presented with the requirements of the applications side for which solutions have to be produced. Knowledge about the inner workings of distribution platforms helps applications programmers make optimal use of the functions available. The concept of the two viewpoints runs through the book like a thread. Our objective is to provide a comprehensive look at the architecture and the design of middleware.

1.2 THEMATIC ORGANIZATION

Many different middleware technologies are available today, among them CORBA (Common Object Request Broker Architecture) and Web Services. In this book we emphasize the concepts for designing and implementing a middleware platform, and the concrete technology is only of a secondary nature. Although Web Services have gained momentum in recent years, we feel that the CORBA specification is still more mature. But the principles explained in this book are universal and apply to all middleware platforms.

CORBA-based middleware

There are many advantages to using CORBA as an underlying basis. For one thing, it allows us to base our examples and explanations on an established industry standard for which numerous products are available. The freely available CORBA specification can be referred to as secondary literature. Also numerous excellent books have been written on CORBA. Finally, knowledge about the internal processes of CORBA platforms is helpful for developing a general understanding about CORBA, and this comes in handy for anyone working with commercial CORBA products.

C++ knowledge a prerequisite

All source code in this book as well as MICO itself is completely implemented in C++. An elementary knowledge of the programming language C++ is therefore essential for understanding the examples. Some of the introductory examples are also presented in Java. We regard a programming language merely as an aid in implementing the concepts we introduce. The reader will find it a useful exercise to map the concepts presented in the book to other programming languages. Along with having C++ experience, the reader will find that experience with a development environment under UNIX or Windows is necessary for understanding the programs presented in this book.

1.3 TARGET GROUP

Target group includes students and professional developers

We have aimed this book at students who are at an advanced stage of their studies and at professional developers who want to use middleware for their work. Different interests motivate these two groups. Students can use this book as a textbook to help them to learn how middleware platforms function. This book has been successfully used in a graduate class on distributed systems, in which the students had to write a distributed application based on CORBA using C++ and Java. As part of their project, the students had to use μORB (described in Chapter 4) to get first-hand experience with the inner workings of a middleware platform. The material used for the term project are available online (see Section 1.5).

The relevance of the topics covered in this book to professional programmers is linked to the success of MICO as an Open Source project. Open Source has become respectable in the commercial world, and more and more companies are now making use of the benefits it offers. The availability of source code enables Open Source to be adapted to meet specific needs—something that comparable commercial products cannot offer. This book lays the foundations for an understanding of the internal workings of MICO—a prerequisite for such adaptations.

1.4 CHAPTER OVERVIEWS

This book is logically structured in several parts. The first part, which includes Chapters 2 through 4, covers the basics and presents an overview of middleware in general and CORBA in particular. All the discussions in these chapters are independent of MICO. The second part, which includes Chapters 5 through 9, then goes into detail about MICO's design and architecture. Chapter 10 gives a broader view on current and future middleware technologies. The final part of this book is composed of the appendices which serve as a brief MICO user manual. The book is structured so that the chapters can be read in sequence. However, the appendices, which explicitly deal with MICO, can be referenced from the index as a direct information source.

Chapter overview of this book

A brief overview of the content of each of the chapters follows:

Chapter 2 introduces the basic concepts required for understanding the content of the book. It also presents a simple sample application to help clarify some of the concepts.

Chapter 3 presents a brief introduction to CORBA. The sample application presented in the previous chapter is implemented on a distributed basis through the use of CORBA.

Chapter 4 describes the μORB. The μORB is a mini ORB that is used to present some components of CORBA-based middleware in a compact form.

Chapter 5 is the first of five chapters that deal solely with the internal details of MICO. This chapter presents the microkernel architecture of MICO's Object Request Broker.

Chapter 6 describes the implementation of CORBA's interoperability framework. In MICO the implementation of IIOP is based on the microkernel approach presented in the previous chapter.

Chapter 7 describes the binding of object implementations to the Object Request Broker on the server side. The CORBA standard introduces its own component, called an *object adapter*.

Chapter 8 discusses the interface between caller and Object Request Broker—this time from the client side. The invocation adapters responsible for this task are likewise integrated in the ORB through the microkernel approach.

Chapter 9 introduces the architecture of MICO's IDL compiler and describes how IDL compilers and interface repositories are closely related.

Chapter 10 concludes this book by giving an overview of emerging technologies in the middleware domain. We also briefly touch on the main differences between CORBA and Web Services.

In addition to the chapters listed, the book includes extensive appendices with further information about MICO:

Appendices contain further technical information

Appendix A provides some information on the installation process for MICO.

Appendix B provides an implementation overview of MICO. It discusses some MICO-specific details such as MICO's Interface Repository and Implementation Repository.

Appendix C gives further information on some specific internals of MICO, including how to integrate new transport mechanisms.

Appendix D reproduces the complete source code for the CORBA sample application presented in Chapter 3.

1.5 ANCILLARY MATERIALS

As an Open Source project, MICO boasts its own home page, which you can find at *www.mico.org*. There you will find the current source code for MICO along with other information about this particular implementation in the form of a user handbook, frequently asked questions (FAQ), and an archive of mailing lists.

Ancillary materials available over WWW

Another thing we have done is to set up a special Web page specifically for this book. You can access this Web page at *www.mico.org/textbook*. In addition to updated references, the Web page includes the complete source code for all sample programs discussed in this book. You will also find a programming project based on μORB and MICO that can be used as a term project for a graduate-level course.

Chapter 2

BASIC CONCEPTS

We start this book with a short chapter on basic concepts. The idea is not to overwhelm the reader with explanations but only to provide as much information as is necessary to understand the content of the following chapters. The reader should check the literature for additional information on the individual topics (for example, see [10], [11], and [34]). We begin by first presenting some basic concepts related to distributed systems. This is followed by a description of an object model that is particularly suitable for modeling distributed applications. We then present a first overview of the structure and tasks of middleware. We conclude the chapter by presenting a simple sample application that is continued in the subsequent two chapters.

2.1 DISTRIBUTED SYSTEMS

The theory behind distributed systems forms the basis for the middleware discussed in this book. This section explains some of the aspects of distributed systems that are necessary for understanding the material discussed in the chapters that follow. We can only provide an overview here of the theory behind distributed systems. The reader should refer to the literature for further information on this subject (for example, see [10] or [26]).

2.1.1 Characterization

Characterization of a distributed system

The literature presents various definitions of what a distributed system is. According to [3], a distributed system is characterized as follows:

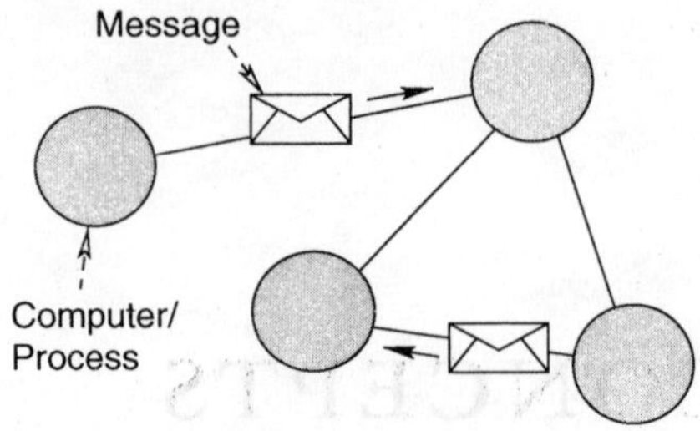

FIGURE 2.1 Structure of a distributed system.

> A *distributed system* is an information-processing system that contains a number of independent computers that cooperate with one another over a communications network in order to achieve a specific objective.

This definition pinpoints a number of aspects of distributed systems. Although the elementary unit of a distributed system is a computer that is networked with other computers, the computer is autonomous in the way it carries out its actions. Computers are linked to one another over a communications network that enables an exchange of messages between computers (see Figure 2.1). The objective of this message exchange is to achieve a cooperation between computers for the purpose of attaining a common goal.

Distribution of state and behavior

A physical view of a distributed system describes this technology. It includes computers as nodes of the communications network along with details about the communications network itself. In contrast, a logical view of a distributed system highlights the applications aspects. Figure 2.1 can therefore also be interpreted as a set of cooperating processes. The distribution aspect refers to the distribution of state (data) and behavior (code) of an application. The process encapsulates part of the state and part of the behavior of an application, and the application's semantics are achieved through the cooperation of several processes. The logical distribution is independent of the physical one. For example, processes do not necessarily have to be linked over a network but instead can all be found on one computer.

Advantages

Distributed systems offer a variety of advantages compared to centrally organized mainframes. Decentralization is a more economic option because networked computing systems offer a better price/performance ratio than mainframe systems. The introduction of redundancy increases availability when parts of a system fail. Applications that can easily be run simultaneously also offer benefits in terms of faster performance vis-à-vis centralized solutions. Distributed systems can be extended through the addition of components, thereby providing better scalability compared to centralized systems.

TABLE 2.1 Advantages and disadvantages of centralized versus distributed systems

Criteria	Centralized system	Distributed system
Economics	low	high
Availability	low	high
Complexity	low	high
Consistency	simple	difficult
Scalability	poor	good
Technology	homogenous	heterogenous
Security	high	low

Disadvantages

The advantages offered by distributed systems are also countered by some disadvantages. The more components in a system, the greater the risk that the rest of the system will suffer unless special measures are taken in the event that one of the components fails. Special mechanisms are needed to avert these failures and make them transparent to the user. Moreover, the many components that make up a distributed system are potential sources of failures. Due to the physical and time separation, consistency (for example, with distributed databases) is more of a problem than with centralized systems. Leslie Lamport presents a (cynical) alternative characterization that highlights the complexity of distributed systems (the complete email and quote can be found at the following URL: *http://research.microsoft.com/users/lamport/pubs/distributed-system.txt*):

> A distributed system is one in which the failure of a computer you didn't even know existed can render your own computer unusable.

Another problem with these systems lies in the heterogeneity of their components. The larger the geographical area over which a distributed system is used, the greater the probability that different types of technology will be incorporated. Special mechanisms are needed to link together the different technologies in a network. The sprawling nature of a distributed system also raises a question about security, because the parts of a system that cannot be controlled are vulnerable to hackers and the like. Consequently, special mechanisms have to be introduced to safeguard security.

Table 2.1 summarizes the key advantages and disadvantages of distributed systems compared to centralized systems. Each application has to be looked at separately to determine whether there is a benefit to running it as a distributed application. Nevertheless, new concepts and tools are always required for working with distributed systems.

2.1.2 Transparency

The above characterization of distributed systems introduces them as a set of mutually cooperating processes. This aspect places the emphasis on the separation and, consequently, the possible distribution of the components of a system. This can prove to be a disadvantage to the applications programmer because of the additional complexity involved in dealing with distributed systems compared to centralized systems. It is desirable to conceal the complexity of distributed systems. In the literature this characteristic is described as *transparency*. Thus the complexity resulting from the distribution should be made transparent (i.e., invisible) to the applications programmer. The aim behind this is to present a distributed system as a centralized system in order to simplify the distribution aspect.

Transparency criteria

The literature cites numerous criteria for the transparency of distributed systems, with most of these criteria based on those from the Advanced Network Systems Architecture (ANSA) (see [2]). The following criteria for transparency are important for the context for this book:

Location transparency: Components can be accessed without having to know where they are physically located.

Access transparency: The ways in which access takes place to local and remote components are identical.

Failure transparency: Users are unaware of a failure of a component.

Technology transparency: Different technologies, such as programming languages and operating systems, are hidden from the user.

Concurrency transparency: Users are unaware that they are sharing components with other users.

It is costly and complicated to implement the mechanisms needed to meet the transparency criteria. For example, distributed systems have new types of fault situations that have to be dealt with that do not occur in centralized systems. As the degree of desired failure transparency increases, the mechanisms that implement the transparency (also see Section 2.1.5) become more complex. One of the main objectives of a middleware platform is to offer mechanisms that help to implement the above transparency criteria.

2.1.3 Communication Mechanisms

Cooperation based on message exchange

Processes are active components with a state and a behavior. The state consists of the data that is managed by the process. The behavior corresponds to the implementation of the applications logic. The processes cooperate with one another through message exchange. A message consists of a sequence of bytes that

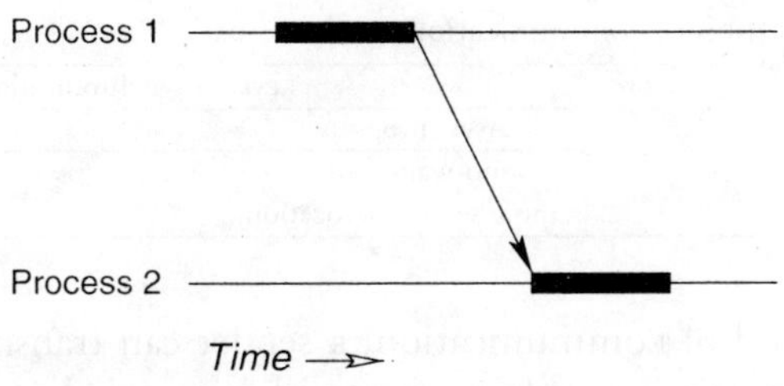

FIGURE 2.2 Message exchange between two processes.

are transported between two processes via a communications medium. Certain rules apply to the way in which a message is structured internally so that it can be interpreted by the process received.

We limit our discussion to the communication that takes place between two processes. The subject of group communication between more than two processes is not appropriate to the context of this book. In message exchange one process assumes the role of sender and another process that of receiver. A space-time diagram can be used to visualize the process during a communications procedure. In Figure 2.2, time runs from left to right. Process 1 is the sender, and process 2 is the receiver.

A process is either in an active or a passive state (the active state is indicated in Figure 2.2 by the thick black lines). A process can only carry out calculations during an active state. Various events, such as the receipt of a message, can change the state of a process. In Figure 2.2, the sender is making some calculations and changes to the passive state when it sends a message. If the message arrives at the receiver, the receiver changes to an active phase and makes calculations based on the content of the message.

Classification

A simple classification scheme of communication mechanisms is the following (also see [27]). We first look at different patterns in the message flow between sender and receiver. The message exchange shown in Figure 2.2 is an example of *message-oriented communication*: The sender transmits a message to the receiver but does not wait for a reply. Message exchange takes place in only one direction. In the case of *request-oriented communication*, the receiver responds to the sender with a reply message. The communications process is not complete until the sender has received a reply to his request.

Communication patterns

Degree of synchronization

The synchronicity of a communication mechanism is orthogonal to the communications patterns from a message-oriented and request-oriented standpoint. The synchronicity describes the time separation between sender and receiver. In *synchronous communication* the sender is passive during the communications process until the message has arrived at the receiver. Conversely, during *asynchronous communication* the sender remains active after a message has been

TABLE 2.2 Classification of communication mechanisms

Communications pattern	Level of synchronization: Asynchronous	Synchronous
Message-oriented	no-wait-send	rendezvous
Request-oriented	remote service invocation	remote procedure call

sent. With this kind of communication, a sender can transmit messages more quickly than the receiver is able to accept them, and thus the transport system must be capable of buffering messages. Although the buffering of messages in the transport system is not necessary in the case of synchronous communication, sender and receiver are still coupled to one another timewise. Asynchronous communication is better, however, at supporting the parallelism of processes.

The two communications patterns and two types of synchronization produce four categories for the classification of communication mechanisms (see Table 2.2).

Remote procedure call (RPC) is an example of synchronous request-oriented communication. The sender sends a request to the receiver and is passive until the receiver delivers the results of the request. An example of asynchronous request-oriented communication is *remote service invocation* (RSI). During this type of communication, the sender remains active while the receiver is processing the request. Although RSI makes better use of the parallelism offered in distributed systems, RPC is based on popular programming paradigms and is therefore intuitive in its interpretation.

Datagram services are an example of asynchronous message-oriented communication. The sender transmits a message to the receiver without waiting for a reply or changing to the passive state. The rendezvous, however, is used in the synchronization of two processes and is an example of synchronous message-oriented communication. Synchronous communication is used in the rendezvous to establish a common (logical) time between sender and receiver.

2.1.4 Client/Server Model

Client and server as roles of objects

The client/server model introduces two roles that can be assumed by processes: the role of *service user* (client) and the role of *service provider* (server). The distribution of roles implies an asymmetry in the distributed execution of an application. The server offers a service to which one or more clients has access (see Figure 2.3). Here processes act as natural units in the distribution. In the context of distributed systems, the communication between client and server can be based on one of the mechanisms mentioned in the previous section. The

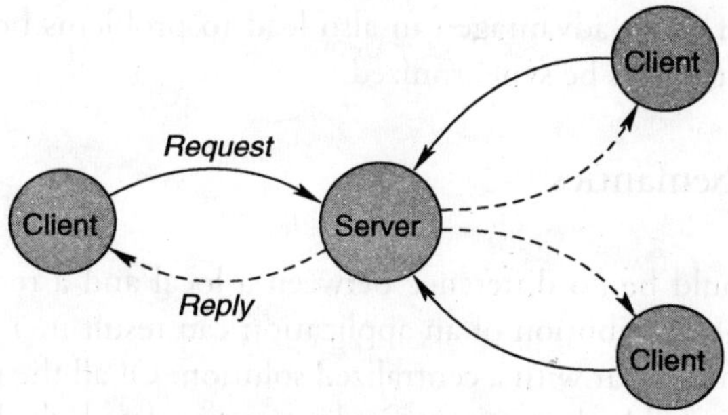

FIGURE 2.3 Client/server model.

client/server model only introduces roles that can be assumed by a process. At a given point in time, a process can assume the role of both client and server. This scenario occurs, for example, when the server is carrying out a task and delegates a subtask to a subordinate server.

The RPC introduced in the last section offers a fundamental communication mechanism for client/server interaction. The client is the initiator of an RPC, and the server provides the implementation of the remotely executed procedure. The request message in Figure 2.3 contains all current input parameters for the procedure call. Conversely, the response message contains all results for the corresponding request produced by the server. The advantage of using remote procedure call as a communication mechanism for the client/server model is that it incorporates procedural programming paradigms and is therefore easily understood. The implementation of the procedure is an integral part of the server, and the invocation of the procedure is part of the application running in the client.

Advantages

An advantage of the client/server model is the intuitive splitting of applications into a client part and a server part. Based on conventional abstractions such as procedural programming, it simplifies the design and the development of distributed applications. Over and above this, it makes it easy to migrate or integrate existing applications into a distributed environment. The client/server model also makes effective use of resources when a large number of clients are accessing a high-performance server. Another advantage of the client/server model is the potential for concurrency.

Disadvantages

From a different point of view, all these advantages could also be considered disadvantages. For example, the restriction to procedural programming paradigms excludes other approaches such as functional or declarative programming. Furthermore, even procedural paradigms cannot always ensure that transparency is maintained between local and remote procedure calls since transparency can no longer be achieved in the case of radical system failure. The concurrency mentioned earlier as an advantage can also lead to problems because of its requirement that processes be synchronized.

2.1.5 Failure Semantics

Ideally, there should be no difference between a local and a remote procedure call. However, the distribution of an application can result in a number of failures that would not occur with a centralized solution. Of all the possible failures that can occur, we will look at two particular types in detail: the loss of messages and the crash of a process. The different failures are shown in Figure 2.4.

Loss of request message (1): If a request message is lost, the client must retransmit the message after a timeout. However, the client cannot differentiate between different types of failures. For example, if the result message is the one that is lost, a retransmission of the request message could result in the procedure being executed twice. The same problem occurs with long procedures when too short a timeout is selected.

Loss of result message (2): The procedure was executed on the server, but the result message for the client is lost. The client retransmits the request after a timeout. If the server does not recognize what happened, it executes the procedure again. This can cause a problem with procedures that change the state of the server.

Server breakdown (3): If the server breaks down due to a failure, it has to be determined whether a partial execution of the procedure had already produced side effects in the state. For example, if the content of a database is modified during the procedure, it is not trivial to allow the execution to recover and continue in an ordered way after the crash of the server.

Client breakdown (4): A client process that breaks down during the execution of a remote procedure call is also referred to as an *orphaned invocation*. The

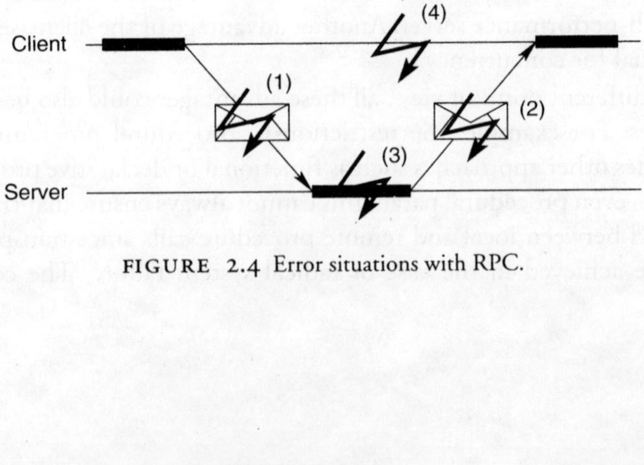

FIGURE 2.4 Error situations with RPC.

question here is what the server does with the results or where it should send them.

Ideally, a remote procedure call should implement *exactly once* semantics—the invocation by a client will result in exactly one execution on the part of the server and also only delivers one result. However, it is not easy to achieve these semantics. Different applications have different requirements for quality of service in terms of failure detection and recovery. For instance, exactly once semantics are particularly desirable for bank transactions. However, repeated executions and numerous result messages would not be a problem in the case of a simple information terminal that only calls up data from a remote server without changing the state of the server (also referred to as *idempotent operations*). In this case, weak assurances of quality of service are sufficient in certain failure situations.

Exactly once semantics

Maybe semantics provide no mechanism for lost messages or process breakdowns. Depending on the particular failure, the procedure can be carried out zero times or once on the server side. Consequently, the client receives at most one result. Maybe semantics essentially provide no guarantees. So long as no failures occur, the remote procedure call is properly carried out. These semantics are also referred to as *best-effort*.

Maybe semantics

At-least-once semantics guarantee that a remote procedure call will be executed on the server side at least once in the event of message loss. After a timeout, the client repeats the remote procedure call until it receives a response from the server. What can happen as a result, however, is that a procedure will be carried out several times on the server. It is also possible that a client will receive several responses due to the repeated executions. At-least-once semantics do not provide a confirmation if the server breaks down. At-least-once semantics are appropriate with idempotent procedures that do not cause state changes on the server and therefore can be executed more than once without any harm.

At-least-once semantics

TABLE 2.3 Failure semantics with RPC

Failure semantics	Fault-free operation	Message loss	Server breakdown
Maybe	Execution: 1 Result: 1	Execution: 0/1 Result: 0	Execution: 0/1 Result: 0
At-least-once	Execution: 1 Result: 1	Execution: $\geqslant 1$ Result: $\geqslant 1$	Execution: $\geqslant 0$ Result: $\geqslant 0$
At-most-once	Execution: 1 Result: 1	Execution: 1 Result: 1	Execution: 0/1 Result: 0
Exactly once	Execution: 1 Result: 1	Execution: 1 Result: 1	Execution: 1 Result: 1

At-most-once semantics

At-most-once semantics guarantee that the procedure will be executed at most once—both in the case of message loss and server breakdown. If the server does not break down, exactly one execution and exactly one result are even guaranteed. These semantics require a complex protocol with message buffering and numbering. Table 2.3 summarizes the failure semantics discussed along with their characteristics.

2.2 OBJECT MODEL

The information technology systems that are the subject of this book are characterized by an inherent complexity. This complexity is due quantitatively to the growing size of these systems and qualitatively to demands for greater functionality. Such systems require a methodical structuring to deal with this complexity. The principles of object modeling are particularly suitable for representing complex problem areas.

2.2.1 Characterization

Tasks of a model

A *model* is the systematic representation of a problem domain to make it possible or easier to examine or research. The model describes which principles are used to produce this representation during the modeling. Concepts that reflect the philosophy behind the approach to a problem area are anchored in the model. Each model defines concepts that focus on specific aspects of the problem area being modeled. The aim of an *object model* is to provide a systematic representation of the problem area on the basis of the concepts *abstraction*, *modularity*, *encapsulation*, and *hierarchy* (see [8] and [30]).

Abstraction: Abstraction is a description of a problem area in which a distinction is made between relevant and nonrelevant aspects. Simplification of a representation is necessary in dealing with the complexity of a problem area. Different abstractions can be generated from one problem area. The decision regarding which aspects are relevant for a particular abstraction depends on the subjective viewpoint of the observer. Furthermore, the abstraction determines the terminology used to describe the relevant characteristics of a problem area.

Modularity: A problem area is partitioned through modularization. This partitioning can be dealt with in different ways depending on a subjective view. The subsets defined by the partitioning reflect the different aspects of the problem area and are distinguished from other subsets by well-defined boundaries. A subset of the problem area represents its own problem area.

Encapsulation: Encapsulation is used to hide all details that are classified as not relevant to a representation. Whereas abstraction describes an outer view, the encapsulation conceals the interior view of the implementation of the behavior established by the abstraction. Encapsulation guarantees that no dependencies between components can occur due to internal implementation details. A consequence of encapsulation is the necessity for an interface that separates the outer view from the inner one. All information that an observer can derive from the outside of a representation is exclusively combined in the interface to the representation.

Hierarchy: A hierarchy establishes the relationship between abstractions of different problem areas. Two hierarchies used in an object model are *specialization (is-a)* and *aggregation (part-of)*. A specialization relationship exists between two abstractions if one of the abstractions has all the characteristics of the other one. The aggregation relationship allows an abstraction to refer to another abstraction for part of its own definition.

The structuring of a problem area according to an object model is based on the four concepts of abstraction, modularity, encapsulation, and hierarchy. The representation of the problem area resulting from the modeling allows levels of freedom that depend on the subjective viewpoint of the observer. A canonical representation of a problem area based on the concepts of an object model does not exist.

2.2.2 Terminology

The concepts of an object model presented in the last section are applied in structuring complex problem domains. The result of the modeling is a representation that is used as the point of departure for other studies and discussions. Standardized terminology is required for the systematic representation.

OBJECT

The main concept of object models is the *object*. The decomposition of a problem domain using the concepts incorporated in the object model results in a set of objects (see Figure 2.5). An object is a thing of our imagination that can be abstract or even concrete in nature. Although the choice of granularity for an object is relative to the observer, an object distinguishes itself from other objects solely on the basis of its definition by well-defined interfaces. The granularity

Object

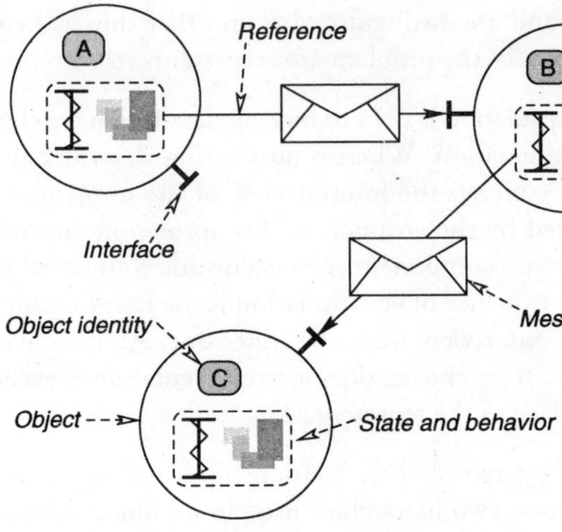

FIGURE 2.5 Decomposition of a problem domain into a set of objects.

in the approach to the problem area determines the level of abstraction. The demarcation between objects creates the modularization needed in the object model. An object is therefore a self-contained problem area.

Identity

Objects are carriers of an *identity*. All objects are differentiated on the basis of their unique identity. According to the concept of identity, objects are sufficiently distinguishable by their inherent existence and not necessarily by their individual characteristics. As well as by its identity, an object is characterized by its *state* and its *behavior*. These two characteristics need not be orthogonal to one another since behavior is usually influenced by the state. State and behavior define the *functionality* an object provides and which can be used by other objects. The *implementation* realizes the functionality of an object based on a programming language.

State and behavior

The concepts of an object model have to be supported in the programming language by conventions or special language constructs. For example, the concepts of state and behavior in an imperative programming language correspond to the programming language constructs data and functions.

Interface

As a result of the encapsulation required in object models, an object needs a well-defined *interface* that can be used as an access point by other objects, thus enabling access to its functionality. The interface separates an inner and an outer view of an object. The outer view provides information about the functionality of an object; the inner view reveals the implementation details. The interface as a fixed access point reduces the dependencies between objects. Implementations can be interchanged so long as the outwardly apparent functionality is preserved.

MESSAGES

The identity enables the unique addressing of an object via its interface (see Figure 2.5). Queries to an object can be sent in the form of *messages* to its interface, which in turn responds to it through messages. A message consists of a *selector* and a finite number of *parameters*. The selector is used to select the functionality offered by an object. The parameters included in a message are identified as *input parameters* if they are contained in a request or *output parameters* if they are contained in a reply. *Selector*

An object model does not stipulate a precise structure for selectors or parameters. Rather the structure is normally based on a programming language paradigm. For example, if the structure of a message is based on an imperative programming language, the selector consists of the function name together with an ordered sequence of parameter types of the function. The selector is then also denoted as the *signature* of a message and the interface as an *operational interface*. The part of the implementation that provides the functionality of a message in an object is referred to as a *method* or an *operation*. The process of directing an incoming message to an implementing method is called *method dispatching*. *Signature* *Method selection*

In the object model, communication between objects typically follows the synchronous, request-oriented communication pattern introduced in Section 2.1.3. A prerequisite for communication process is that the sender of a message has a *reference* to the addressee. The reference embodies knowledge about the object identity that is necessary for unique addressing. It manifests the *view* an object has of a referenced object. An *expression* describes the use of a message to a referenced object. For example, the expression *a.deposit*(100) indicates the use of a message on an object with an operational interface, which can be referenced over the identifier *a* (see Figure 2.6). *Reference* *Expression*

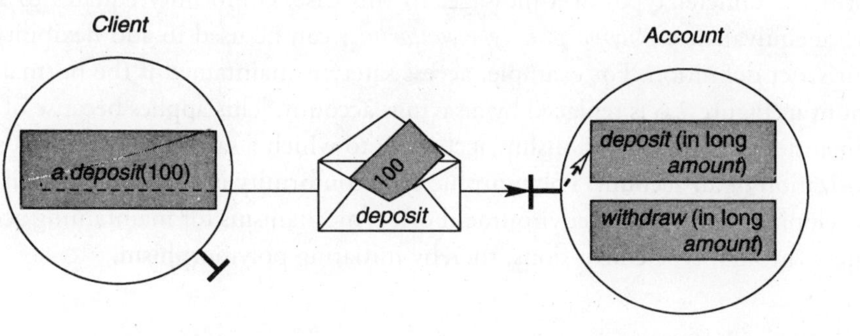

FIGURE 2.6 Method selection using the signature of a message.

The message in this example has the signature *deposit*(`in long`). The keyword `in` stands for an input parameter of the operation. When an operation is invoked, input parameters are bound to concrete values (such as the value 100 in Figure 2.6). The expression *a.deposit*(100) is part of the implementation of the client object. The identifier *a* references the operational interface of an account object. Based on the signature of the incoming message, the method *deposit*(`in long` *amount*) is selected. The actual parameter 100 is bound to the formal parameter *amount* of the method, and the implementation is executed.

TYPE AND TYPE CONFORMITY

Type

Types enable objects to be classified according to prescribed criteria. Subsets of objects can therefore be categorized according to certain characteristics. A type is a specification of conditions. If the conditions apply to an object, the object belongs to a type. If the conditions formulated in the type apply to the object, then this object is an *instance* of the type.

Instance

The view defined through a reference to an object can be specified through a *reference type*. The reference type does not necessarily have to be identical with the object type because the view defined through the reference for its part represents an abstraction based on certain details of the object type. To guarantee *access safety* to the functionality offered by an object, the reference type has to have a certain relationship to the object type. *Type conformity* defines the criteria that can be applied to determine if two types conform with one another so that access safety is guaranteed.

Access safety

Monomorphic and polymorphic type conformity

Monomorphic type conformity demands an exact agreement between reference and object type, which constitutes conformity between the current and the formal parameter types of a message. In this case, conformity equates to syntactic equivalence. *Polymorphic type conformity* can be used to add flexibility to this strict definition. For example, access safety is maintained if the normal account in Figure 2.6 is replaced by a savings account. This applies because of the semantics of the *is-a* relationship according to which a savings account is a specialization of an account. Polymorphic type conformity is only achievable if the development or runtime environment offers mechanisms for maintaining access safety through type conversions, thereby initiating polymorphism.

2.3 MIDDLEWARE

The preceding sections showed that distributed systems create new problems that do not exist in centralized systems. The question is how suitable concepts and mechanisms can be used to develop and execute applications in distributed systems. It is obvious that new concepts and mechanisms are necessary, but not at which level they should be embedded. In principle, different options exist—from support at the hardware level all the way to the extension of programming languages to enable support of distributed applications. Software solutions typically provide the greatest flexibility because of their suitability for integrating existing technologies (such as operating systems and programming languages).

These conditions lead to the concept of *middleware*. Middleware offers general services that support distributed execution of applications. The term *middleware* suggests that it is software positioned between the operating system and the application. Viewed abstractly, middleware can be envisaged as a "tablecloth" that spreads itself over a heterogeneous network, concealing the complexity of the underlying technology from the application being run on it.

2.3.1 Middleware Tasks

We start this section by looking at the tasks carried out by middleware. We will limit the discussion to the middleware support of an object-based application because the concepts of an object model ideally reflect the characteristics of distributed systems. An object encapsulates state and behavior and can only be accessed via a well-defined interface. The interface hides the details that are specific to the implementation, thereby helping to encapsulate different technologies. An object therefore becomes a unit of distribution. Recall that objects communicate with each other by exchanging messages.

Tasks of middleware

For the context of this book, we define the following middleware tasks:

Object model support: Middleware should offer mechanisms to support the concepts incorporated in the object model.

Operational interaction: Middleware should allow the operational interaction between two objects. The model used is the method invocation of an object-oriented programming language.

Remote interaction: Middleware should allow the interaction between two objects located in different address spaces.

Distribution transparency: From the standpoint of the program, interaction between objects is identical for both local and remote interactions.

Technological independence: The middleware supports the integration of different technologies.

2.3.2 The Structure of a Middleware Platform

As we mentioned earlier, middleware is conceptually located between the application and the operating system (see Figure 2.7). Because an object model serves as the underlying paradigm, the application is represented as a set of interacting objects. Each object is explicitly allocated to a hardware platform (i.e., we do not consider cases in which an object logically extends beyond computer boundaries).

Types of heterogeneity

The middleware hides the heterogeneity that occurs in a distributed system. This heterogeneity exists at different places:

Programming languages: Different objects can be developed in different programming languages.

Operating system: Operating systems have different characteristics and capabilities.

Computer architectures: Computers differ in their technical details (e.g., data representations).

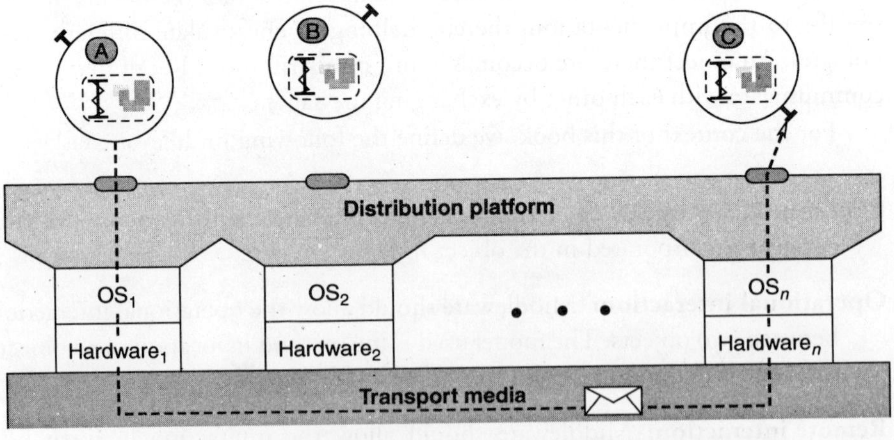

FIGURE 2.7 Middleware for the support of object-based applications.

Networks: Different computers are linked together through different network technologies.

Middleware overcomes this heterogeneity by offering equal functionality at all access points. Applications have access to this functionality through an Application Programming Interface (API). Because the API depends on the programming language in which the application is written, the API has to be adapted to the conditions of each programming language that is supported by the middleware.

An applications programmer typically sees middleware as a program library and a set of tools. The form these take naturally depends on the development environment that the programmer is using. Along with the programming language selected, this is also affected by the actual compiler/interpreter used to develop a distributed application.

2.3.3 Standardization of a Middleware

If we were to project a middleware to a global, worldwide network, we would find special characteristics that differ from those of a geographically restricted distributed system. At the global level, middleware spans several technological and political domains, and it can no longer be assumed that a homogenous technology exists within a distributed system.

Due to the heterogeneity and the complexity associated with it, we cannot assume that one vendor alone is able to supply middleware in the form of products for all environments. From the standpoint of market policy, it is generally desirable to avoid having the monopoly on a product and to support innovation through competition. However, the implementation of middleware through several competing products should not result in partial solutions that are not compatible.

Compatibility is only possible if all vendors of middleware adhere to a standard. The standard must therefore stipulate the *specification* for a product—an abstract description of a desired behavior that allows a degree of freedom in the execution of an implementation. It serves as a blueprint according to which different products (i.e., implementations) can be produced.

Products that conform to a standard

A specification as a standard identifies the verifiable characteristics of a system. If a system conforms to a standard, it is fulfilling these characteristics. From the view of the customer, standards offer a multitude of advantages. In an ideal situation a standard guarantees vendor independence, thereby enabling a customer to select from a range of products without having to commit to one particular vendor. For customers this means protection of the investments they have to make in order to use a product. The following characteristics are associated with *open standards:*

Characteristics of an open standard

Nonproprietary: The standard itself is not subject to any commercial interests.

Freely available: Access to the standard is available to everyone.

Technology independent: The standard represents an abstraction of concrete technical mechanisms and only defines a system to the extent that is necessary for compatibility between products.

Democratic creation process: The creation and subsequent evolution of the standard is not ruled by the dominance of one company but takes place through democratic processes.

Product availability: A standard is only effective if products exist for it. In this respect a close relationship exists between a standard and the products that can technically be used in conjunction with the standard.

2.3.4 Portability and Interoperability

Two different interfaces in middleware

In the context of middleware, a standard has to establish the interfaces between different components to enable their interaction with one another. We want to distinguish between two types of interface: horizontal and vertical (see Figure 2.8). The horizontal interface exists between an application and the middleware and defines how an application can access the functionality of the middleware. This is also referred to as an *Application Programming Interface* (API). The standardization of the interface between middleware and application results in

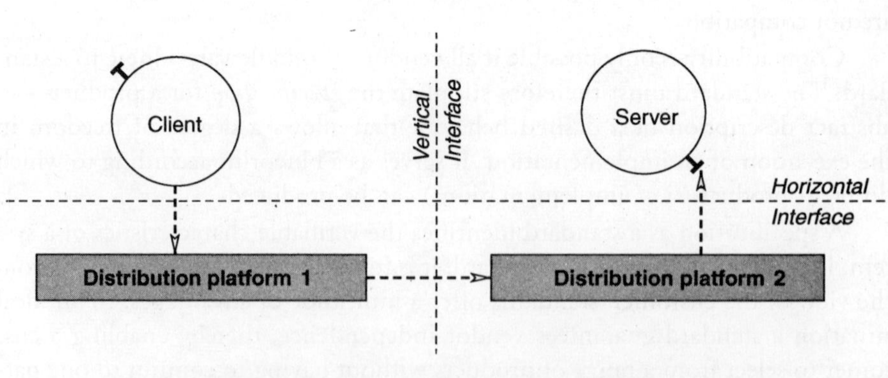

FIGURE 2.8 Portability and interoperability.

the *portability* of an application to different middleware because the same API exists at each access point. *Portability*

In addition to the horizontal interface, there is a vertical interface that defines the interface between two instances of a middleware platform. This vertical interface is typically defined through a protocol on the basis of messages, referred to as *protocol data units* (PDUs). A PDU is a message sent over the network. Both client and server exchange PDUs to implement the protocol. The vertical interface separates technological domains and ensures that applications can extend beyond the influence area of the product of middleware. The standardization of this interface allows *interoperability* between applications. *Interoperability*

Applications programmers are typically only interested in the horizontal interface because it defines the point of contact to their applications. From the view of the applications programmer, the vertical interface is of minor importance for the development of an application. Yet an implicit dependency exists between vertical and horizontal interfaces. For example, coding rules for the PDUs have to exist in the vertical interface for all data types available in the horizontal interface of an application.

2.4 SAMPLE APPLICATION

In this section we will present a simple application that serves as the basis for the examples appearing in the subsequent two chapters. The degree of completeness of the example is of minor importance for our discussion. It is intentionally kept simple in order to focus on middleware issues. In the two chapters that follow, we will then show how this application can be distributed across address space boundaries.

2.4.1 The Account Example

The first steps in any software development process are the analysis and design of the problem domain. The result of this process is a formal description of the application that is to be developed. One possible way to describe the application is through the *Unified Modeling Language* (UML). In the following we introduce a simple application where the design is trivial. Our emphasis is the distribution of the application with the help of a middleware, not the analysis and design process itself.

The application that will be used in this and subsequent chapters models a customer who wishes to do operations on a bank account. Here we are not con-

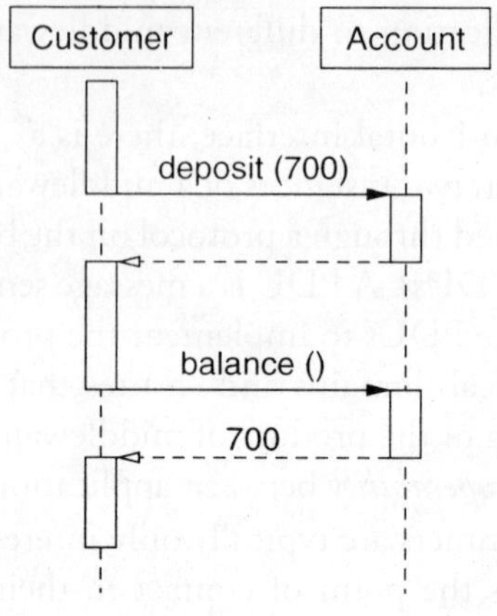

FIGURE 2.9 Sequence diagram for account use case.

cerned with different types of accounts, or how accounts are created by a bank. In order to keep the scenario simple, we assume that only one customer and one account exist, each represented through an object. The account maintains a balance, and the customer can deposit and withdraw money through appropriate operations. The customer can furthermore inquire as to the balance of the account.

Sequence diagram

We use UML to further formalize the account application. UML introduces the notion of a *sequence diagram* that describes a use case of our application. For example, one possible use case might be that the customer deposits 700 units and then asks the account for the current balance. Assuming that the previous balance was 0, the new balance should be 700. This is only one of many possible use cases. For complex applications we would have several such use cases to describe the behavior of the application.

The use case described in the previous paragraph is depicted in Figure 2.9. The notation is based on the UML notation for sequence diagrams. The two actors—the customer and the account—are listed horizontally. Time flows from top to bottom. The arrows show invocations and responses between the two actors. The white bars indicate activity. In combination, the white bars and the arrows show clearly how the thread of execution is passed between the customer and the account.

Class diagram

The next step in designing the application is to decompose the problem domain into classes. UML offers another notation for class diagrams. For our simple account application, we will only introduce one class: `Account`. Figure 2.10 shows the class diagram for the account application.

A class is represented by a rectangle that is further divided in three sections. The top section contains the name of the class. The middle section contains the

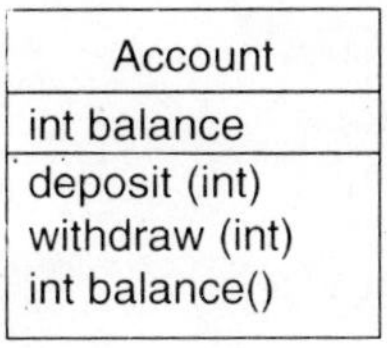

FIGURE 2.10 UML class diagram for the account example.

description of the state. For the account class we only need one variable representing the balance of the account. Sometimes the state is not explicitly mentioned in the class diagram, especially if we only want to highlight the interface. The bottom section of the class diagram lists all the operations that instances of this class accept. The signature describes the input/output behavior of each operation, similar to prototype definitions in C++.

2.4.2 C++ Implementation

The UML diagrams in the previous sections describe a design for the bank account scenario. The class structure for an object-oriented programming language such as C++ is derived directly from the design. Our initial interest in the following is the conversion of the UML diagram into a stand-alone (i.e., not distributed) application. When UML classes are mapped to C++ classes, we introduce a naming convention according to which the C++ class name is assigned the suffix _impl. The following code fragment shows the implementation of the account application based on the programming language C++:

C++ implementation of account application

```
// File: account.cc

#include <iostream>
#include <assert.h>

using namespace std;

// Implementation for interface Account
class Account_impl
{
private:
  int _balance;

public:
```

```
  Account_impl ()
  {
    _balance = 0;
  }

  void deposit (int amount)
  {
    cout << "Server: deposit " << amount << endl;
    _balance += amount;
  }

  void withdraw (int amount)
  {
    cout << "Server: withdraw " << amount << endl;
    if (_balance >= amount)
      _balance -= amount;
    else
      cout << "Server: withdraw failed" << endl;
  }

  int balance ()
  {
    cout << "Server: balance " << _balance << endl;
    return _balance;
  }
};

int
main (int argc, char *argv[])
{
  int balance;
  Account_impl* account = new Account_impl();
  account->deposit (700);
  balance = account->balance ();
  cout << "Client: balance is " << balance << endl;
  account->withdraw (50);
  balance = account->balance ();
  cout << "Client: balance is " << balance << endl;
  account->withdraw (200);
  balance = account->balance ();
  cout << "Client: balance is " << balance << endl;
```

```
56:
57:     return 0;
58: }
```

Since we assume C++ knowledge, the above code should be trivial to understand. The one point to make is that the application can be broken up into a client and a server portion. Lines 9–40 define the server (i.e., the account), and lines 42–58 define the client (i.e., the customer). In the following section we show how this stand-alone program residing in one address space can be distributed across different address spaces.

2.4.3 Distribution of the Sample Application

The sample application as presented in the last subsection is completely processed within one address space. Figure 2.11 shows the different components of the bank scenario in the form of a layer model in which the higher layers use the functionality of the layers below them. The interfaces between the layers are defined by the API, which in our example is the declaration of class `Account`. The server layer contains the account object. The client layer accesses this object through references (i.e., C++ pointers). It is important to note that the layers express a dependency relationship. Higher layers depend on lower layers. In that sense, the client depends on the server, but not vice versa.

The separation of client and server into different address spaces assumes that the actual parameters are being transmitted between processes since a common address space no longer exists. All data belonging to the parameters of an interaction between a client and a server must therefore be transmitted explicitly to the address space of the server. The data must be self-contained; that is, it is not allowed to contain a pointer that is only valid in the context of the client.

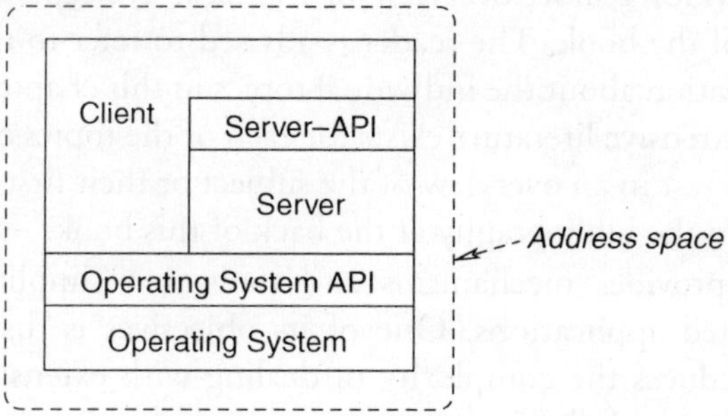

FIGURE 2.11 Complete application in an address space.

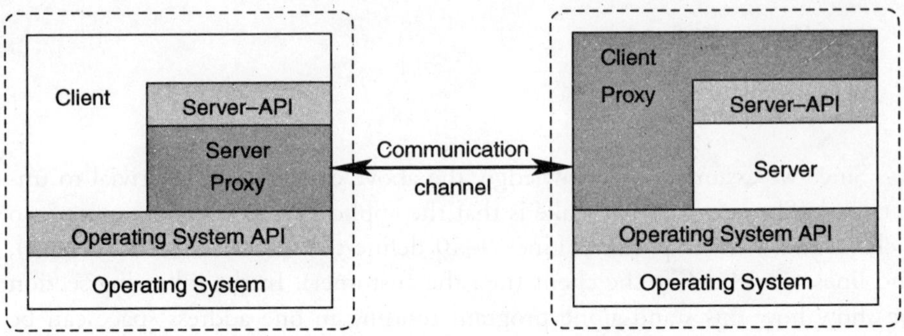

FIGURE 2.12 Distributed execution of the application.

Figure 2.12 illustrates the principle with the client and server in different address spaces. A proxy of the server (component in dark gray shading) exists on the client side. This proxy offers the same API as the server itself. Its tasks include transmitting all current parameters over a communications channel to the remote address space.

In the remote address space, a proxy of the client accepts the data and executes the actual invocation on the server. Outwardly it is not possible to distinguish the proxies from their "originals," so the distribution of client and server is transparent. The arrangement of the components in Figure 2.12 is derived through a simple transformation of Figure 2.11. The client and server portions of the stand-alone application in Figure 2.11 are separated. The proxies are used to fill the gaps on either side so that client and server are unaware of the separation.

2.5 SUMMARY

This chapter provides a short overview of the basic concepts that are important for the rest of the book. The reader is advised to refer to the literature for additional information about the individual topics in this chapter. A separate research area with extensive literature exists for each of the topics covered. Readers with a further interest in an overview of the subject or their first introduction to a topic can refer to the bibliography at the back of this book.

Middleware provides mechanisms and tools that simplify the development of distributed applications. One of its objectives is distribution transparency, which reduces the complexity of dealing with extensively distributed systems. We devote the following chapters to the architecture, design, and implementation of middleware. We start by presenting a CORBA-based middleware platform from the view of an applications programmer and showing how the bank application described in this chapter can be executed on this platform.

Chapter 3

INTRODUCTION TO CORBA

This chapter deals with the fundamental concepts of CORBA (see [28]). This chapter could have been written using any middleware technology; however, we have chosen CORBA because of its maturity and significance in the marketplace. The specification for CORBA, published by the OMG, is based on an object model described in the Object Management Architecture (OMA). We start by looking at the characteristics of the OMA in Section 3.1 and then those of CORBA in Section 3.2. Those sections provide a high-level overview of CORBA. While this part is more theoretical, it will provide the foundation for the rest of the chapter that is devoted to CORBA from the view of an applications programmer. Section 3.3 demonstrates the development process of a CORBA application. A complete CORBA application, based on the bank account scenario introduced in the last chapter, is then presented in Section 3.4.

ORB, product-independent introduction to CORBA

This chapter is an introduction to CORBA, and presents all the background information necessary for understanding the material presented in the subsequent chapters. The view of CORBA presented corresponds to that of an applications programmer and is largely independent of Mico. It should be pointed out that the explanations in this chapter by no means cover all aspects of CORBA. Readers should refer to secondary literature for further information (for example, see [14]). Although we only dedicate one chapter to the introduction to CORBA, it also features a complete CORBA application written in C++ and Java.

3.1 OBJECT MANAGEMENT ARCHITECTURE

OMG is the publisher of the CORBA specification

The Object Management Group (OMG) was founded in 1989 as an international, nonprofit consortium and has many members from the field of information technology worldwide. The task of the OMG consists of publishing and updating specifications that describe an object-oriented infrastructure as the basis for information processing. The OMG functions as the publisher of the freely available specification and coordinates contributions and modifications to the standard submitted by members of the consortium.

We will be dealing with two standards published by the OMG. The first standard is the Object Management Architecture (OMA), which describes a general platform for the development of distributed, object-oriented applications. The second standard is the Common Object Request Broker Architecture (CORBA), which is a specialization of OMA and describes an actual middleware platform. We will be looking at CORBA in detail in the following section, but we will first start with an overview of OMA.

Object Management Architecture

The main features of the OMA are an abstract *object model* and a *reference architecture*. The OMA object model differentiates between *object semantics* and *object implementation*. The object semantics describe the object characteristics

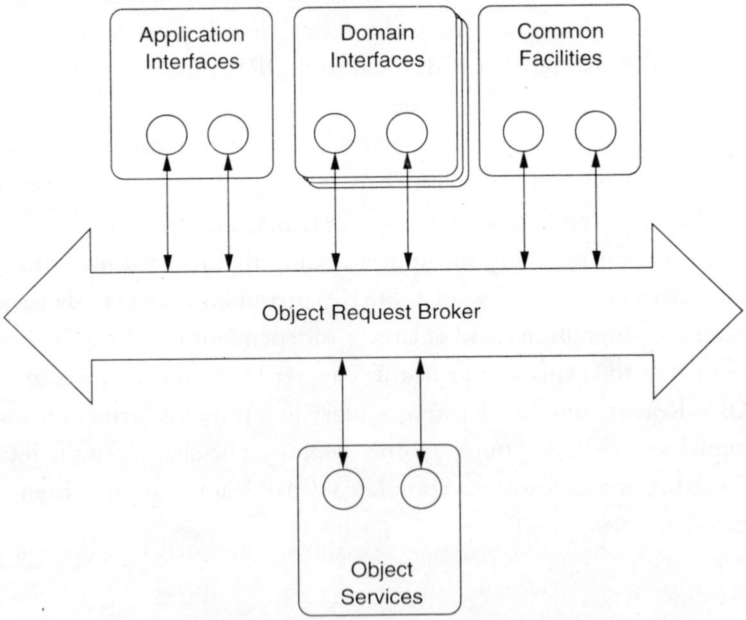

FIGURE 3.1 OMA reference architecture.

that are outwardly visible to clients; the object implementation deals with the concepts needed to execute objects. The OMA puts the main emphasis on the object semantics, and the aspect of object implementation is only defined in broad terms to enable maximum flexibility in the implementation of objects.

Whereas the OMA object model provides an abstract characterization of objects, the *reference architecture* defines relationships between objects. Figure 3.1 shows the structure of the reference model. The main component is the *Object Request Broker* (ORB), which functions as a software bus that enables communication between objects in four different categories:

Object services: This category combines the horizontal system services that are application-independent and can be used in different contexts. Examples of object services include naming, trading, and security services.

Common facilities: The common facilities provide horizontal end user services that are typically required in different application contexts. An example is the printing service.

Domain interfaces: The domain interfaces represent vertical services for special application areas. Examples of domain interfaces are medical, telecommunications, and financial services.

Application interfaces: The application interfaces represent application-specific services. In contrast to the three other categories, application interfaces are not included in the OMG standardization efforts.

Object framework

Object frameworks, which represent a type of distributed class library for a specific application area, can be created by the OMG or a user through an implementation of the interfaces specified. In the process the implementation of an object can access the functionality of objects in other categories. Figure 3.2 shows the structure of such a framework. In this example, the implementation of common facilities makes use of the object services.

3.2 OVERVIEW OF CORBA

CORBA

The *Common Object Request Broker Architecture* (CORBA) is derived from an instantiation of the OMA presented in the last section. Figure 3.3 presents an overview of the key CORBA components. The components that are part of CORBA are shaded in gray, and the components of the embedded application

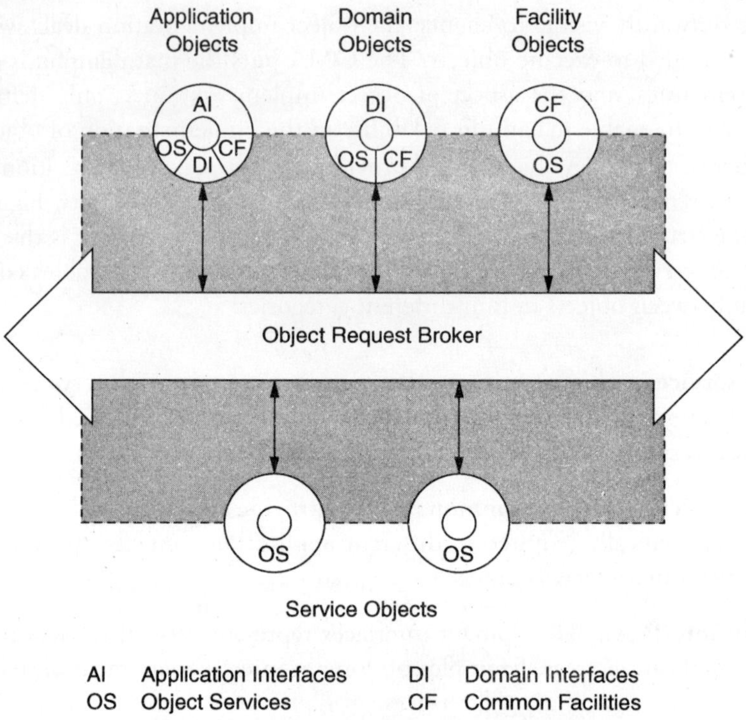

FIGURE 3.2 Object framework.

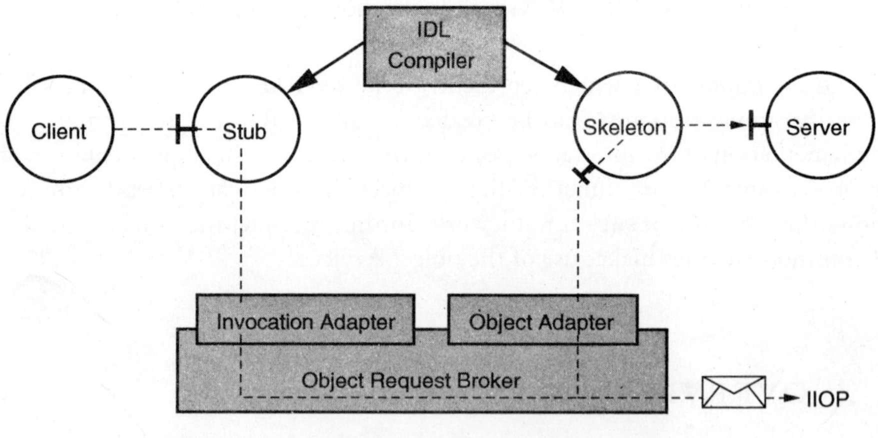

FIGURE 3.3 Components of a CORBA-based middleware.

are those with a white background. The following sections look at the different building blocks of a CORBA platform.

3.2.1 CORBA Object Model

CORBA object model

The difference between the CORBA object model and the OMA object model is that the CORBA object model transforms the abstract object model of the OMA into a concrete form. For example, in contrast to the OMA, the CORBA object model defines a number of basic types (`Boolean`, `Char`, `Long`, etc.) as well as constructed types (`struct`, `union`, `sequence`, etc.). Moreover, the CORBA object model defines the signature and the invocation semantics of the operations defined in an interface. The signature of an operation consists of

Invocation semantics: Specifies which failure semantics are used for an operation (supported are *best-effort* or *at-most-once*).

Result type: Defines the type of return value, which can also be *void*. The return value is the same as an output parameter.

Operation name: Indicates the name of an operation. A name consists of an identifier and must be unique within an interface.

Parameter list: Each parameter has a type as well as a *tag* that identifies the parameter as an input or an output parameter or a combined input/output parameter.

Exception list: An optional list of exception types that can occur during the processing of an operation. An exception signals an error to the caller of the operation.

Context list: An optional list of context information. The context information consists of implicit input parameters that are defined by the client before an operation invocation and transmitted along with the actual parameters to the invoked entity.

The CORBA object model briefly outlined above is based on the *Interface Definition Language* (IDL), which enables a formal specification of the types of the object model and, particularly, the interfaces from objects.

3.2.2 Interface Definition Language

The *Interface Definition Language* (IDL) is used to specify object interfaces independently of a specific programming language. This makes IDL the basis for the separation of the interface and the implementation of an object. CORBA-IDL is a *declarative* language—it contains no algorithmic constructs for the description of loops, branching, and so forth. Its syntax is extensively based on that of C++, but it includes some additional constructs to accommodate the special characteristics of distributed environments (for example, the identification of parameters as input or output parameters).

CORBA-IDL permits description of object interfaces

The elements of CORBA-IDL permit the definition of types that are conformant to the CORBA object model. IDL provides the mechanism of *interface inheritance* to enable existing types to be reused in the construction of new ones. Many object-oriented programming languages typically use *implementation inheritance*, which enables the inheritance of interfaces and their implementations. Interface inheritance, in contrast, only allows the reuse of interfaces. However, appropriate mechanisms of the implementation language (for example, inheritance, delegation, and aggregation) can be used so that existing program code can be reused in the construction of new CORBA objects.

3.2.3 IDL-Language Mappings

Connection between IDL and a high-level programming language

The mapping of IDL interfaces to a particular programming language such as C++ is defined by an IDL language mapping. The OMG currently defines language mappings for C, C++, Smalltalk, Python, Ada 95, COBOL, PL/1, and Java. *IDL compilers* automate the use of this language mapping by translating an IDL specification to the corresponding code in one of the programming languages mentioned.

The basic types and constructed types of CORBA-IDL are mapped to the corresponding data types of the target language. Each IDL interface is mapped to two proxies: a *stub* and a *skeleton*. Similar to an RPC, the stub is located in the client and behaves like a remote CORBA object in relation to the caller. The skeleton is in the server and behaves like the remote caller in relation to the local CORBA object.

Language mappings depend on the programming language

The details of the IDL language mapping heavily depend on the programming language being considered. For example, in object-oriented programming languages, IDL interfaces are mapped to classes; in procedural programming languages, functions and procedures take on these tasks. However, the CORBA standard makes no statements about the internal implementation of the proxies; it only states that the interface of the proxy objects is subject to the rules of IDL language mapping.

3.2.4 Object Request Broker

ORB is the central component in CORBA

The Object Request Broker (ORB) transmits operation invocations from a client to a server that can be located in the same address space, in different address spaces on the same computer, or on different computers. It therefore ensures that communication between objects in a distributed environment is transparent for the objects.

Special components are used as the interface between the ORB and the application. On the client side the invocation adapter enables an operation to be generated and invoked. In a similar way, the object adapter on the server side allows an invocation to be delivered to the object implementation. The task of the ORB is to accept operations at the invocation adapter and to forward and deliver them to the appropriate object adapter.

3.2.5 Invocation and Object Adapters

Client-side interface to ORB

Clients use invocation adapters either indirectly through stub objects or directly in order to transfer method invocations to the ORB. Invocation adapters are components that are separate from the ORB because the functionality needed to initiate method invocations can vary considerably. A special invocation adapter can be used for certain requirements.

Server-side interface to ORB

Similar to invocation adapters, object adapters form the connection between ORB and object implementations. They too are separate components from the ORB because different types of object implementations place different demands on object adapters. Object adapters manage the life cycles of CORBA objects and handle the execution of operation invocations. Consequently, object implementations are bound to an object adapter through *skeletons*.

3.2.6 Interoperability

The CORBA standard specifies *inter-ORB protocols* that have to be supplied by each compliant CORBA implementation in order to guarantee cooperation between different CORBA products. The standard defines an interoperability framework that is independent of a concrete transport mechanism. This framework is defined in the standard through the *General Inter-ORB Protocol* (GIOP). The interoperability framework must be adapted to the peculiarities of the transport mechanism. This applies to technical details, such as the addressing of a communication end point. The CORBA specification defines an inter-ORB protocol that is based on TCP as the transport mechanism. In the standard this protocol is referred to as the *Internet Inter-ORB Protocol* (IIOP).

3.3 THE CREATION PROCESS OF A CORBA APPLICATION

Different implementations of ORB

In this section we examine the development of a CORBA application from the view of an applications programmer. As was explained in the last section, CORBA is a specification that allows freedom in its implementation. For example, the standard does not prescribe a specific way to implement the ORB. One possibility to implement the ORB could be to integrate the ORB into the operating system. The functionality of CORBA would thus be made available through an API, analogous to the socket or any other API being offered by the operating system. Another way to implement the ORB would be to augment a high-level programming language compiler. For example, a C++ compiler could be changed in such a way that it natively understood the aforementioned IDL.

The majority of all known CORBA implementations, including MICO, use another approach to implement the CORBA specification: as a set of libraries and tools. This approach is the most flexible because the ORB developer can use compiler and operating systems without having to change those. Figure 3.4 depicts a typical configuration of a CORBA client and server. Both server and client are processes executing on an operating system. The server listens on a TCP socket, and the client opens a TCP connection to the remote server. The "language" spoken over this TCP connection is IIOP.

It is worth mentioning that this configuration is typical for client/server applications running on the Internet. The World Wide Web is one example: a browser on the client side "speaks" with a Web server via HTTP (HyperText Transfer Protocol). As with any such application, client and server need not be written in the same programming language. For example, the client in Figure 3.4 could be written in Java and the server in C++. The only important thing is that client and server agree on a protocol. Of course, using a different programming language usually means using a different tool chain. MICO only supports C++, and we will have to use a Java-ORB to implement the sample application in Java.

The first step in developing a CORBA application typically involves identifying the object interfaces using the IDL. The IDL specification serves as an

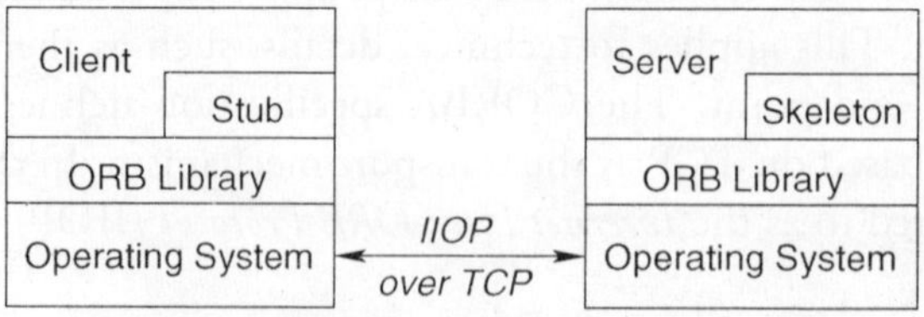

FIGURE 3.4 A CORBA application in context.

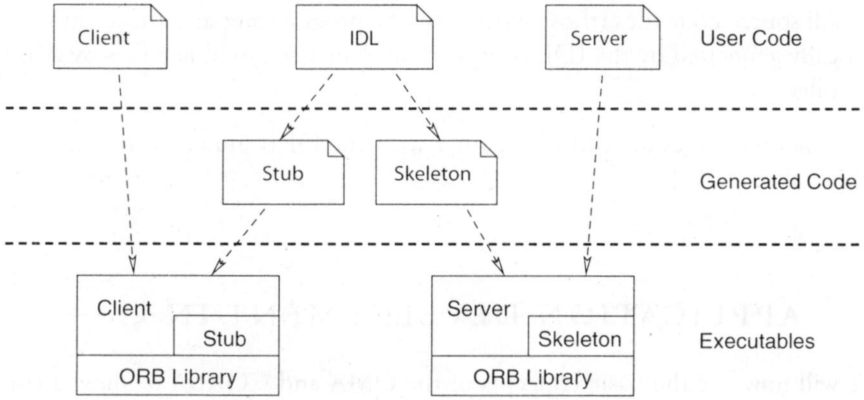

FIGURE 3.5 The creation of a CORBA application.

agreement between client and server. Once the IDL specification is determined, developers can independently develop the client and the server in their preferred programming languages. It is important to note that the IDL specification serves as a contract between client and server. The contract states what operations the server is offering at the interface and what therefore the client can expect in terms of functionality.

To look at it from a different perspective, the IDL fulfills the requirement of encapsulation postulated in the object model. The IDL is language independent, and the client does not need to know in which language the server is implemented. The IDL language mappings of the respective programming language control the binding to the respective ORB on both the client and the server sides.

Once the implementations (i.e., source code) of the client and the server are available (top layer in Figure 3.5), they are translated and bound to an executable file (lowest layer in Figure 3.5). The IDL compiler is used to generate the proxy objects from the IDL specifications. In this case, the stub is generated in the same programming language as the client, and the skeleton in the same programming language as the server. The IDL compiler of the corresponding ORB is the one that must be used to generate the proxy objects.

Steps involved in creating a CORBA application

The process of creating a CORBA application consists of four steps.

1. The application-specific part is contributed by the developer and implements the application's logic.

2. The proxy objects are generated automatically from an IDL specification through the use of an IDL compiler.

3. All source code files (those written by the programmer and those automatically generated by the IDL compiler) are translated to object files by a compiler.
4. The object files are linked together with the ORB library to the final executables.

3.4 APPLICATION DEVELOPMENT IN C++

We will now use the basic concepts of the OMA and CORBA to show a complete CORBA application. The application is the account scenario presented in the previous chapter. It is not our aim to explain all details of a CORBA platform because this is not within the scope of this book. Instead our goal is to show a complete application from the view of a developer. We will present the implementation for both C++ and Java.

Account scenario under CORBA

The application described below exclusively uses CORBA-compliant functionality. This means that the application is portable to other ORB implementations. We start by describing the IDL specification of the account application and then separately show the implementation of the server and of the client. All code fragments used appear in their entirety in Appendix D. The complete source code has consecutive line numbers to facilitate the relationship between code fragments presented in this chapter.

3.4.1 IDL Specification

The first step in developing a CORBA application is to specify the interfaces. We have identified only one interface in the account scenario presented in the last chapter: the interface of an account object. This interface has to be defined on the basis of CORBA IDL. The IDL syntax resembles that of C++. It should again be noted that IDL is a specification language and not an implementation language. Only the interfaces of the objects identified in the system are specified. The implementation follows later and is based on the higher programming languages such as C++ or Java. The IDL specification of our account object is fairly straightforward:

Interface `Account`

```
interface Account {
  void deposit (in long amount);
  void withdraw (in long amount);
  long balance ();
};
```

Note that the syntax of those few lines follows that of CORBA-IDL. At a first glance, the specification of interface `Account` resembles that of a C++ class declaration. The keyword `interface` signals the introduction of a new CORBA interface. The three main operations (deposit, withdraw, balance) of an account are specified in this definition. Each operation has a signature that defines the input/output behavior of that operation. Again, it resembles the signature in C++. The type `long` is one of many built-in types provided by CORBA. `long` is a signed, 32-bit long integer value. The keyword `in` declares the formal argument as an input parameter (i.e., a parameter that is transmitted from client to server). Besides `in`, CORBA also supports `out` and `inout` (a parameter that is an input as well as an output parameter).

3.4.2 IDL Language Mapping for C++

The CORBA standard describes IDL language mappings for various programming languages. In the following we first focus on C++; we will look at Java in a later section of this chapter. The language mapping rules define how different IDL constructs are to be mapped to C++ constructs. Because every compliant ORB implementation has to adhere to these rules, the portability of an application is largely guaranteed.

The details of the IDL language mapping prescribed by CORBA are complex and cannot be fully covered here. We have limited our discussion to some general comments that are sufficient for the purposes of our account application. The IDL basic type `long` is mapped to the C++ type `CORBA::Long` defined in the ORB library along with an integer value range of -2^{31} to $2^{31} - 1$. The question is why the IDL type `long` is not mapped to one of the built-in types of C++ (e.g., `int`). The surprising reason is that the C++ language does not define a value range for type `int`; that is, `sizeof(int)` may yield different results for different C++ compilers. Since we need to ensure that the IDL type `long` always has the value range -2^{31} to $2^{31} - 1$, the CORBA specification solves this problem by introducing the type `CORBA::Long`. It is the ORB's responsibilty to `typedef` this type to something that has the exact same value range.

For each interface described in IDL, the CORBA language mapping rules for C++ define several C++ classes that the IDL compiler needs to generate. These classes basically make up the stub and skeleton and support the programmer in dealing with remote objects. The IDL language mapping for C++ defines some naming conventions for the class names. For example, the IDL compiler generates the following C++ classes for the IDL interface `Account`:

Classes created from an IDL interface

`Account` is an abstract base class that contains all local definitions for the interface `Account`. This class also includes the class method `_narrow`, which will be discussed later. As all interfaces, the C++ class `Account` is derived from the class `CORBA::Object`, which is part of the CORBA library.

`POA_Account` is the skeleton of the interface `Account`. The prefix `POA_` is a convention in accordance with the *Portable Object Adapter* (POA), which is an object adapter described in the CORBA specification. The implementation of the interface `Account` provided by the developer is derived from `POA_Account`.

`Account_var` is a helper class whose instances represent pointers to a CORBA object. The client uses this class to hold a reference to a remote CORBA object. Note that an instance of `Account_var` represents a reference to the CORBA object, not the CORBA object itself. That is, when the `Account_var` instance is destroyed because the flow of execution leaves the current scope, this does not affect the life cycle of the remote CORBA object that will continue to exist.

All IDL interfaces are derived from the C++ class `CORBA::Object`. In some situations the type of an object has to be specialized. The IDL compiler generates the C++ class method `_narrow` for type-safe downcasting. If type-safe specialization is not possible, this method returns a null pointer. Examples in the following sections clarify this point.

3.4.3 C++ Server Implementation

The IDL specification describes only the interface of objects, not the implementation of their behavior. An interface needs to be implemented in a high-level programming language such as C++ or Java. In this section we first introduce the implementation of the account interface using C++. A later section will show the implementation based on Java.

The developer first needs to implement the skeleton generated by the IDL compiler. As mentioned in the previous section, the IDL compiler generates for each IDL interface an abstract base class in C++. In order to implement the abstract base class, we need to derive a class that provides the implementation for each operation specified in the interface (the complete source code for the server appears in Section D.3 on page 293):

Implementing the interface

```
// Implementation for interface Account
class Account_impl : virtual public POA_Account
{
```

```
77: private:
78:   CORBA::Long _balance;
79:
80: public:
81:   Account_impl ()
82:   {
83:     _balance = 0;
84:   }
```

Similar to the naming conventions presented in the last chapter, the implementation of an interface is identified by the suffix `_impl`. The C++ class `Account_impl` inherits from the class `POA_Account`, which represents the skeleton of the interface `Account` that is generated by the IDL compiler. Incoming operation invocations are forwarded from the object adapter to the skeleton, which is responsible for the invocation of the respective operation. The account object maintains a balance, which is the state of that object (line 78). When instantiating a new account object, the balance is initialized to 0 in the constructor (line 83).

The definition of class `Account_impl` continues by providing implementation for the three operations that are specified in interface `Account`. Those three methods are defined as pure virtual in the base class `POA_Account`, and implementing these makes the derived class concrete. The following code excerpt shows the implementation of the method `withdraw`:

```
92:   void withdraw (CORBA::Long amount)
93:   {
94:     cout << "Server: withdraw " << amount << endl;
95:     if (_balance >= amount)
96:       _balance -= amount;
97:     else
98:       cout << "Server: withdraw failed" << endl;
99:   }
```

The implementation of the other two operations `deposit` and `balance` are equally simple. The signature of operation `withdraw` follows the language-mapping rules for C++. In IDL, the operation `withdraw` was declared with just one input parameter of type `long`. This input parameter is mapped to the C++ type `CORBA::Long`. Note that the definition of this type is part of the ORB library.

Initialization on server side

The implementation of the interface `Account` is only part of what is required for a CORBA server. What is still missing on the server side is the main program that initializes the ORB, creates an account object, and then waits for incoming operation invocations. Following is an extract that demonstrates the initialization of the ORB and the object adapter:

```
108:  int
109:  main (int argc, char *argv[])
110:  {
111:    // Initialize the ORB
112:    CORBA::ORB_var orb = CORBA::ORB_init (argc, argv);
113:
114:    // Obtain a reference to the RootPOA and its Manager
115:    CORBA::Object_var poaobj =
116:            orb->resolve_initial_references ("RootPOA");
117:    PortableServer::POA_var poa =
118:            PortableServer::POA::_narrow (poaobj);
119:    PortableServer::POAManager_var mgr =
120:            poa->the_POAManager();
```

As is customary in C++, the entry point of the program is defined through the function `main` (line 109). The initialization of the ORB using the class method `ORB_init` defined in the ORB library is found in line 112. For the input parameters the ORB requires the command line parameters where ORB-specific parameters are automatically processed and removed during initialization.

Bootstrap mechanism to reach first object reference

The return value of class method `ORB_init` is a pointer to the ORB. The ORB is used to access certain functionality of the CORBA platform. For example, the method `resolve_initial_references` in line 116 serves as a simple bootstrap mechanism for obtaining object references for certain services specified in the standard. Each of these services has a unique identification string ("`RootPOA`" in the case of the POA object adapter). It may look a bit awkward, but this is the way to obtain a pointer to the POA. It is interesting to note that the object adapter is treated like a CORBA object. What makes it different from a normal CORBA object is the locality: the reference to a POA object cannot be transmitted as a parameter to another address space.

Type-safe downcast in CORBA

The return value of the method `resolve_initial_references` is of the `CORBA::Object` type, the abstract base class of all CORBA objects. However, the invocation in line 116 actually returns a reference to the POA object that is defined through the type `PortableServer::POA` derived from `CORBA::Object` in the ORB library. Consequently, the reference type must be specialized from `CORBA::Object` to `PortableServer::POA`. This corresponds to a *downcast* in the language C++. A downcast changes the type of a pointer, without changing where the pointer points to. In CORBA, each CORBA object defines a class method `_narrow` that permits type-safe downcast (line 118). Note that variables `poa` and `poaobj` both point to the same object, but they are of different type.

According to the CORBA specification, a POA manager exists for each POA. We will deal with the tasks of the POA manager later. However, a pointer to the POA manager is already stored in variable `mgr` in line 119 for later use. Once the ORB has been initialized, an account object can be instantiated and accessed by remote clients. The following code fragment shows the procedure required:

```
122:   // Create an Account
123:   PortableServer::Servant account_servant =
124:           new Account_impl;
125:
126:   // Activate the Account
127:   CORBA::Object_var the_account =
128:           account_servant->_this();
129:
130:   // Write the object's IOR to a file
131:   CORBA::String_var ior =
132:           orb->object_to_string (the_account);
133:   ofstream of ("account.ior");
134:   of << ior;
135:   of.close ();
```

Servant

The POA distinguishes between an object and a *servant.* A servant provides the implementation of an object. A CORBA object cannot execute operation invocations until it is assigned to a servant. This process is called *activation.* In line 123 only an account servant is initially created. At this point a CORBA object does not yet exist. The life cycles of servants and CORBA objects are independent of one another. Due to the distinction between object and servant, they are not even polymorphic to each other (i.e., the class `POA_Account` is not derived from the class `CORBA::Object`). A call of method `_this` (line 128) generated by the IDL compiler activates the CORBA account object. The invocation of `_this` produces the following results:

Implicit object activation with POA

1. The object is activated by the association between servant and object; that is, it can receive and process incoming operation invocations.

2. A reference to the object is produced and returned. This reference can be forwarded to the client.

Interoperable object reference

This raises the question of how a client obtains the reference to the account object. A portable solution that works with all compliant CORBA implementations is the generation of an *Interoperable Object Reference* (IOR). This IOR must then be forwarded to clients over a transport mechanism that is located outside of CORBA. The reference to the account object is converted into an IOR using the ORB method `object_to_string` (line 131). Then the IOR of the account object is written to a file called "account.ior" (lines 133–135).

Main loop of ORB

After the new CORBA object has been created and activated, the ORB on the server side enters an event loop that waits for incoming operation invocations:

```
139:    mgr->activate ();
140:    orb->run();
```

First, however, like other CORBA objects, the object adapter must be activated (line 139). The POA manager mentioned earlier has the task of activating the POA object. The only thing that is still required is the invocation of the method `run` of the ORB, whereupon the ORB enters an event loop that waits for incoming operation invocations. In our sample application, the execution of the method `run` never returns. The server process responds to client requests until it is terminated manually.

3.4.4 C++ Client Implementation

The server explained in the previous section runs in its own UNIX process. As we saw earlier, it has its own main function. The last part of our CORBA application is the implementation of the client. In this section we demonstrate the implementation done in C++. It is important to note up front that the client has its own main function and will run as a separate UNIX process. The complete source code for the client can be found in Section D.4 on page 295. Again the entry point is defined by the function `main`. The following code fragment shows the ORB initialization on the client side:

```
int
main (int argc, char *argv[])
{
  // Initialize the ORB
  CORBA::ORB_var orb = CORBA::ORB_init (argc, argv);
```

The initialization is identical to that of the server. However, unlike the server, the client does not need to initialize the object adapter. The POA only needs to be initialized when the process contains server objects that can be accessed by remote clients. Since this is not the case for our account client, there is no need for POA initialization. Once the ORB is initialized, the IOR of the account object is read from a file:

Client connects to an account object

```
162:    // Connect to the Account
163:    ifstream f ("account.ior");
164:    string ior;
165:    f >> ior;
166:    CORBA::Object_var obj =
167:            orb->string_to_object (ior.c_str());
168:    Account_var account = Account::_narrow (obj);
```

Note that the file "account.ior" is the same as the server. Therefore, the client reads the content of that file that the server wrote before. This is how the client obtains the knowledge of where the server is located. As we will see later, this information is contained in the IOR, which itself is stored in the file "account.ior". The ORB is used to transform the IOR into an object reference (line 167). The result is a reference of the type CORBA::Object. Similar to what happens for a POA object on the server side, the reference type has to be downcast because the IOR actually refers to an account object. For type-safe downcast the IDL compiler generates a class method with the name _narrow for each interface (line 168).

Once a reference to the bank object exists, operation invocations can be executed on it. The following code fragment demonstrates a possible scenario:

```
170:    // Deposit and withdraw some money
171:    account->deposit (700);
172:    cout << "Client: balance is "
173:         << account->balance () << endl;
174:    account->withdraw (50);
175:    cout << "Client: balance is "
176:         << account->balance () << endl;
177:    account->withdraw (200);
178:    cout << "Client: balance is "
179:         << account->balance () << endl;
```

In lines 170–179 some deposit and withdraw operations are being carried out on the remote account. After each operation, the client prints out the current account balance. Our sample application does not provide an explicit mechanism for the deletion of objects. The question arises of what happens with the account object within the server process when a client process is terminated. Because CORBA does not provide a distributed garbage collection, the account object continues to exist after the client is terminated. If the client is run a second time, it will connect to the same account objects.

CORBA has no distributed garbage collection

3.5 COMPILING AND EXECUTING THE APPLICATION

Now that the sample application has been described, we continue this chapter with a look at some of the practical aspects of application programming under CORBA. The generation of executable program files and their subsequent execution are explained in the following two subsections. The descriptions are specific to MICO but can easily be applied with little modification to other CORBA implementations. The following explanations assume that MICO is installed on the system where the application is compiled.

3.5.1 Compiling the Application

Files of sample application

The individual source files of the application are stored in different files according to functionality. The following files are relevant to the account application:

account.idl: IDL specification of the interfaces (see Section 3.4.1).

account.cc: Contains stubs and skeletons of object interfaces. This file is generated automatically by the IDL compiler.

server.cc: Implementation of the server (see Section 3.4.3).

client.cc: Implementation of the client (see Section 3.4.4).

Compiling and linking the application

This decomposition of the application into different translation units enables the account application to be generated through the following command sequence based on MICO:

```
idl account.idl
mico-c++ -I. -c account.cc -o account.o
mico-c++ -I. -c server.cc -o server.o
mico-c++ -I. -c client.cc -o client.o
mico-ld -o server server.o account.o -lmicoX.Y.Z
mico-ld -o client client.o account.o -lmicoX.Y.Z
```

The command `idl` invokes the IDL compiler (line 1). The execution of the command results in the creation of the file `account.cc`, which contains the proxy objects. The shell scripts `mico-c++` and `mico-ld` are part of the MICO installation and encapsulate invocations of the C++ compiler and the linker under UNIX. The object files of the individual translation units are created in lines 2–4. The executable program of the server is linked in line 5 and the program of the client in line 6. The library `micoX.Y.Z` contains the ORB library of MICO. The placeholder `X.Y.Z` represents the three-digit version number of the MICO installation.

3.5.2 Executing the Application

The compilation and linking of the account application produce two executable program files: one each for the client and the server. The server first has to be called up before the client can be started. As explained earlier, the server writes the IOR of the account object it creates to a file called "`account.ior`". Note that the IOR will be different every time the server is executed. This is done on purpose to make sure the client notices a server crash. If the IOR were the same with every server execution, the client might not notice if the server crashes and restarts. The following dump shows a possible content of file "`account.ior`":

```
IOR:010000001000000049444c3a4163636f756e743a312e30\
00010000000000002c000000010100000a0000003132372e\
302e302e3100168514000000 2f31393938332f313036313334\
373034342f5f30
```

Except for the prefix `IOR:`, the IOR is a sequence of hexadecimal values. The exact content of the IOR depends on the system on which the server is started. MICO has the tool `iordump` that can be used to decode the IOR and display it in a readable form. For the above IOR the tool shows the following information:

```
    Repo Id:  IDL:Account:1.0

IIOP Profile
    Version:  1.0
    Address:  inet:127.0.0.1:34070
        Key:  2f 31 39 39 38 33 2f 31 30 36 31 33 34 37 30 34
              34 2f 5f 30
```

The repository ID indicates the interface type of the object referred to by the IOR. In CORBA the interface type is represented by a character string con- *Repository ID* sisting of three components. The prefix `IDL` indicates that the interface is based on CORBA IDL. The character string `Account` is the name of the interface that is implemented by the referenced object. The suffix `1.0` provides the version number of the interface.

Transport address

Another IOR component is the information about the transport address. In our example the address is a TCP address, which is indicated by the prefix `inet`. It is followed by the TCP address, which consists of an IP address and a port number.

The IP address and port number are not sufficient to locate a CORBA object because they only address one process on a specific host. But this one process can contain several CORBA objects. Another component of the IOR, called the *object key*, is required to locate a CORBA object with respect to a process. The triple (IP address, port number, object key) uniquely identifies a CORBA object. From the client's perspective, the object key is just a sequence of octets. The client does not need to understand the inner structure of this byte sequence. Only the server that created the object key uses it to locate the target object.

Object key

The client can be executed once the server has been started and the IOR has been written to the file "`account.ior`". The client reads the content of this file to establish a connection to the remote account object located in the server. Note that it is possible to copy the IOR to a different system (e.g., via FTP or email) and run the client from a remote machine. Since the TCP/IP address is contained in the IOR, the client will be able to establish a connection with the server. Running the client yields the following output on the console:

Client output

```
Client: balance is 700
Client: balance is 650
Client: balance is 450
```

As the client produces the above messages, the server also writes some log messages to its console:

```
Server: deposit 700
Server: balance 700
Server: withdraw 50
Server: balance 650
Server: withdraw 200
Server: balance 450
```

Note that the output of the nondistributed version of the account implementation introduced in Section 2.4.2 on page 27 is just an interleaved version of the console output written by the client and the server. The client can be restarted any number of times as long as the server is running. Since the account object in the server saves the balance between successive invocations of the client, the output of client and server will change slightly with each run of the client. With each execution the client first deposits 700, and then withdraws 50 followed by 200, so that the final balance of the server will be effectively increased by 450.

3.6 APPLICATION DEVELOPMENT IN JAVA

The previous section demonstrated how to implement the account scenario in C++. Both client and server were implemented in the same language. One of the strengths of CORBA is that it supports heterogneity at the programming language level. In the following we will reimplement the same application in Java. The resulting Java code will compile on any CORBA-compliant Java ORB. Here we will use the free JDK Java platform released by Sun.

3.6.1 Java Server Implementation

We start our explanations of the Java version with the server. Just like in the C++ version, the implementation of the server is based on an IDL specification. It is important to note that the Java version is based on the same IDL specification used for the C++ implementation; that is, the Java implementation of the account server is also based on the IDL introduced in Section 3.4.1. It should become clearer now why the IDL specification is also referred to as a contract: the contract is binding no matter what programming language or what CORBA implementation is used.

Since C++ is obviously quite different from Java, different IDL language-mapping rules have to be used. As explained earlier, the CORBA standard defines different language-mapping rules for different programming languages. This will become immediately evident by looking at the implementation of the IDL interface `Account` (the complete source code of the Java server-side implementation can be found in Section D.5 on page 296):

```
class AccountImpl extends AccountPOA
{
  private int _balance;

  public AccountImpl ()
```

```
195:   {
196:     _balance = 0;
197:   }
```

This code fragment resembles the server implementation for C++. Here again the implementation class inherits from the skeleton generated by the IDL compiler. But in contrast to C++, the name of the skeleton class is different. In C++, is called `POA_Account`; in Java it is called `AccountPOA` (line 190). These differences often have historic reasons. Apart from that difference, the Java version also defines a private member variable for the account balance (line 192) that is initialized to 0 in the constructor (lines 194–197). The implementations of the three account operations `deposit`, `withdraw`, and `balance` are as one would expect. Just as for the C++ version, we show the implementation of the operation `withdraw` in Java:

```
203:   public void withdraw (int amount)
204:   {
205:     System.out.println ("Server: withdraw " + amount);
206:     if (_balance >= amount)
207:       _balance -= amount;
208:     else
209:       System.out.println ("Server: withdraw failed");
210:   }
```

The only noteworthy detail to point out is the language mapping of the IDL type `long`. Whereas in C++ the type `CORBA::Long` was used to represent this IDL type, Java simply uses the integral type `int` as can be seen in the signature of the operation `withdraw` (line 203). Since Java is identical for all platforms, it is guaranteed that the Java type `int` has the same value range as the CORBA type `long`.

We turn our attention to the implementation of the main function, which is defined in Java by the static class method `main`:

```
219: public class Server {
220:
221:   public static void main (String args[])
222:   {
223:     try {
224:       // Initialize the ORB
225:       ORB orb = ORB.init (args, null);
226:
```

```
        // Obtain a reference to the RootPOA and its Manager
        org.omg.CORBA.Object poaobj =
            orb.resolve_initial_references ("RootPOA");
        POA poa = POAHelper.narrow (poaobj);
        POAManager mgr = poa.the_POAManager();
```

This code excerpt is identical in functionionality to the C++ version. There are only some noteworthy comments with regards to the IDL-to-Java language mapping. First, the language mapping does not prescribe the generation of _var pointers. In C++ the IDL generated a C++ type Account_var from the IDL interface Account. The purpose of Account_var was to serve as a smart pointer that automatically disposes of any local memory when no longer needed. Since Java has a garbage collector, this behavior is given for free by the Java runtime system.

Second, the way type-safe downcasts are done is different in Java. The IDL-to-Java language mapping mandates that a so-called *helper class* is to be generated for each IDL interface. For example, the helper class of IDL interface Account is the Java class AccountHelper, which is automatically generated by the IDL compiler. Likewise, the helper class of class POA is called POAHelper. The familiar narrow method that was used in C++ is declared as a static class member method of this helper class.

Following the ORB initialization, an account object can be instantiated and accessed by remote clients. The following code fragment shows the procedure required:

```
233: // Create an Account servant
234: AccountImpl account_servant = new AccountImpl ();
235:
236: // Activate the Account object
237: org.omg.CORBA.Object the_account =
238:                         account_servant._this();
239:
240: // Write the object's IOR to a file
241: String ior = orb.object_to_string (the_account);
242: java.io.FileWriter file =
243:     new java.io.FileWriter ("account.ior", false);
244: file.write (ior + "\n", 0, ior.length() + 1);
245: file.flush();
246: file.close();
```

This code excerpt is again very similar to the C++ version. An account servant is created (line 234), activated by calling the _this() method (line 238) and the IOR of the account object written to a file called "`account.ior`" (lines 240–246). After the new CORBA object has been created and activated, the ORB on the server side enters an event loop that waits for incoming operation invocations:

Main loop of ORB

```
250: mgr.activate();
251: orb.run();
```

3.6.2 Java Client Implementation

We complete our short CORBA tutorial by presenting the client-side implementation of the account application. The following code is identical in terms of functionality with the C++ version of the client presented in Section 3.4.4 on page 49. The code fragment below is included in its entirety in Section D.6 on page 298:

Reimplementation of client in Java

```
account.deposit (700);
System.out.println ("Client: balance is " +
                    account.balance ());
account.withdraw (50);
System.out.println ("Client: balance is " +
                    account.balance ());
account.withdraw (200);
System.out.println ("Client: balance is " +
                    account.balance());
```

3.6.3 Compiling and Executing the Java Implementation

The way to compile the application presented in the previous two subsections depends on which Java CORBA implementation is being used. Sun's reference implementation of the Java language also includes a complete CORBA implementation. This implementation, known as the Java Developer Kit (JDK), can be downloaded for free from Sun's Java Web site *java.sun.com*. Using the JDK, the Java version of the account example can be compiled as follows:

```
idlj -fall Account.idl
javac Client.java
javac Server.java
```

`idlj` is Sun's IDL compiler that generates all the necessary stubs and skeletons out of the IDL specification. Note that because every public Java class has to reside in its own source file, the IDL compiler generates numerous files. It is sufficient to compile the files `Client.java` and `Server.java`. The Java compiler will automatically compile all other dependent `.java` files.

After the application is successfully compiled, it can simply be executed by first running the server and then the client. The server writes the IOR of the account object to a file called "`account.ior`", which the client subsequently reads.

Just before concluding the discussion of the account example, there is one point worth mentioning again. We have explained the implementation of the account application in the languages C++ and Java. It is important to note that the resulting client and server implementations can be arbitrarily mixed. There are two clients and two servers, each one written in Java and in C++. This results in four different permutations to combine a client and a server (e.g., Java client with Java server, Java client with C++ server, etc.). Since all clients and servers speak IIOP over the network, all those permutations are permissible. This is the very core of interoperability.

3.7 THE BOOTSTRAPPING PROBLEM

The problem of how the client obtains the first object reference of a server is called the *bootstrapping problem.* The problem with bootstrapping a CORBA application is how the client is given an initial object reference. In order to solve this problem, information has to flow from server to client (i.e., this information is the object reference to the server). But since the client does not yet know about the server, this flow of information has to happen outside of the CORBA framework. This means that we cannot use CORBA to transmit the initial object reference.

A subsequent section will introduce the CORBA naming service. A naming service maps symbolic names to CORBA object references, just like the Domain Naming Service (DNS) of the Internet maps DNS names to IP addresses. But when carefully thinking about the bootstrapping problem, the question arises how the client knows about the naming service. We always end up at a point where a client needs to obtain an initial object reference. There are different solutions to this problem, and it is essential to understand all of the alternatives. There are several, and there is no "best" one; you can choose which one fits your expectations best.

3.7.1 File-Based Bootstrapping

In our sample application we introduced in this chapter, we have used what is called *file-based bootstrapping.* The initial reference to the server object was relayed to the client by way of a file. The object reference is stringified and written to a file. The client can then read the content of that file and convert it back to an object reference. File-based bootstrapping is very attractive if server and client share a file system, either a local one or via NFS. Otherwise, the file has to be transported over the network, for example, by FTP, WWW, or email.

3.7.2 Object URLs

CORBA now offers the use of "object URLs" instead of stringified object references. The term URL stands for *Uniform Resource Locator*. A URL is the standard way to name resources in the World Wide Web. CORBA has adopted this naming schema to obtain an initial object reference. The two object URLs we describe here have the prefix `file:` or `http:`. The former allows us to read a stringified object reference from a file; the latter allows to read a stringified object reference from a Web server. With `file:`, we can bypass reading a string out of a file, but directly use a `file:` URL with `string_to_object`, as in

```
obj = orb->string_to_object ("file:///tmp/account.ior");
```

Unfortunately, `file:` URLs require an absolute file name. If the client expects a file in the current directory, it would have to construct an absolute file name with the help of the `getcwd` system call. When using an `http:` URL, the server's administrator puts a file holding the stringified object reference up on a Web server, and you can directly reference it from everywhere, as in

```
obj = orb->string_to_object ("http://www.acme.org/account.ior");
```

which loads the object reference from the Web site *www.acme.org*. The benefit of the `http:` URL is that client and server do not need to share the same file system.

3.7.3 Command Line Arguments

One of the problems in bootstrapping a CORBA application is that the initial object reference is often hardcoded in the client application. This makes the client application dependent on many factors such as file name and location.

A better way is to pass the initial object reference as a command line argument to the client. The CORBA specification offers a standard way to do this via the `-ORBInitRef` option. As with all command line parameters that begin with `-ORB`, this option is processed during the initialization of the ORB (this is the reason the command line arguments are passed as parameters to the `ORB_init()` method). An IOR can be passed in the following way:

```
client -ORBInitRef Account=file:///tmp/account.ior
```

The application can then read the argument using the `resolve_initial_references()` method offered by the ORB. Here is a little code excerpt:

```
CORBA::Object_var obj =
    orb->resolve_initial_references ("Account");
```

The argument `Account` that is passed as an argument to `resolve_initial_references()` is the same as was used with the `-ORBInitRef` command line option. This way, several initial references can be passed to the application if necessary.

3.8 NAMING SERVICE

The naming service is an essential component of any distributed application. Since virtually all applications will need this service, we give some details on how to use it. The CORBA standard contains a specification of a naming service. The explanations and examples presented in this section are independent of a specific implementation and should work with all CORBA-compliant ORBs. We first provide a short overview of the CORBA naming service and then augment the familiar account application to make use of the naming service.

3.8.1 Overview

In a distributed environment, you need to address the problem of propagating references from server objects to clients. Earlier in this chapter we have introduced different solutions to this bootstrapping problem. The only portable and CORBA-compliant solution is to pass stringified object references in one way or another. But even after passing the initial object reference, finding an object is a nontrivial task. A solution to this problem is the topic of this section.

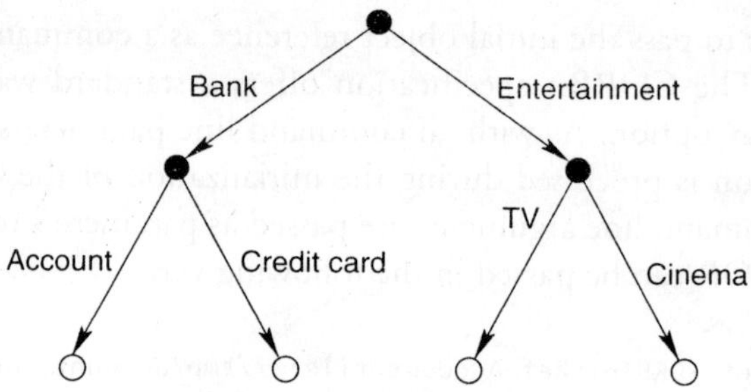

FIGURE 3.6 A naming graph.

Naming service

The CORBA standard as issued by the OMG describes a *naming service* as part of the Common Object Services Specification (COSS). In order to understand this standard, we need to introduce a bit of terminology. As already mentioned earlier, a naming service maps names to addresses. This mapping is called a *binding* in CORBA. The addresses actually are object references or, to be more specific, instances of the IDL type `Object`.

Naming context

Naming graph

A name always exists relative to a *naming context*. A naming context is itself an object that can be assigned a name. This way a hierarchical namespace can be constructed. In a mathematical sense, all bindings in a CORBA environment can be modeled by a directed graph, also called a *naming graph* in CORBA terminology. The nodes in Figure 3.6 denote objects, and the labeled vertices denote references. The black nodes are naming-context objects maintained by the naming service, and the white nodes are application-specific objects.

There is no need for a unique root, but all vertices stemming from one node need to be unique. A name is always relative to a naming context; there are no absolute names in CORBA. A name is therefore an ordered sequence of components relative to a naming context. Since naming contexts are themselves CORBA objects, the naming graph can span host boundaries.

Name consists of identifier and kind attributes

A component of a name is a tuple consisting of an *identifier attribute* and a *kind attribute* (this distinction is not shown in Figure 3.6). The purpose of the kind attribute is to distinguish between different kinds of names with the same identifier. Both identifier and kind attributes are represented in the CORBA naming service through IDL type `string` and are not interpreted by the naming service.

3.8.2 Name Server Daemon

While the CORBA specification defines the interface to the naming service, it does not prescribe how to implement it. The most common approach is to

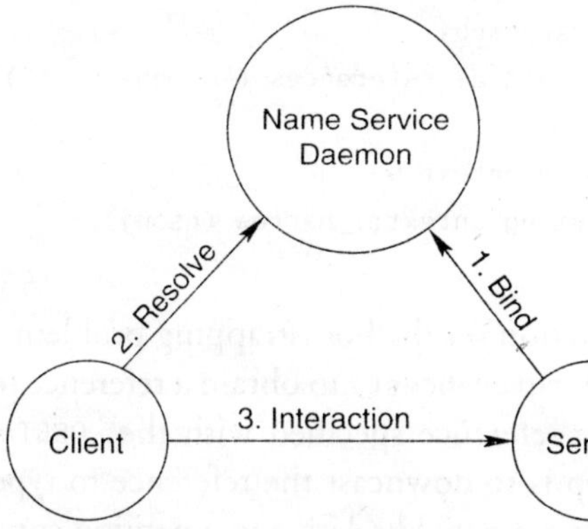

FIGURE 3.7 The trading triangle.

implement the service through a so-called daemon process. This daemon runs as a separate process and replies to queries from clients and servers.

The so-called trading triangle of naming service daemon, client, and server is depicted in Figure 3.7. As the first step, the server binds its object reference under a certain name with the naming service. In the second step, the client resolves a name to an object reference using the appropriate interface offered by the naming service. Once the client has obtained a reference to the server as a response from the naming service, it starts to interact with the server. In the following sections we present a step-by-step approach to show how the trading triangle works in practice.

3.8.3 Example

This section provides a little example of how to make use of the naming service. It augments the account application discussed in previous sections to make use of the naming service. Since there are only minor changes to the source code discussed so far, we have not included the complete versions in the appendix. The home page for this book includes the complete version.

SERVER SIDE

First, we discuss the server implementation using the naming service. Conceptually, the server creates an account object as discussed earlier. Then the server binds the reference to this object with the naming service. Since the naming service is itself implemented as a CORBA object, the first step is to obtain a reference to this object, which is shown in the following code excerpt: *Server implementation*

```
CORBA::Object_var nsobj =
  orb->resolve_initial_references ("NameService");

CosNaming::NamingContext_var nc =
  CosNaming::NamingContext::_narrow (nsobj);
```

As discussed in the section on the bootstrapping problem, we use the ORB method `resolve_initial_references()` to obtain a reference to the naming service. This will return the reference specified with the `-ORBInitRef` command line option. The next step is to downcast the reference to type `NamingContext`. Remember that all objects are named relative to a naming context.

The next step is to establish a new binding for the account object. We chose "`myAccount`" for the name, but without a specific kind attribute. The predefined type `CosNaming::Name` corresponds to an ordered sequence of tuples consisting of identifier and kind attributes, as described earlier. Here is the IDL specification of `Name` as defined in the COSS standard. This excerpt is taken straight from the CORBA specification for the naming service:

Specification of `CosNaming::Name`

```
// IDL
module CosNaming {
  typedef string Istring;

  struct NameComponent {
    Istring id;
    Istring kind;
  };
  typedef sequence <NameComponent> Name;
};
```

Now that we have defined a name for the account object, all that is left to do is to create a binding. This is simply done using the `bind()` operation of the naming-context object. The account object will become known under the name "`myAccount`". Here is the code for the bind operation:

```
CosNaming::Name name;
name.length (1);
name[0].id = (const char*) "myAccount";
name[0].kind = (const char *) "";
nc->bind (name, the_account);
```

Once the bind operation has completed, the naming service daemon has stored the binding for "myAccount" to the new account object. The server then completes its initialization as previously outlined and enters the event loop waiting for client requests.

CLIENT SIDE

Once the server has created a new binding for the account object, a client can query the name server. This operation is called resolve(). The only two things the client needs to know are the initial reference to the naming service and the name of the object. The former is passed as a command line argument in a similar way as shown for the server, and the latter is the name "myAccount", which must be known to the client. The following code excerpt shows how the resolve operation happens after the ORB initialization:

```
CORBA::Object_var nsobj =
  orb->resolve_initial_references ("NameService");

CosNaming::NamingContext_var nc =
  CosNaming::NamingContext::_narrow (nsobj);

CosNaming::Name name;
name.length (1);
name[0].id = (const char*) "myAccount";
name[0].kind = (const char *) "";

CORBA::Object_var obj;
obj = nc->resolve (name);

Account_var account = Account::_narrow (obj);
```

The name, which is again of IDL type Name, must match the name that the server used during the creation of the binding. Now we use the operation resolve() to query the name server for an appropriate object. Since a binding maps names to object references, we need to downcast the result of the resolve operation to type Account.

The home page for this book contains the complete source code of the account example with all the variations discussed here. Also included are UNIX shell scripts that facilitate the execution of the application. In particular there is one script that launches the naming service daemon as well as the client and server to demonstrate how the trading triangle works in practice.

3.9 SUMMARY

This chapter presented an overview of the CORBA specification published by the OMG. Only some of the details of the specification could be highlighted. We recommend that the reader refer to secondary literature on the subject. We also suggest that you take a look at the original specification for the CORBA standard. Although the standard is not a substitute for a textbook on CORBA, it offers valuable information that is not available in many books. The CORBA specification is available free of charge from the OMG Web site at *www.omg.org*.

The example we used in this chapter presented the CORBA application from the point of view of an applications programmer. The CORBA standard specifies the interface to middleware for compliant ORB implementations. Even if the technology used in the different ORB implementations is not the same, the applications (such as our account application) created on them are portable. In the remaining chapters of this book, we will be looking at middleware from the point of view of the systems programmer instead of an applications programmer. We first present μORB in detail and then MICO.

Chapter 4

μORB

We use this chapter to present μORB—a mini-CORBA implementation. Because μORB implements a subset of CORBA, the technical terms used in this chapter are CORBA based. However, the concepts introduced translate to other middleware technologies as well. The goal is to use a compact, easy-to-understand version to describe the elementary components of a middleware platform. Although μORB only comprises a few hundred lines of program code, it is still possible to execute the bank application on it. Moreover, the bank application under μORB is interoperable over IIOP to its CORBA counterpart; that is, the clients and servers of μORB and CORBA can be combined in any combination.

μORB understands a limited IIOP

Our aim is to keep the implementation of μORB as compact as possible. Consequently, we have limited its functionality considerably compared to CORBA-compliant middleware. Despite these limitations, we are able to explain the key concepts that are helpful in understanding the Mico architecture. Moreover, μORB is suitable as an experimental platform for other modifications. The complete source code for μORB is available at *www.mico.org/textbook/*.

4.1 μORB ARCHITECTURE

From a programming standpoint, μORB is a C++ program library that is linked to an application. Figure 4.1 shows the relationship between μORB, an application that is run on μORB, and the underlying operating system. The internal structure of μORB, which is highlighted in Figure 4.1 by a black border, is

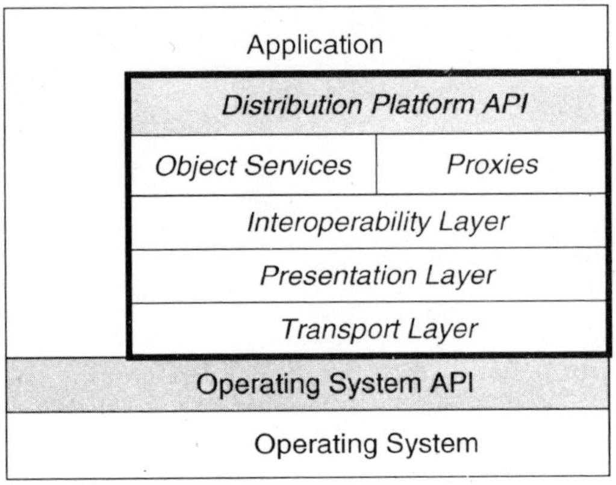

FIGURE 4.1 Components of μORB.

based on a layered model. The arrangement of the components over the layering shows their interdependency. A layer offers the layer above it a service and in turn uses the functionality of the layer below.

Layers of μORB

μORB consists of five separate layers:

Transport layer: The transport layer allows the exchange of data beyond address space boundaries. Its functionality is typically based on that of the operating system.

Presentation layer: The presentation layer structures a byte sequence and hides the differences between hardware architectures in terms of how they present data.

Interoperability layer: The interoperability layer implements a reduced version of the IIOP protocol.

Proxies: The proxy objects include the application-specific stubs and skeletons that guarantee type-safe access to objects of the bank application.

Object services: This layer offers generic object services, such as the management of object references.

4.2 TRANSPORT LAYER

A *transport layer* is required for transporting data beyond the boundaries of an address space. From the point of view of the transport layer, the data being transported consist of unstructured byte sequences. The transport layer is implemented by a concrete *transport mechanism*. The task of the transport layer is to abstract from platform-specific transport mechanisms and to offer a homogeneous interface to the presentation layer. The transport layer is typically merely a wrapper of the network functions offered by an operating system. Similar to the introduction of the bank scenario, an analysis of requirements presents the characteristics of the transport layer that form the basis for a design:

Transport layer links address spaces

1. The transport layer guarantees a reliable end-to-end connection between precisely two address spaces.
2. Data can be sent bidirectionally in the form of unstructured byte sequences of any length.
3. Different transport mechanisms should be supported.

The transport layer offers reliable end-to-end connections; that is, details of the underlying transport mechanism are hidden above the transport layer. Many transport mechanisms, such as TCP, already offer reliable connections. However, implementation of the transport layer using an unreliable transport mechanism makes it more difficult to guarantee suitable semantics above the transport layer.

The requirement that the transport layer should link exactly two address spaces together is aimed at reducing the complexity of the middleware. If this restriction did not exist, the administration of the transport channels between various address spaces would be complex. As a consequence, μORB only permits the objects belonging to an application to be distributed among exactly two address spaces.

The transport layer views data that are exchanged between a client and a server over the transport layer as unstructured, variable-length byte sequences. However, the transport layer is not expected to transmit continuous media, a capability required by multimedia applications. On the other hand, the assumption is that it will support different transport mechanisms.

The following use case suggests the type of modeling required at the class level:

Applications scenario of the transport layer

1. The server establishes a communication end point and waits for a connection setup request.

2. The client creates a communication end point and connects it to the server.

3. The client sends data and waits for a response.

4. The server receives the data of the client and then sends a response.

5. After the client receives the response from the server, both close their communication end points.

Note that in this use case the words "client" and "server" do not refer to objects. They refer instead to roles taken in interaction with the transport layer, thus indicating an asymmetry in the use of the transport layer. Clients and servers define a communications channel on the basis of the corresponding communication end points. The communication end points are specified by an address that represents a mutual consent between client and server. An address of the transport layer typically contains a network address that refers to the actual transport mechanism. Different transport mechanisms can have different address formats and details. Thus a generally valid format does not exist.

Classes `Buffer`, `Address`, and `Transport` model transport layer

Three classes are introduced for modeling the transport layer: `Buffer`, `Address`, and `Transport`. The class `Buffer` represents the storage area associated with a chunk of memory. Instances of this class are used as containers for the unstructured byte sequences that are transmitted between address spaces via a transport mechanism. The interface of the class `Buffer` offers methods for setting up and managing a memory chunk.

`Address` serves as a factory for `Transport` instances

The class `Address` represents the address of a particular transport mechanism, and the class `Transport` represents the transport mechanism itself. The address here is used as a *factory* for the transport mechanism. The two classes themselves are abstract because they only form the interface for the actual transport mechanism. Therefore, two concrete classes have to be defined for each transport mechanism: one for the address and one for the transport mechanism itself. These classes are derived from the abstract base classes `Address` and `Transport`. Figure 4.2 shows a TCP-based transport mechanism in UML notation.

The preceding use case clarifies the use of the transport layer and can be translated into the following C++ code fragment:

```
// Server
TCPAddress saddr ("localhost", 1234);
Transport *server_transport = saddr.create_transport ();
```

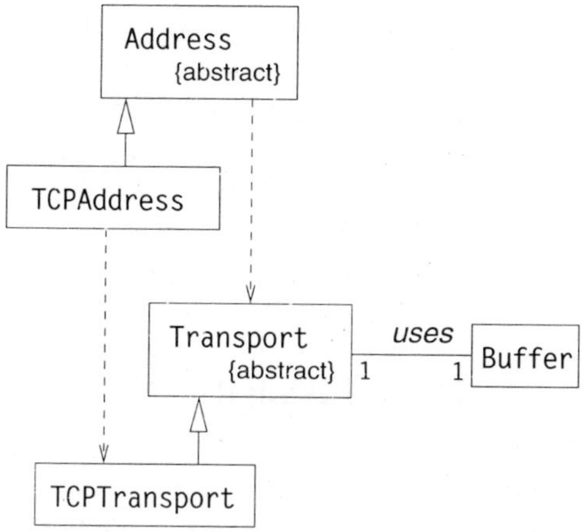

FIGURE 4.2 UML class diagram of transport layer.

```
 4:  server_transport->accept ();
 5:
 6:  Buffer* recv_buf = new Buffer;
 7:  int r = server_transport->recv (recv_buf, 10);
 8:  server_transport->close ();
 9:
10:  // Client
11:  Buffer* buf = ...
12:  TCPAddress caddr ("localhost", 1234);
13:  Transport *client_transport = caddr.create_transport ();
14:  client_transport->open ();
15:  client_transport->send (buf);
16:  client_transport->close ();
```

Transport mechanism on server side

The transport mechanism used here is based on TCP/IP, which explains why instances of the class TCPAddress are used. A tuple (*computer name, port number*) establishes the communication end point for client and server (lines 2 and 12). The server generates the communication end point from the address in line 3, and using the method accept() waits for a connection setup request from the client. This method blocks the server until the client sets up a connection. The server then creates a data area using the class Buffer (line 6) and waits until a maximum of 10 bytes are received (line 7). The maximum number of bytes to be received is indicated as a parameter of the method recv(). The result that this method returns is the exact number of bytes received. The method close() is then used on the server side to terminate the connection to the client (line 8).

Transport mechanism on client side

The client proceeds in a similar way. However, instead of waiting for an incoming connection setup request, it initiates the connection to the server using the method `open()` (line 14). The method `send()` then transports a previously created data area to the server in line 15. The entire data area is sent without any transformation of the data. In line 16 the client terminates the connection to the server.

4.3 PRESENTATION LAYER

Presentation layer structures a byte sequence

The task of the transport layer presented in the last section is to transport unstructured byte sequences between address spaces. The byte sequence naturally has an inner structure since the actual parameters of remote operation invocations are coded in it. The task of the presentation layer is to structure byte sequences. The class `Buffer` that has already been discussed serves as the link between the presentation and the transport layers.

Common Data Representation

μORB implements conventions of the CORBA standard to be interoperable with CORBA-based middleware. The presentation layer is defined within the CORBA specification through the *Common Data Representation* (CDR), the rules of which we discuss below.

4.3.1 Value Ranges of Types

The presentation layer must be able to represent instances of different data types in the form of byte sequences. Some data types were already used in the bank scenario, such as the type `ULong` for representing a sum of money. Until now it has been implicitly assumed that there is an agreement about the semantics of the data types. This agreement is independent of any specific programming language and is valid in the entire domain where the middleware is used. For each programming language the mapping of the types used in the middleware to the types defined in the programming language has to be provided.

Elementary and constructed types

The first step in defining the presentation layer therefore consists of a specification of the data types occurring in the system. A distinction is usually made between *elementary* and *constructed* types. Elementary types, also called *basic types*, define atomic types, such as `Long`, `Short`, and `Char`. In addition to the atomic or indivisible types, there are constructed types such as `struct`, `union`, `array`, and `sequence`. The value ranges of constructed types is dependent on the value ranges of the basic types because in the end the definition of a constructed type is always a composition of a sequence of basic types. Table 4.1 summarizes

TABLE 4.1 Value ranges

Type	Value range
`Boolean`	Binary value
`Char`	8-bit ISO Latin 1 8859.1 characters
`Octet`	8-bit value
`Short`	Integer value in interval $[-2^{15} \cdots 2^{15}-1]$
`UShort`	Integer value in interval $[0 \cdots 2^{16}-1]$
`Long`	Integer value in interval $[-2^{31} \cdots 2^{31}-1]$
`ULong`	Integer value in interval $[0 \cdots 2^{32}-1]$
`String`	Sequence of `Char` instances
`sequence`	Sequence of instances of an arbitrary type
`struct`	Aggregation of arbitrary types
`enum`	Enumeration with maximum 2^{32} elements

the types used here along with their respective value ranges. No types other than those listed in Table 4.1 are permitted in μORB. The value ranges match the ones that the CDR defines for the corresponding types.

4.3.2 Representation of Type Instances

The stipulation of the range of values for the types that occur in a system says nothing about how they are represented physically. The following factors have to be considered in the context of the presentation layer:

Endianness: Hardware architectures differ from one another in their physical representation of basic types.

Alignment: The alignment of basic types affects the performance of storage access.

Complex types: How are instances of constructed types represented?

We will deal with each of these points below.

ENDIANNESS

Hardware architectures may specify different coding rules for simple numeric values. For example, due to its range of values, the type `ULong` from Table 4.1 requires 4 bytes for its representation. If b_1, b_2, b_3, and b_4 are these 4 bytes, then the represented value of the type `ULong` is derived from the formula $b_1 \times 2^0 + b_2 \times 2^8 + b_3 \times 2^{16} + b_4 \times 2^{24}$. Depending on the order of $b_1 \cdots b_4$ in memory, the architecture is called either *Little Endian* or *Big Endian* (see Figure 4.3).

Little Endian and Big Endian

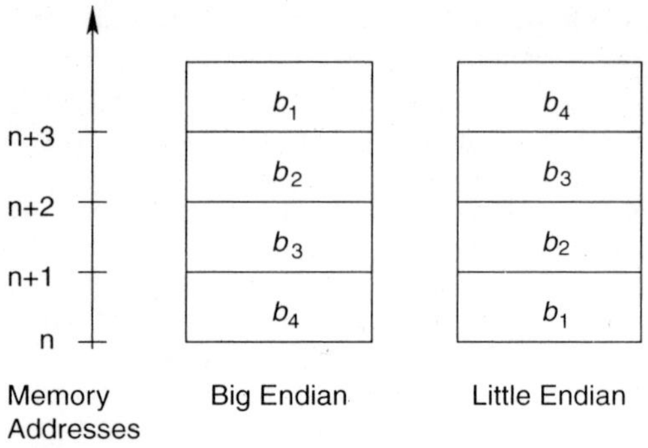

FIGURE 4.3 Different arrangements in the representation of a ULong.

The following portable C++ code fragment establishes whether the hardware architecture it was executed on is a Little or a Big Endian system. The idea is to find out whether the order in memory is the byte sequence 1,0,0,0 (Little Endian) or 0,0,0,1 (Big Endian) for the value 1.

```
union {
  long l;
  char c[sizeof (long)];
} u;
u.l = 1;
if (u.c[0] == 0)  // Host is big endian
```

The CDR in the CORBA specification specifies support for the coding procedures Little Endian and Big Endian. The presentation layer of μORB must therefore be able to deal with both coding procedures.

ALIGNMENT

It is not only how data are ordered in the main memory of a computer but also their alignment that is important. Typically, it is not individual bytes but precisely defined groups of the bytes that are read from memory through a read operation. The reason is that the memory blocks of a system are not arranged in individual bytes but in multiples thereof. Therefore, it makes sense to align an instance of a ULong at a boundary because otherwise two read operations would be required from main memory. Consequently, the usual procedure is to use padding when coding more extensive data in order to guarantee the data are aligned at integer multiples. Although this effectively increases the length of the byte sequence being transmitted, it makes access to the individual data

Padding

TABLE 4.2 Size and alignment of base types

Type	Size	Alignment
`Boolean`	8 bits	1
`Char`	8 bits	1
`Octet`	8 bits	1
`Short`	2 bytes	2
`UShort`	2 bytes	2
`Long`	4 bytes	4
`ULong`	4 bytes	4
`enum`	4 bytes	4

more efficient. Table 4.2 illustrates the alignment of basic types as defined in the CDR. For example, an alignment of 2 means that the corresponding data has to be aligned at an even address in main storage.

COMPLEX TYPES

The complex types supported by μORB include `string`, `struct`, and `sequence`. All these types are represented as a composition of basic types. No special markers that could be used to detect complex data types within a byte sequence are introduced.

Coding of constructed types

The representation of a `struct` in the presentation layer is the sequence of its member variables. If the member types are complex types, then the same principle is applied to them recursively. The coding of a `string` instance begins with a `ULong`, which indicates the length of the character string—including a terminating null character. The individual characters that make up the character string follow it—again including the terminating null. A `sequence` instance is represented in a similar way. First the `ULong` indicates the number of elements in the sequence. Then the elements themselves are coded.

The following IDL data type clarifies the CDR coding:

```
// IDL
struct S {
  sequence<octet> x;
  long            y;
};
```

An actual instance of this data type shall define a length of 3 for the `sequence` of the variable x. The elements of the sequence shall be the hex values 0x11, 0x22, and 0x33. The content of the variable y is 0x12345678. The byte sequence created for this `struct` instance based on Little Endian coding is as follows:

TABLE 4.3 Sample coding of the struct `S`

Pos.	Hex	Description
0	03 00 00 00	Length of sequence
4	11 22 33	Content of sequence
7	00	Padding
8	78 56 34 12	`ULong` value

Hex sequence:	03 00 00 00 11 22 33 00 78 56 34 12
Position:	0 1 2 3 4 5 6 7 8 9 10 11

Table 4.3 shows the byte sequence in a structured form. Note that the individual basic types used for the coding are aligned on their corresponding multiples. This explains the padding before the representation of the variable y.

4.3.3 Modeling of the Presentation Layer

Requirements of the presentation layer

The following analysis summarizes the requirements of the presentation layer of μORB:

1. The presentation layer should be able to code and decode basic types.
2. Constructed types are represented as a sequence of basic types.
3. Both Little Endian and Big Endian coding should be permitted.
4. Data are aligned at their natural boundaries.

The introduction of an abstract basic class `Codec` (stands for "**co**ding, **dec**oding"), which defines the interface required of the presentation layer (see Figure 4.4), would support different coding procedures. The presentation layer manages unstructured byte sequences using the class `Buffer` introduced in Section 4.2. Whereas the class `Codec` processes a byte sequence using a `Buffer` instance, the class `Transport` presented earlier transmits the byte sequence to a different address space.

Example of CDR coder

Different coding procedures are derived from the basic class `Codec`. According to the rules of the CDR, there are two different coders (`LECodec` and `BECodec`) that always file data in a Little Endian or a Big Endian format, irrespective of the computer's hardware architecture. The following code fragment, showing the coding of the instance of `struct S` given in the preceding section, helps to explain the use of classes at the C++ level:

```
Buffer* buf = new Buffer;
Codec* encoder = new LECodec (buf);
```

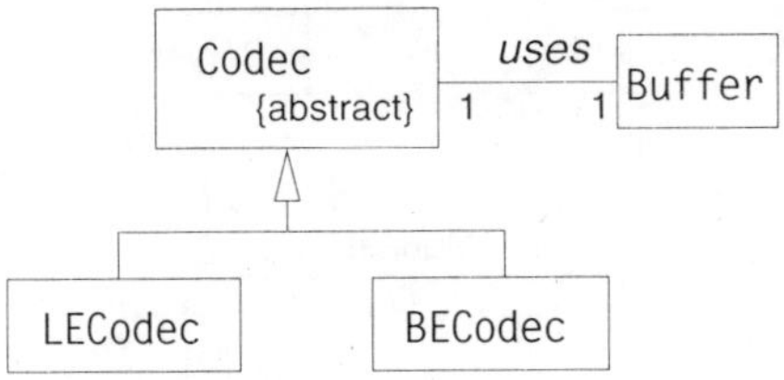

FIGURE 4.4 UML class diagram of data coder/decoder.

```
3:
4:  encoder->put_ulong (3);
5:  encoder->put_octet (0x11);
6:  encoder->put_octet (0x22);
7:  encoder->put_octet (0x33);
8:  encoder->put_ulong (0x12345678)
```

The variable `encoder` is used to code the parameters (line 2). First the number of elements of `sequence` are coded, followed by the three `octet` instances. The `ULong` of the `struct` is then filed (line 8). The class `Codec` automatically adds the filler bytes (padding) to the data stream where they are required. Note that the byte sequence filed after line 8 in the `Buffer` instance does not contain any type information. The developer is responsible for ensuring that the decoding takes place in the same order as the information was written.

4.4 INTEROPERABILITY LAYER

The components of μORB presented so far have been responsible for the exchange between address spaces and representation of data. This section examines how messages that flow between sender and receiver must be structured for the execution of a remote operation invocation.

4.4.1 Protocol for Remote Operation Invocation

We will now develop a protocol for remote operation invocation using the presentation layer discussed in the last section. Because of our compliance with the conventions of the CORBA standard, μORB is interoperable with the CORBA application that was introduced in the last chapter. Again we begin with an analysis of requirements, this time for an interoperability protocol:

Requirements of interoperability protocol

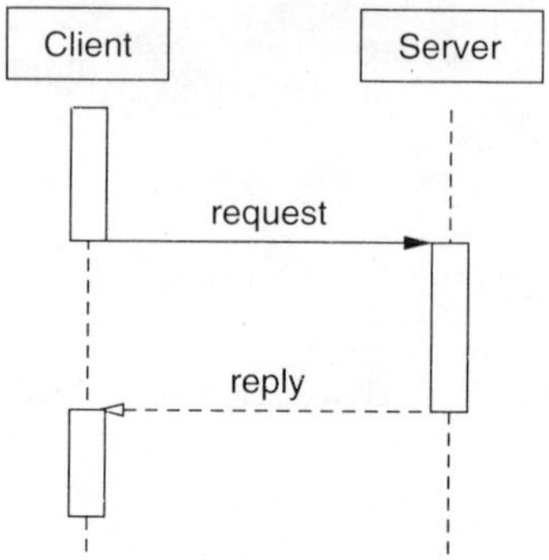

FIGURE 4.5 Protocol between client and server.

1. The protocol is based on a reliable, end-to-end transport layer.
2. The protocol decouples the different technological domains that exist at the communication end points.
3. The protocol enables interaction between two objects that exist in different address spaces, based on an abstraction of the operation invocation.
4. The sender determines the coding rules.

Request

From the point of view of an object-oriented application, the interaction between a client and a server consists of two messages (see Figure 4.5). The first message is used by the client to transmit the actual parameters of an operation to the server, thus initiating the execution of the operation (*request*). In addition to the actual parameters, the server also needs information about which operation is to be executed on which object. The message sent by the client to the server must include appropriate information for addressing the target object and the target operation.

Reply

Once the server completes the operation, the results must be transmitted in the reverse direction to the client (*reply*). It should be noted that, based on the analysis of requirements listed in Section 4.2, the transport layer guarantees a reliable end-to-end connection. This is the only reason why two messages are sufficient. An unreliable connection would require the use of additional messages (such as acknowledgment messages).

Sender selects coding procedure

As we explained in the last section, there are two different coding rules. The question is how the sender and the receiver reach agreement on a uniform coding rule. According to the solution proposed by CORBA, the sender selects the coding, and the receiver is responsible for translating it into its local representation. Consequently, a special flag is added to each data packet. This flag enables the receiver to detect whether the data in this packet is in a Little Endian or in a Big Endian format. The advantage of this procedure is that the sender and the receiver do not explicitly have to negotiate any coding. If both sides use the same format, there is no need for any conversion of the data being transmitted.

4.4.2 Structure of Protocol Data Units

The General Inter-ORB Protocol (GIOP) in CORBA defines a number of Protocol Data Units (PDUs) that are used in the interaction of objects in distributed systems. In the context of μORB, we are only interested in the request and reply PDUs that enable basic remote operation invocation. The general structure of these PDUs is shown in Figure 4.6. The structure of the first 12 bytes (also called the *header*) is identical for both PDUs. The header is then followed by a body that is different for each PDU. In the CORBA standard the structure of PDUs is specified through IDL. The coding rules established in the CDR ensure that a PDU is correctly mapped as a byte sequence. The definition of the PDU header follows:

```
 1: // IDL
 2:
 3: struct Version {
 4:   octet major;
 5:   octet minor;
 6: };
 7:
 8: struct MessageHeader {
 9:   char           magic[4];
10:   Version        GIOP_version;
11:   boolean        byte_order;
12:   octet          message_type;
13:   unsigned long message_size;
14: };
```

Each GIOP PDU begins with an identification consisting of the four letters `GIOP`, which enables valid GIOP messages (line 9) to be recognized. The version number of the protocol follows the identification. μORB exclusively uses GIOP Version 1.0, which we use for the structure of the request and reply PDUs. The next component provides the format of the coding of the respective PDU (line 11). The value TRUE stands for Little Endian, and the value FALSE stands for Big Endian. The next piece of data distinguishes between request and reply

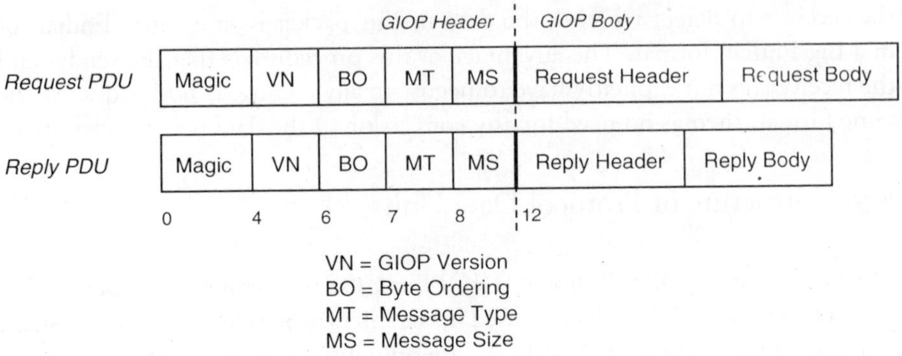

FIGURE 4.6 Structure of protocol data units.

messages (line 12). The value 0 refers to a request PDU, and the value 1 to a reply PDU. The length of the GIOP body is the last information supplied in the header (line 13). The coding of this value is already based on the format given in line 11.

We continue by describing the structure of the body of a GIOP message. The structure of the body depends on whether it is a request PDU or a reply PDU. The body of both PDU types is in turn divided into a header and a body. We will first look at the header of a request PDU:

Header of a request PDU

```
 1:  // IDL
 2:
 3:  struct RequestHeader {
 4:    ServiceContextList service_context;
 5:    unsigned long      request_id;
 6:    boolean            response_expected;
 7:    sequence<octet>    object_key;
 8:    string             operation;
 9:    Principal          requesting_principal;
10:  };
```

The information given in lines 4 and 9 is not of interest to us in the context of μORB, but it has to be provided to prevent a violation of CORBA interoperability. In both cases these are `sequence` instances that are always simply coded with 0 elements in μORB. The other information in the request header is relevant. The request ID is used for the explicit numbering of all outgoing request PDUs (line 5). The request ID can be used to match a later-arriving reply PDU to a request. Line 6 allows the sender of a request PDU to indicate whether it expects a reply. In μORB this field is always set to TRUE.

Line 7 indicates the object key for the operation invocation (see Section 3.5.2). The object key is specified as a sequence of octets and addresses an object on the receiver side. The final information in the request header gives the name of the operation that is to be executed (line 8). This parameter is coded as a character string. The request header is followed by the request body, which contains all current input parameters for the operation.

Header of a reply PDU

Following is the structure of the reply header, which is less complex:

```
 1: // IDL
 2:
 3: enum ReplyStatusType {
 4:   NO_EXCEPTION,
 5:   USER_EXCEPTION,
 6:   ...
 7: };
 8:
 9: struct ReplyHeader {
10:   ServiceContextList service_context;
11:   unsigned long      request_id;
12:   ReplyStatusType    reply_status;
13: };
```

In μORB the information in line 10 is always coded as a sequence with 0 elements, similar to the request PDU. The request ID in line 11 must agree with the one of the corresponding request PDU. This enables the receiver to match request and reply PDUs to one another. The reply status in line 12 signals either a normal execution (NO_EXCEPTION) or an error triggered by the application (USER_EXCEPTION) to the client. Consequently, the body of the reply PDU contains either all output parameters of the operation or the coding of an exception.

4.4.3 Modeling of Protocol Data Units

Instances of the class PDU pictured in Figure 4.7 manage request and reply PDUs. A PDU is linked to a communication end point over which it sends and receives protocol data units. For the coding of PDU-specific data, such as the current parameters of an operation invocation, a PDU entity provides a Codec and a Buffer instance that edit the data outside the PDU.

Sending a GIOP message

The following C++ code fragment from the implementation of the PDU::send() method shows the actions carried out when a PDU is sent:

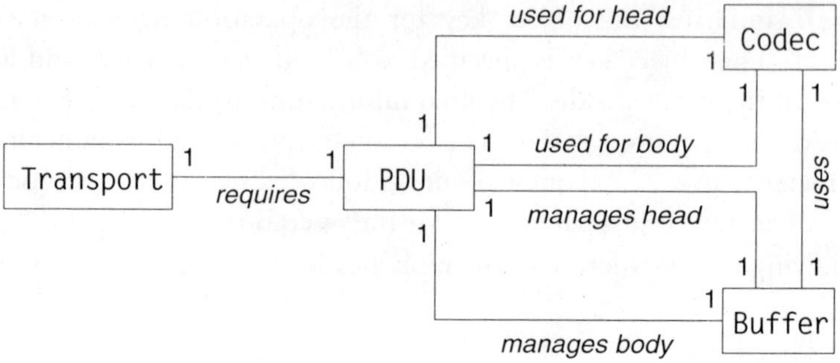

FIGURE 4.7 UML class diagram of PDU.

```
void PDU::send ()
{
  Buffer* giop_header = new Buffer;
  Codec *codec;

  if (Codec::is_little_endian())
    codec = new LECodec (giop_header);
  else
    codec = new BECodec (giop_header);

  codec->put_char ('G'); // magic cookie
  codec->put_char ('I');
  codec->put_char ('O');
  codec->put_char ('P');

  codec->put_octet (1);  // GIOP Version 1.0
  codec->put_octet (0);

  codec->put_octet (Codec::is_little_endian() ? 1 : 0);
  codec->put_octet (_pdu_type);
  codec->put_ulong (_giop_body->length ());

  _transp->send (giop_header);
  _transp->send (_giop_body);
}
```

The GIOP body of the PDU being sent was constructed in the `Buffer` instance `_giop_body` before the `PDU::send()` method was invoked. The code fragment above essentially shows how the GIOP header is structured. First a

`Codec` instance that supports the native coding of the system is created (lines 6–9). Then the GIOP header with its components is built up (lines 11–21). Once this is completed, first the GIOP header and then the GIOP body are sent to the remote communication end point. The communication end point is referenced through a `Transport` instance with the variable `_transp` (lines 23 and 24).

4.5 PROXIES

The μORB components presented so far are already sufficient for the execution of a simple distributed operation invocation between two objects. The proxies close the gap between the middleware and the bank application. To keep the complexity of μORB to a minimum, we have not included the implementation of an object adapter. As can be gleaned from Figure 2.12, each object that can be accessed from another address space requires two proxies, one each to represent both the client and the server in their address spaces. This section concerns itself with how these proxies are structured. We again begin with an analysis of requirements:

Requirements of a proxy

1. The proxies are to execute an operation invocation between address spaces.
2. There should be no syntactic difference between a local operation invocation and a remote one.
3. It is not necessary to realize the architectural object adapter component.

Figure 4.8 shows the class structure for the interface `Account` of our bank application. All classes can be divided into three categories, which are separated by a dotted line in Figure 4.8. First are some generic classes that are used as base classes for all proxies. The generic classes are part of the μORB library. These classes are followed by the classes of proxy objects, which are naturally dependent on the application. In CORBA these classes are normally generated through an IDL compiler; in μORB they are written by hand. The last classes are the ones the applications programmer provides as an implementation of the interface. All these classes are examined in detail below:

`Request` represents a remote operation invocation on the client side. This class is essentially a wrapper for the PDU class presented in the last section.

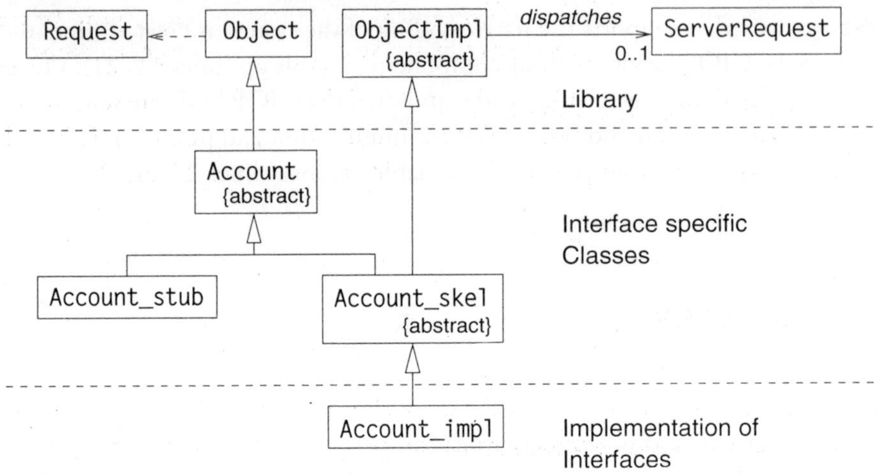

FIGURE 4.8 UML diagram of proxy classes for the interface Account.

ServerRequest represents a remote operation invocation on the server side and is also a wrapper for the PDU class.

Object is the common base class of all proxies. The class Object is used as a factory for Request objects.

ObjectImpl is the common base class of all object implementations. This class receives ServerRequest instances and forwards them to the right skeleton.

Account serves as an abstract base class and contains the signatures and type definitions of the interface.

Account_stub is the stub on the client side that creates the Request object and fills it with the current parameters.

Account_skel is the skeleton on the server side. It forwards an incoming operation invocation to the appropriate operation.

Account_impl contains the implementation of the interface Account.

μORB has no object adapter

Since μORB does not implement a POA, there is a different naming convention for designating the skeleton (suffix _skel instead of prefix POA_). The class ObjectImpl incorporates a pure virtual method invoke that forwards an incoming operation invocation, represented by an instance of the class ServerRequest, to the skeleton. The operations dispatcher is found in the implementation of the `invoke` method in the skeletons. Based on the operation name, the skeletons decide whether the corresponding operation belongs to their interface.

The class `Account` is an abstract base class because all the operations defined in the interface `Account` are defined there as pure virtual methods. The class `Account_stub` provides implementations for these pure virtual methods that essentially create a `Request` object. The skeleton `Account_skel`, however, continues to be an abstract base class, and the implementations of the operations of the interface `Account` are not provided until the derived class `Account_impl`.

4.6 OBJECT SERVICES

The last component of μORB is the object services. These deal with general functions for the objects managed by μORB, including support of the life cycle of an object, management of object references, and server-side support of object implementations. These three areas are examined in detail below.

4.6.1 Life Cycle of an Object

Objects experience a life cycle: they are created, they process operation invocations for a period of time, and then they are finally deleted. Until now we have only discussed the active phase, during which an object reacts to incoming operation invocations. Before an object reaches this state, it first has to be created. When an object is created, it is also registered within the middleware so that the system is notified of the existence of the new object. A distinction is made in μORB between the following phases of an object life cycle:

Life cycle of an object

Nonexistent: The object does not exist and therefore no references can yet be assigned.

Active: The object exists and is ready to accept and to process operation invocations. References can only be assigned to active objects.

Terminated: The object is no longer able to accept operation invocations.

The two states "nonexistent" and "terminated" are not identical because in a terminated state references may still exist to objects that are no longer active. An object passes through the three states in the sequence indicated above.

The events that activate or terminate an object lie outside the μORB. Typically it is the context of an application that determines when an object is acti-

Distributed garbage collection is not implemented

vated or terminated. Some programming languages, such as Smalltalk and Java, automatically terminate objects as soon as no reference to them exists. This method is referred to as *garbage collection* in the literature and in principle can be applied to distributed systems. However, due to the complexity associated with garbage collection, it is not easy for a CORBA-compliant implementation to support distributed garbage collection.

4.6.2 Object References

Object reference gives type and address of an object

An object reference represents the client's view of a referenced object. The view is defined by the type of the reference as well as by the address over which the object can be reached. The address is defined through an instance of the class `Address` and an object key (also see Section 3.5.2). In μORB the object key identifies an object relative to its address space. The CORBA standard defines the structure of an object reference through the Interoperable Object Reference (IOR). The definition of an IOR is also based on CORBA's own IDL:

```
 1: // IDL
 2: typedef unsigned long ProfileId;
 3: const ProfileId TAG_INTERNET_IOP = 0;
 4:
 5: struct TaggedProfile {
 6:   ProfileId tag;
 7:   sequence<octet> profile_data;
 8: };
 9:
10: struct IOR {
11:   string type_id;
12:   sequence<TaggedProfile> profiles;
13: };
```

An IOR essentially consists of a type identification (line 11), which indicates the type of the referenced object, and information providing the communication end points over which the object can be reached (line 12). Note that an object potentially can be reached over various communication end points based on different transport mechanisms. These transport mechanisms are all listed separately through a sequence in the IOR. In the case of μORB, we are only interested in communication end points based on TCP. CORBA defines a separate identification for a TCP-based address (line 3) for this protocol. The following information is important for TCP-based transport mechanisms:

Information in a TCP-based address

```
14:  // IDL
15:  struct Version {
16:    octet major;
17:    octet minor;
18:  };
19:
20:  struct ProfileBody {
21:    Version          iiop_version;
22:    string           host;
23:    unsigned short   port;
24:    sequence<octet> object_key;
25:  };
```

The structure `ProfileBody` in line 20 gives the complete address of an object in a distributed system. This includes the IP address (line 22), the port number (line 23), and the object key (line 24). The structure `ProfileBody` from line 20 is coded as a normal CDR stream, and the resulting byte sequence is embedded in the structure `profile_data` in line 7. This type of embedding enables new transport mechanisms with their own address conventions to be supported at a later time, without necessitating any changes to the underlying structure of the IOR. The CORBA specification refers to this technique as *encapsulation.*

If a reference is sent as the parameter of an operation in a CORBA-based middleware platform, it is represented as an instance of the structure `IOR` from line 10. The representation of an IOR as a character string shown on page 51 is also based on this structure. The byte sequence that originates during the coding of the structure `IOR` is simply indicated in the form of hexadecimal values. The first octet of the IOR presents the Endian format of the remaining coding. During embedding (as it occurs, for example, with an IOR for the structure `ProfileBody` (line 20) as an element of the sequence `profile_data` in line 7), a separate Endian format can be specified for the coding of the embedding. Table 4.4 shows the byte-by-byte coding of the IOR shown on page 51.

In μORB the class `ObjectReference` converts the attributes of an IOR (see Figure 4.9). However, the complexity is reduced because this class can manage the information for only one communication end point. As indicated in Figure 4.9, an object reference in μORB consists of a type identification, a communication end point for the transport layer, and an object key.

TABLE 4.4 Coding of IOR on page 51

Position	Hex.	Description
0	01	Little Endian coding
1	00 00 00	Padding
4	0d 00 00 00	Length type_id = 13
8	49 44 4c 3a 41 63 63 6f	"IDL:Account:1.0\0"
	75 6e 74 3a 31 2e 30 00	
24	01 00 00 00	A tagged profile
28	00 00 00 00	TAG_INTERNET_IOP
32	2c 00 00 00	Length profile_data = 44 octets
36	01	Little Endian coding
37	01 00	IIOP Version 1.0
39	00	Padding
40	0a 00 00 00	Length host = 10
44	31 32 37 2e 30 2e 30 2e	"127.0.0.1\0"
	31 00	
54	16 85	TCP Port = 34070
56	14 00 00 00	Length object_key = 20 octets
60	2f 31 39 39 38 33 2f 31	Object key
	30 36 31 33 34 37 30 34	
	34 2f 5f 30	

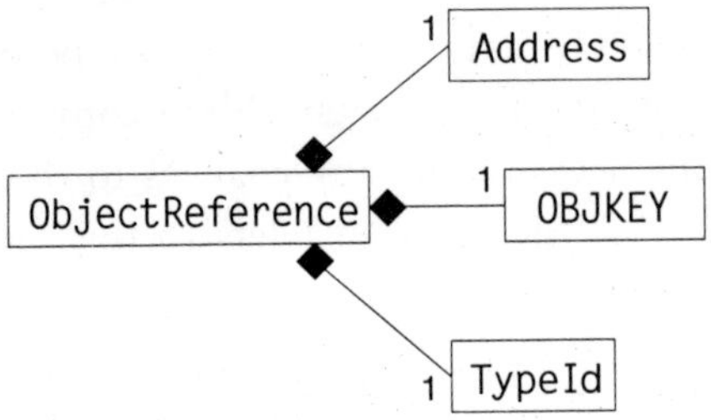

FIGURE 4.9 UML diagram of class ObjectReference.

4.6.3 Services on the Server Side

Several objects that are managed by the middleware are typically found in one address space. The ORB's tasks on the server side include registering active objects and forwarding incoming operation invocations to the appropriate ObjectImpl instances. The following requirements are placed on the server-side services of μORB:

Requirements of server-side services

1. Management of several object implementations.
2. Forwarding of incoming operation invocations to correct object implementations.

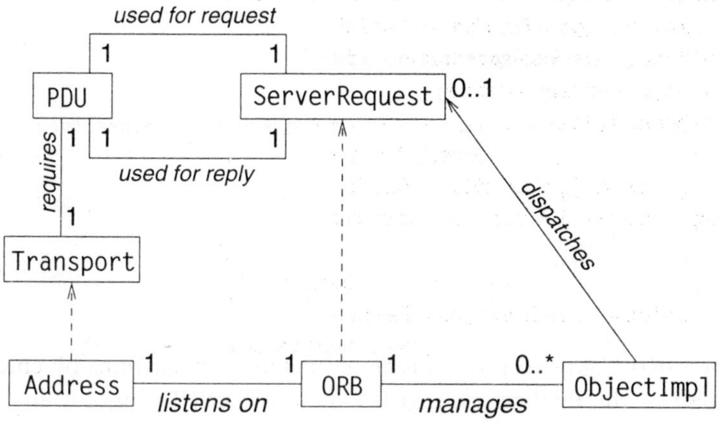

FIGURE 4.10 UML diagram of class ORB.

3. Acceptance by the middleware of incoming operation invocations at precisely one communication end point.

Figure 4.10 presents the class diagram for the support of server-side object services within μORB. At the center is the class `ORB`, based on the Object Request Broker of the CORBA architecture. The class `ORB` manages several `ObjectImpl` instances that can register and deregister with the ORB at any time. The ORB waits for a connection setup request at a transport address. Therefore, exactly one connection can be established with μORB from another address space.

If a connection is set up at the transport level, the ORB receives and processes incoming operation invocations. An incoming operation invocation is represented by an instance of the class `ServerRequest`. This class manages two PDU instances: one for the request PDU and one for the corresponding reply PDU. The task of the ORB is to forward a `ServerRequest` instance to the correct object implementation. The following code fragment shows the main loop of μORB:

Main loop of μORB

```
void ORB::run ()
{
  // ...
  _transp->accept ();

  while (1) {
    PDU pdu (_transp);
    PDUType pdu_type = pdu.recv_next_pdu ();
```

```
 9:
10:      ServerRequest req (&pdu);
11:
12:      _obj_key_impl_map [req.obj_key ()]->invoke (req);
13:
14:      req.send_reply ();
15:    }
16:    // never reached
17:  }
```

The ORB begins to process remote operation invocations by entering the main loop in the method `ORB::run()`. First the ORB waits for an incoming connection at the transport address that it received as a parameter (line 4). It then moves into an endless loop in which incoming operation invocations are continually processed. The first step consists of receiving a request PDU (line 8). Based on the incoming request PDU, a `ServerRequest` instance is set up in line 10.

`ServerRequest` represents an incoming operation invocation

The `ServerRequest` instance serves as a parameter for the invocation of the object implementations. The ORB manages the mapping of object keys to `ObjectImpl` instances in order to provide the correct object implementation. The method `ServerRequest::obj_key()` supplies the object key of the request PDU that arrives, which is then used as the index for this mapping. The instruction in line 12 leads to the invocation of the method `ObjectImpl::invoke()` of the correct object implementation. The method `ObjectImpl::invoke()` in turn invokes the appropriate skeleton, which in turn invokes the appropriate operation implementation. After the invocation the results (i.e., output parameters, return value, or exceptions of the remote operation) are transmitted back to the client over a reply PDU (line 14).

4.7 SUMMARY

Middleware handles a variety of tasks. This chapter showed the design of μORB, which enables the distributed execution of applications. We especially emphasized the design of the individual components of middleware. The result is a complete middleware in the sense that it guarantees the distribution transparency of the bank application introduced in a previous chapter. It should be noted that some functional modifications were needed in order to reduce the complexity of the presentation. These modifications apply specifically to the following points:

Transport layer: μORB limits the distribution of objects to exactly two address spaces. This is, of course, not a realistic limitation, and a procedure involving a complicated management of several transport channels must be used.

Nested callbacks: An operation invocation on the client side blocks μORB until the server sends the results. During this time the μORB on the client side cannot accept any other operation invocations, which makes sense with many applications.

Interoperability protocol: μORB only understands two messages of the GIOP (request and reply messages). However, the CORBA interoperability protocol provides eight messages for different requirements in the case of distributed object communication.

Object adapters: In μORB, proxy objects directly link an object implementation to the ORB. CORBA, however, provides for the use of object adapters that allow better flexibility on the server side.

Proxy objects: Proxy objects that are generated manually are prone to error. It is more effective to use appropriate tools for an automatic generation of stubs and skeletons.

It is evident from this list that a "complete" middleware requires considerably more effort. However, the concepts introduced in this chapter should provide the foundation for an understanding of MICO's architecture.

Chapter 5

ORB DESIGN

The Object Request Broker (ORB) is the key component of the CORBA architecture. Its key responsibility is to forward method invocations from a client to an object implementation, including the tasks associated with this process in heterogeneous environments. In particular, invoked objects may be located in the same process as the caller, in a different process on the same computer, or on a remote computer. Also, objects can be implemented using different programming languages, running on different operating systems and hardware, and connected by diverse types of networks. The ORB has to provide a consistent interface to invoke these different types of objects.

Expandability

Because the ORB is closely linked with the other components of a CORBA system (partially through proprietary interfaces), the developers of specialized ORBs were forced to develop new versions of these components of the CORBA system or not to provide them at all. This happens with some research projects in the integration of *Quality of Service* (QoS) aspects into CORBA ([25] and [32]).

Microkernel architecture

So this is the starting point for MICO as a platform for research and training projects: the development of an extendible and modifiable ORB. The microkernel approach from the area of operating systems has been applied to CORBA for this purpose. For this, the minimal necessary ORB functionality has to be identified, such that modifications and extensions can be implemented outside the ORB as *services*.

Consequently, the following sections start by compiling the tasks of an ORB. An analysis will be undertaken to determine which components are required for fulfilling these tasks, which of these components can be implemented as ORB core components, and which as services. Lastly, an overview of the design of a microkernel ORB will be presented.

5.1 ORB FUNCTIONALITY

From a conceptual standpoint, an ORB offers all the functionality that is independent of certain types of objects. The object adapter carries out object-specific tasks. The ORB is in a sense the smallest common denominator in functionality among all conceivable types of objects. Its responsibilities include

- Object generation
- Bootstrapping
- Method invocation

  —Object localization

  —Invocation forwarding

  —Demultiplexing between object adapters

Object references

Object references contain addressing information along with the type and the identity of the object. The generation of type and identity is the task of object adapters, and the ORB provides the addressing information. Object adapters and the ORB must therefore cooperate closely in the creation of object references.

Bootstrapping

Once the objects are created, there is the question of how a client is informed of the object reference. A commonly used approach is the use of a naming service. Because the naming service itself is realized as a set of CORBA objects, the question is how the client finds out the object reference of the naming service. To solve this bootstrapping problem, the ORB offers clients an integrated bootstrapping service.

Method invocation

From the view of an ORB, a method invocation consists of three tasks: First, after an invocation adapter (see Section 3.2.5) initiates a method invocation, the location of the target object has to be looked up based on the target object reference. Second, in the event that the target object is not located in the address space of the caller, the method invocation must be forwarded to the address space of the target object through the use of suitable transport mechanisms. Third, the object adapter responsible for the target object is identified on the basis of the object reference of the target object. The object adapter then invokes the method on the target object. Any results are returned to the caller on the reverse path.

5.2 ORB ARCHITECTURES

ORB implementations

Conceptually, the ORB is a cross-address system, like the one shown in Figure 5.1. It permits transparent communication between objects in different address spaces.

So there are many opportunities for converting this conceptual idea into an implementation. A distinction is essentially made between a centralized approach and a distributed approach (see Figure 5.2). With a distributed approach the ORB is implemented as a library that is linked to each CORBA application. The ORBs in different address spaces then communicate with one another on a direct path. For security, reliability, and performance reasons, this library could also be located directly in the underlying operating system. The distributed approach is characterized by the following:

Distributed approach

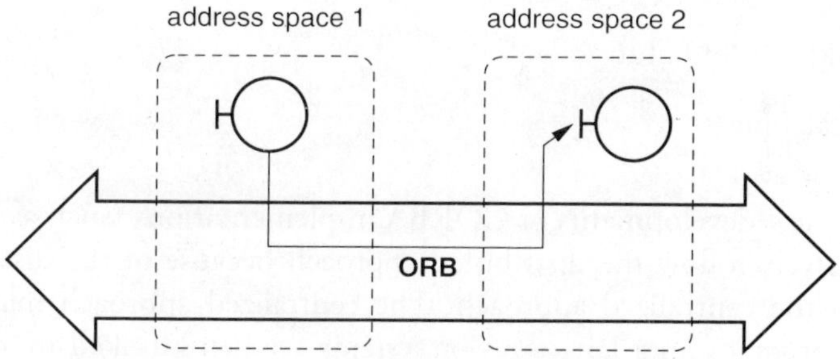

FIGURE 5.1 ORB as a cross-address object bus.

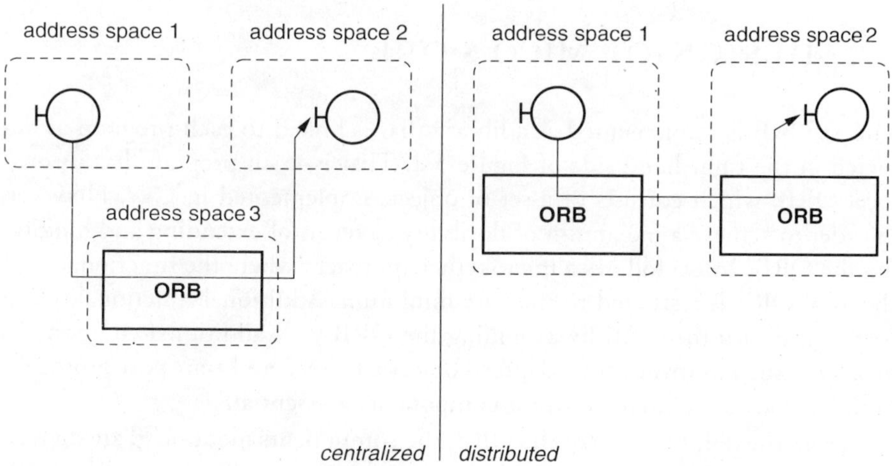

FIGURE 5.2 Centralized versus distributed ORB implementation.

- ⊞ Good performance because clients and server communicate directly with one another
- ⊟ Complex management because information is distributed over local ORBs

Centralized approach

In a centralized solution the ORB is implemented as a separate process. All communication between two CORBA applications takes place over this server. Of course hybrid solutions are also possible. In this case, part of the communication avoids the indirect route over the central ORB. The centralized approach is characterized by the following:

- ⊞ Simple management because all information is available in a central location
- ⊟ Reduced performance because communication between clients and servers is not on a direct route
- ⊟ Central point of failure
- ⊟ Poor scalability

Totally new developments of CORBA implementations (such as MICO) almost exclusively follow the distributed approach because of the disadvantages inherent in the centralized approach. The centralized approach may be used when new programming languages or systems are being linked to an existing ORB.

5.3 DESIGN OF MICO'S ORB

Requirements for expandability

MICO's ORB is implemented as a library that is linked to each program as depicted in the right-hand side of Figure 5.2. That is, each program has its own local ORB, which consists of a set of objects implemented in C++. However, in order to achieve a maximum of flexibility in terms of extending and modifying the ORB, MICO follows a microkernel approach, where the functionality of the local ORB is restricted to the bare minimum. Additional functionality can be plugged into the ORB by extending the ORB with additional components or *services* such as invocation adapters, object adapters, and transport protocols. Simultaneous use of many of these components is essential.

From the point of view of the ORB, the components mentioned are divided into two categories: components that request method invocations to the ORB and components that execute method invocations on behalf of the ORB:

- Components that trigger method invocations:
  - —Invocation adapters
  - —Server-side transport modules (receive network packets and request a method invocation to the ORB)
- Components that execute method invocations:
  - —Object adapters
  - —Client-side transport modules (take over method invocation from ORB and send network packet)

Invocation and object adapters

So it suffices for an ORB to be equipped with a generalized *invocation adapter interface* as well as a generalized *object adapter interface*. In addition to these interfaces, the ORB has an *invocation table* in which it keeps a record of the method invocations currently being executed.

Scheduling

Because a CORBA system has many subtasks that have to be processed simultaneously (see Section 5.3.4), an ORB also has a scheduler. The scheduler itself is implemented as a service outside the ORB due to the variety of demands placed on it (multithreaded versus single-threaded, real-time-enabled). Again the ORB only supplies a suitable *scheduler interface*.

Generation of object references

Section 5.1 pointed out that the creation of object references requires a close cooperation between object adapter (provides type and identity) and ORB (provides address). Due to the arrangement of transport modules outside the ORB, it is the transport module and not the ORB that has the addresses where an object can be found. Therefore, the ORB must supply a mechanism for communication between the transport modules and the object adapters.

Loadable modules

All interfaces are designed so components can be registered and deregistered with the ORB anytime during runtime. Because a microkernel ORB offers an interface for loading modules, it can even be extended through the addition of new object adapters, transport modules, and so forth during runtime.

Figure 5.3 presents an overview of the major components in a microkernel ORB. The individual components and interfaces of the ORB will be covered in detail in the following sections.

5.3.1 Invocation Adapter Interface

The *invocation adapter interface* is used to initiate a remote method invocation on an ORB. To execute method invocations, stub objects indirectly use this

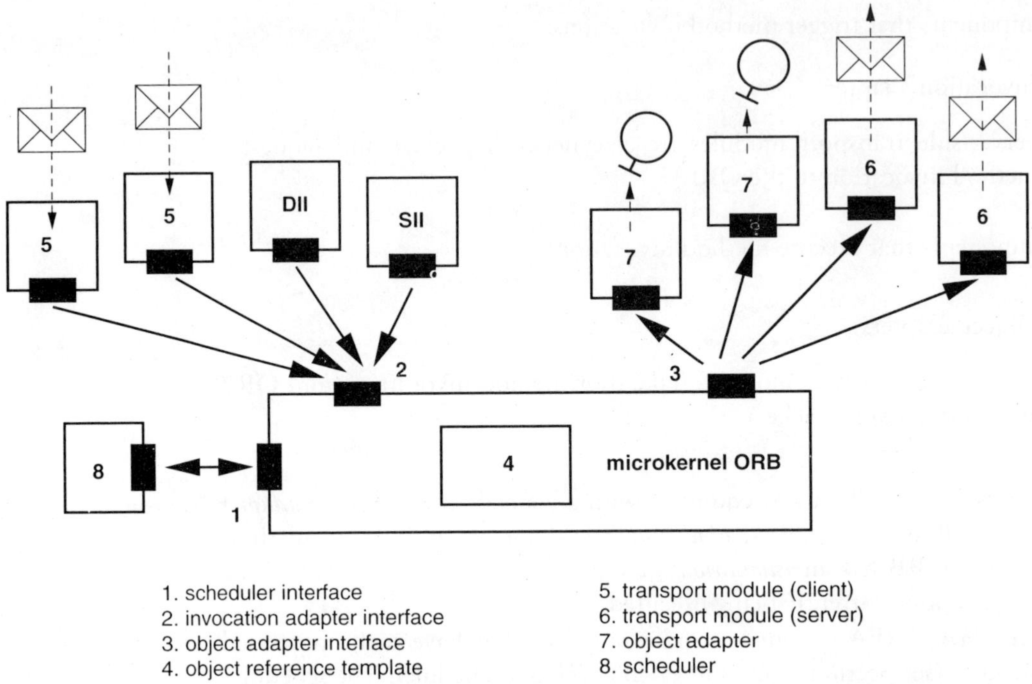

FIGURE 5.3 Microkernel ORB.

interface via the Static Invocation Interface (SII). Method invocations generated via the Dynamic Invocation Interface (DII) by CORBA applications also indirectly use this interface. Transport modules on the client side (box 5 in Figure 5.3) receive messages from ORBs in other address spaces and transform these messages into invocations to the invocation adapter interface of the local ORB.

Invocation adapters require type information

The difficulty in designing an invocation adapter interface is that the components directly using this interface do not have equal detail of information about the method invocation being executed. The signature of the invoked method, including the parameter types, is usually known to invocation adapters such as DII and SII, but this is usually not the case with transport modules on the server side. The reason for this is that inter-ORB protocols such as IIOP try to minimize the amount of information being transmitted. Therefore, they only supply the object reference, the method name, and the values of the parameters, but not their types, because the invoked object is able to reconstruct this information from the method name. The transport module on the server side could theoretically use the interface repository to obtain the type information. The problem is that, first, it is entirely possible that no type information for a particular method is available in the repository and, second, the level of performance would be impacted considerably because a repository other than the local one might have to be consulted for each method invocation.

As a consequence, due to the lack of type information, server-side transport modules normally cannot reconstruct the values of parameters of method invocations from the byte streams of coded parameters. This reconstruction is not possible until much later when the method invocation reaches the target object that knows the signature of the invoked method, as described above. At the same time it should be transparent to the target object whether the method invocation was initiated locally from DII, SII, or a transport module.

Lazy evaluation

The principle of *lazy evaluation* is used to resolve this problem. Here evaluation of the expressions of a programming language is deferred until the value of the expression is actually needed and all input values for the evaluation are available. A *thunk object*, which contains the expression itself and all the information needed to evaluate it, is created for each expression requiring lazy evaluation. The thunk is not evaluated until the value of the expression is required.

Thunk objects

Lazy evaluation was included in Algol 60 as a method for passing parameters *by name*. Another important application of this technology is the lazy evaluation of data streams in Lisp, first described in [21]. The name *thunk* originates from the implementation of the name invocation in Algol 60. The origin of the word is unknown, but it is said that it resembles the sound produced by data in a running Algol 60 system when it is being written to the stack [1].

What this means to the invocation adapter interface of an ORB is that a special thunk object containing the coded parameters and other information important to the decoding (such as a reference to the decoding procedure to be used) is generated for the method invocation. The thunk object is not supplied with the known type information or evaluated (i.e., the parameters decoded) until the values of the parameters for invoking the method are actually needed.

Asynchrony

The invocation adapter interface must be asynchronous if several method invocations are to be executed simultaneously. This means that the control flow returns directly to the caller once a method invocation has been initiated in the ORB. The semantics for what under CORBA is usually a synchronous method invocation can therefore be simulated. The interface supports the operations:

$$invoke(O, M, T) \rightarrow H$$

$$cancel(H) \rightarrow \{\}$$

$$wait(\{H_i\}) \rightarrow H$$

$$results(H) \rightarrow T$$

Operations of invocation adapter interface

The operation *invoke* supplies the ORB with a method invocation in the form of a tuple (O, M, T), consisting of a target object O, the method name M, and parameters in the form of a thunk T, and returns a handle H for the initiated method invocation. The method invocation associated with the handle can be canceled by the operation *cancel.* Note, however, that this cancellation is only a local operation that marks the associated record in the ORB for removal. The remote process that actually executed the method invocation is not affected. The operation *wait* waits for the completion of one of the method invocations indicated in the form of a set of handles and supplies the handle of the first completed method invocation as a result. Lastly, the operation *results* can be used to obtain the results of the method invocation in the form of a thunk T from the ORB. Lazy evaluation also has to be used for the results because the types of output parameters, return value, or exception are first known in the stub object that triggered the method invocation.

5.3.2 Object Adapter Interface

An *object adapter interface* is in a sense the opposite of an invocation adapter interface. An ORB uses this interface to forward a method invocation to the component responsible for its execution. This can either be an object adapter that executes the method invocation directly or a transport module that forwards the method invocation to another address space.

The difficulty in designing this interface is that it is supposed to hide the dissimilarities of object adapters and transport modules from the ORB. However, the ORB still must be able to determine from the object reference which transport module is responsible for the execution of a method invocation on the target object.

The way to solve this problem is to allow the object adapter or the transport module—and not the ORB—to make this choice. The interface offered to the ORB by the object adapters and transport modules comprises the following operations:

$$has\_object(O) \rightarrow \{\text{TRUE, FALSE}\}$$

$$invoke(O, M, T, H) \rightarrow \{\}$$

$$cancel(H) \rightarrow \{\}$$

Operations of object adapter interface

The ORB can use *has_object* to query an object adapter or a transport module whether it is responsible for the object reference O. An important requirement of *has_object* is that *has_object*(O) returns TRUE for at most one object adapter or transport module for each possible object reference O. This is the only way that a unique association among object references and object adapters is possible for the ORB. The operation *invoke* transfers a method invocation in the form of a tuple (O, M, T, H), consisting of an object reference O, method name M, parameters in the form of a thunk T, and a handle H to the object adapter or transport module. If necessary, the ORB can cancel a method invocation through *cancel*.

Asynchrony

Object adapter interfaces also have to be asynchronous if several method invocations are to be executed simultaneously. Consequently, in addition to operations for registering and deregistering object adapters, the interface offered by the ORB to object adapters and transport modules also includes the operation *answer_invoke*:

$$register(OA) \rightarrow \{\}$$
$$unregister(OA) \rightarrow \{\}$$
$$answer\_invoke(H, T) \rightarrow \{\}$$

Object adapters and transport modules use *answer_invoke* to inform the ORB through a thunk T of the results of a method invocation specified by the handle H.

5.3.3 Invocation Table

Due to the asynchrony of the object adapter interface, the ORB has to keep a record of currently active method invocations. For this purpose it has a table of these method invocations. The table contains entries of the form (H, O, M, T_{in}, T_{out}), consisting of handle H, object reference O of the target object, method name M, thunk T_{in} for the input parameters, and (sometimes empty) thunk T_{out} for results.

Therefore, from the point of view of an ORB, a method invocation is executed in three steps. First the ORB accepts a method invocation from an invocation-generating component and forwards it to the invocation-executing component:

Method invocation procedures

1. Acceptance of method invocation (O, M, T_{in}) via *invoke*.
2. Generation of a new handle H and entry of (H, O, M, T_{in}, NIL) in the invocation table.

3. Selection of component responsible for executing the invocation and transfer of the method invocation to this component.
4. H is returned as the result of *invoke.*

The component executing the invocation then processes the method invocation and notifies the ORB of the results of the method invocation:

5. Acceptance of T_{out} for the method invocation with handle H at the object adapter interface via *answer_invoke.*
6. Replacement of the associated entry $(H, O, M, T_{in}, \text{NIL})$ in the table of active method invocations with entry $(H, O, M, T_{in}, T_{out})$.

For the third and last step the component generating the invocation may use $wait(\{H_i\})$ to wait for the completion of one of the invocations indicated by the handles $\{H_i\}$. Internally, the ORB then blocks until *answer_invoke* is invoked for one of the handles and then returns this handle to the caller. The component generating the invocation then uses $results(H)$ to fetch the results of the method invocation with handle H at the invocation adapter interface:

7. Find entry with handle H in the invocation table.
8. T_{out} is returned as the result of *invoke,* and the entry with handle H is deleted from the invocation table.

5.3.4 Scheduler

There are various situations in a complex system like an ORB in which many tasks have to be executed simultaneously. The following examples list some of these situations:

EXAMPLE 5.1. An extension of the microkernel ORB implements two transport protocols: the TCP-based IIOP and a special ATM-based *Realtime Inter-ORB Protocol* (RIOP). Both transport protocols must independently wait for and then evaluate incoming TCP and ATM messages. □

EXAMPLE 5.2. Situations exist in which two or more CORBA objects mutually invoke methods to one another. One example of this is a callback, where a client invokes a method in the server, which in turn invokes a method (the callback method) in the client while the original invocation is still pending.

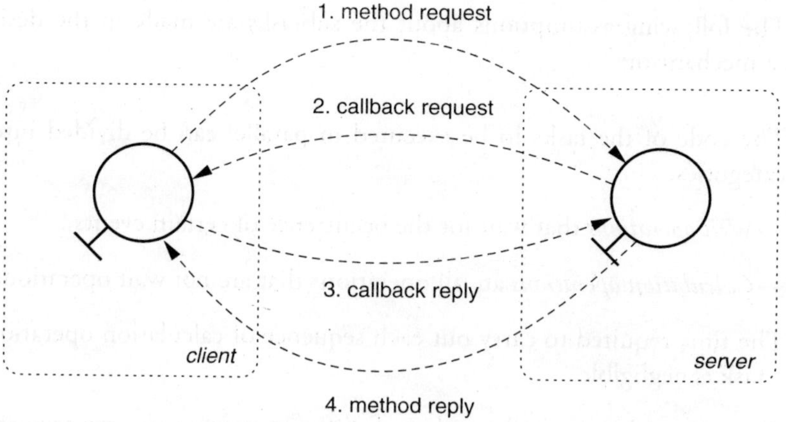

FIGURE 5.4 Nested method invocation.

See Figure 5.4 for an illustration of this scenario. To ensure that this operation functions and does not result in a deadlock, the ORB must be able to wait for both the completion of the method invocation and the arrival of new method invocations (e.g., the callback). □

Challenges

What complicates matters is that the ORB is not always able to foresee these situations because any number of transport modules can be integrated into a system during runtime and then removed again. As an extendable platform, the microkernel ORB should function in both single- and in multithreaded environments. Thus the problem cannot simply be solved by using a thread package. Consequently, the ORB itself must offer some form of scheduler that allocates processing time to the program parts that are to be executed simultaneously. Because scheduling algorithms largely depend on the area of application of an ORB, the scheduler should be interchangeable and therefore must be embedded as a service outside the microkernel ORB.

SCHEDULER ABSTRACTION

What is needed is a scheduling mechanism with the following characteristics:

Requirements of scheduler

- Functions in single- and multithreaded environments
- Allows the implementation of different scheduling algorithms

The following assumptions about the subtasks are made in the design of such a mechanism:

Assumptions

1. The code of the tasks to be executed in parallel can be divided into two categories:

   —*Wait operations* that wait for the occurrence of certain events

   —*Calculation operations* are all operations that are not wait operations

2. The time required to carry out each sequence of calculation operations for a task is negligible.
3. There are only a limited number of different events (e.g., message arrived, timeout).

Breakdown into wait and computing operations

Note the following concerning assumption 1: At first glance some operations cannot easily be classified into one of the two categories and are a combination of both. For example, in some cases input/output operations can block until input/output is completed. However, these hybrid operations can be transformed into a sequence of pure wait and calculation operations.

EXAMPLE 5.3. The operation

```
read_blocking (socket, buffer, buffer_size)
```

reads the number of bytes indicated in `buffer_size` in `buffer` from the network connection that is represented by `socket`. The operation blocks until the number of bytes indicated in `buffer_size` are received. Thus, `read_blocking()` is neither a wait operation nor a calculation operation but is both. The code piece

```
while (buffer_size > 0) {
  wait_for_data (socket);
  read = read_not_blocking (socket, buffer, buffer_size)
  buffer += read;
  buffer_size -= read;
}
```

also reads the number of bytes indicated in `buffer_size` in `buffer` from the network connection `socket`. In this case, use is made of the wait operation `wait_for_data(socket)` that is waiting for the event *Data has arrived on the connection* `socket` and the computing operation `read_not_blocking` that reads what is currently available without blocking. □

Time limits

Referring to assumption 2, "negligible" in this case means that for any prescribed time span $\Delta t > 0$, the time required for the execution of each sequence of computing operations for all subtasks is less than or equal to Δt. This is by no means an obvious assumption. One should note, however, that each sequence of computing operations that does not comply with this condition can be transformed into a set of equivalent computing operations that comply with this condition. All that is needed is the simple insertion of a dummy wait operation in the middle (timewise) of the sequence. This then produces two new sequences of computing operations that either comply with the conditions or not. If the new sequence does not comply, the procedure is repeated until all sequences comply.

Event types

Referring to assumption 3, in principle a single primitive suffices for interprocess communication, such as a semaphore with the associated event *Down on Semaphore X possible*. All conceivable events can be mapped to this primitive [35]. However, some events occur so frequently that it makes sense to make them directly available:

- Input possible on channel X
- Output possible on channel X
- Timeout T expired

Blocks

As shown above, a CORBA runtime system contains different subtasks that basically have to be executed simultaneously. According to assumption 1, subtasks can be divided into blocks consisting of a wait operation followed by calculations. Since each subtask is executed sequentially and execution time of calculations is negligible according to assumption 2, most of the time each subtask waits for the occurrence of a certain event. Scheduling then means waiting for the occurrence of one of those events and executing the respective block.

For many applications, such a nonpreemptive scheduling is sufficient. However, as the scheduling does not only apply to the CORBA runtime system itself, but also to application code (e.g., the method implementations of a CORBA object), splitting long methods into smaller blocks may be inconvenient for the application developer. If the application is additionally subject to real-time constraints (i.e., certain tasks have to be completed with given deadlines), nonpreemptive scheduling may not be sufficient. However, the scheduler abstraction presented here does allow the use of scheduling algorithms that support preemption—for example, using thread packages.

Scheduler functions

MICO's scheduler abstraction basically implements waiting for a given set of events to occur. When a block is "executed," the associated event is registered with the scheduler, which notes which block is associated with the event. Using appropriate mechanisms, the scheduler waits for the occurrence of the next registered event. It then removes the corresponding entry from its list of pending events and executes the block associated with the event. The scheduling algorithm controls what happens when many events occur simultaneously.

EXAMPLE 5.4. Figure 5.5 shows two subtasks, A (consisting of two blocks) and B (consisting of one block). A wait operation occurs at the beginning of each block; the rest of the block (shaded area) consists of calculation operations. The dotted arrows show the control flow between the blocks. The execution of subtasks starts at block A_1 for subtask A and B_1 for subtask B. So initially the associated events E_1 and E_3 are registered with the scheduler. The scheduler uses the method `schedule()` to implement the scheduling. This method is invoked at the start and continues through to the end of the program. The scheduler now waits for event E_1 or E_3 to occur. Assuming that E_1 occurs first, E_1 is removed from the list of the scheduler and block A_1 is executed. In ac-

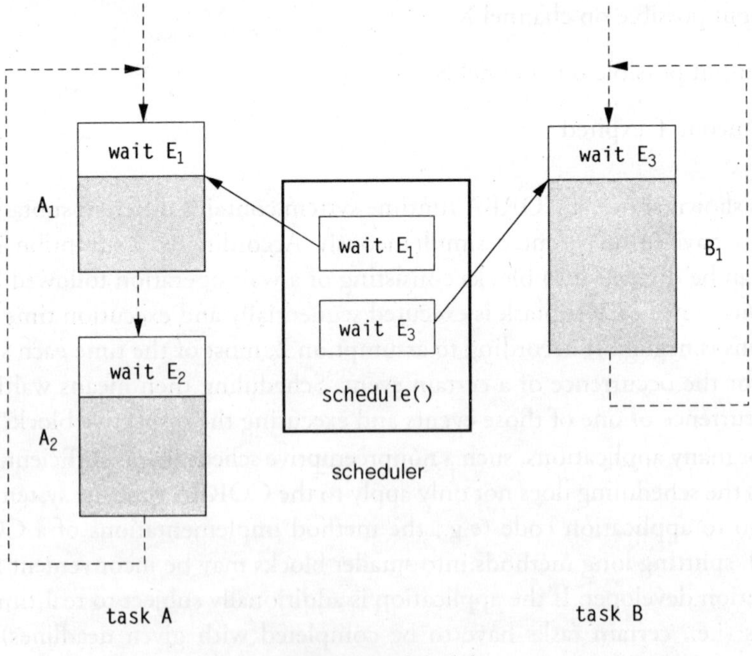

FIGURE 5.5 Scheduler.

cordance with the control flow, block A_2 has to be executed next. This means that event E_2 is registered with the scheduler, and the scheduling starts from the beginning. □

Scheduler characteristics

The characteristics of this approach are as follows:

- ⊞ Complete separation of interface and implementation of the scheduler
- ⊞ Functions in single-threaded environments and can utilize the advantages of a multithreaded environment (for example, one thread per subtask)
- ⊟ Program must be specially structured
- ⊟ No preemption in single-threaded environments

SCHEDULER INTERFACE

What makes it difficult to design a general interface to the scheduler abstraction above is that each scheduling algorithm requires special configuration data. For example, *round robin* requires the duration of a time slice, with *scheduling by priority*, a priority has to be assigned for each subtask. The user must therefore be aware of which scheduling algorithm is being applied, which means that a general interface cannot be used to encapsulate all scheduling algorithms.

Exchange of scheduler

On the other hand, it turns out that using a special scheduler in CORBA systems is often linked to other special components that use the services of the scheduler in the system. For example, for applications in real-time environments, TAO [32] contains special real-time inter-ORB protocols and real-time object adapters that use a real-time scheduler. Therefore, for MICO to be equipped with real-time features, the scheduler *and* the components that use the scheduler would have to be interchanged simultaneously. This would enable the components using the scheduler to know the algorithm used in the interchanged scheduler.

General and specialized interfaces

MICO schedulers therefore offer two interfaces: a general interface independent of algorithms and specific to the configuration data (such as priorities and deadlines) and a specialized interface customized to the algorithm used. When invocations are executed via the general interface, the missing configuration data is replaced by appropriate default values. System components that do require a special scheduling algorithm use the specialized interface. Other components that do not depend on specific scheduler instances use the general interface.

5.3.5 Object Generation

Locator

An object reference is a tuple $(\{L_i\}, T, I)$ consisting of the locators L_i, the type T, and the identity I of an object. A locator describes the mechanism that allows an object to be accessed. Because different mechanisms could be available for accessing an object, each object reference may have not only one but a number of locators.

Locators are closely related to addresses, since a locator identifies the location of an object as does an address. The difference between the two is the more abstract nature of an address. Although an address can provide unique identification of an object, it does not necessarily describe a way to locate the object. Therefore, a tuple [country, city, street, house number] is an address but not a locator. A locator could be a route description.

EXAMPLE 5.5. The locators described above are similar in their function to the *Uniform Resource Locators* (URL) [5], familiar from the WWW world. In the same vein, the syntax of locators in MICO visible to the user is similar to that of URLs. Locators for objects that can be accessed via IIOP follow this format:

```
inet:<ip-address>:<port-number>
```

In comparison, communication between processes on the same computer is supported by *named pipes* that are visible as special files in a file system. The format of the associated locators is

```
unix:<path>
```

The special locator `local:` is used to access objects in the same address space. □

Object reference template

Object adapters work closely with the ORB to create new object references. The object adapter contributes the type and the identity; the locators originate from the server-side transport modules that enable access to the address space from outside. As shown in Figure 5.6, the ORB supplies a template in which the transport modules enter locators; this template is used for the communication between object adapters and transport modules. Through the addition of type and identity to the template, the object adapter generates a new object reference,

5.3.6 Bootstrapping

Service provision

One of the fundamental tasks of distributed systems is *service mediation*—a bringing together of service providers and service users. A fundamental distinc-

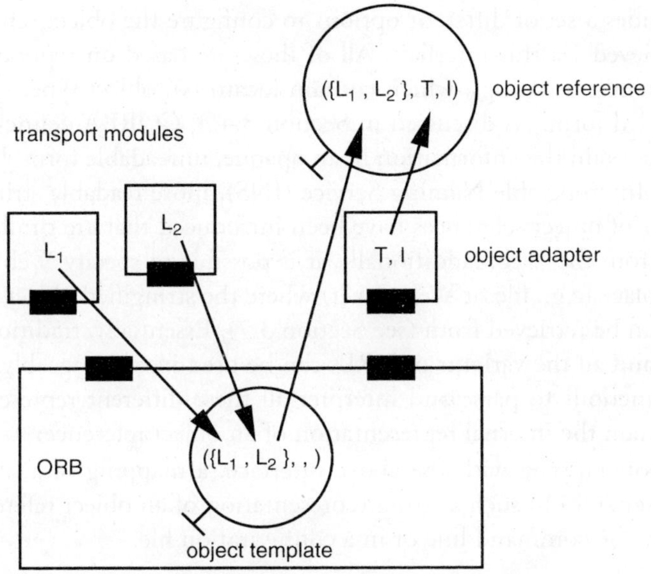

FIGURE 5.6 Generation of object references.

tion is made between two approaches: name-oriented mediation and content-oriented mediation. In the first case, the mediation is carried out through names the user allocates to services. In the second case, the mediation is based on characteristics of the service. The first type of mediators is called *name services*; the second type, *traders*.

In CORBA these mediators are carried out as an object service, which is a set of CORBA objects located outside the ORB core. However, this raises the question of how a service user obtains knowledge about the object reference of the mediator (name service or trader), also referred to as a *bootstrapping problem*.

The CORBA specification offers a solution to this problem with the ORB supplying an interface for querying *initial object references* based on a name (such as `NameService` for the object reference of the name service):

Initial object references

```
// IDL
interface ORB {
  ...
  Object resolve_initial_references (in string name);
  ...
};
```

MICO provides a set of different options to configure the object references that can be retrieved via this interface. All of these are based on representations of object references as strings, which contain locator(s), object type, and identity in an encoded form. As discussed in Section 3.4.3, CORBA defines stringified IORs that contain this information in an opaque, unreadable form. However, as part of the Interoperable Naming Service (INS), more readable stringified representations of object references have been introduced that are similar to URLs as known from the Web. Additionally, it is possible to specify Web URLs that point to a place (e.g., file or Web server) where the stringified object reference is stored or can be retrieved from (see Section 3.7). Essentially, traditional stringified IORs and all the variants of URLs can be used interchangeably. The ORB contains functions to parse and interpret all these different representations in order to obtain the internal representation of an object reference.

For bootstrapping with the above interface, a mapping of a service name (e.g., `NameService`) to such a string representation of an object reference can be specified on the command line or in a configuration file.

5.3.7 Dynamic Extensibility

For some applications it may be desirable to extend an executing CORBA application with new modules (e.g., other transport modules). With many compiled languages such as C++, loading such modules into a running program requires appropriate support by the operating system. In particular, cross-references between the running program and the loaded module must be resolved using a *dynamic linker*. Through its use of the dynamic linker, MICO offers the possibility of extending running CORBA systems through the addition of new modules, such as object adapters.

Dynamic linking

5.4 SUMMARY, EVALUATION, AND ALTERNATIVES

Microkernel approach

The microkernel approach has been applied to CORBA to enable the design of extensible and modifiable CORBA platforms. This has involved dividing the components of a CORBA system into microkernel components and services (components outside the microkernel ORB) and designing the necessary interfaces for the microkernel ORB. What comes to light is that the services can essentially be broken down into *invocation-generating* and *invocation-executing* services, with each group requiring a special interface to the microkernel ORB.

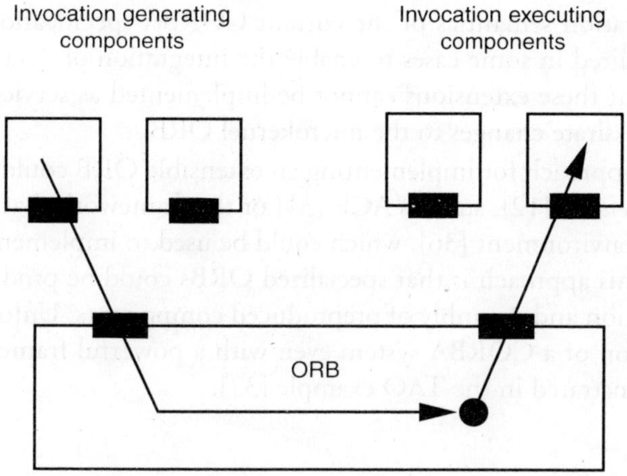

FIGURE 5.7 Microkernel ORB as demultiplexer during method invocation.

As shown in Figure 5.7, in simplified terms the function of the microkernel ORB during method invocation is to select an invocation-executing component.

A microkernel ORB incorporates the following characteristics:

- ⊞ Easy extensibility through the addition or exchange of services
- ⊟ Extensibility restricted to service types that are considered during the design of the microkernel ORB
- ⊟ Additional overheads

The additional overhead required is a disadvantage often associated with generic approaches. Conventional CORBA systems in which a specific communication mechanism, a specific object adapter, and the ORB core are merged to create a monolithic component allow for a great deal of optimization. This type of optimization is not possible when components are separated because a microkernel ORB is used. For example, some conventional CORBA systems incorporate a centralized table that allocates CORBA object servants (see Chapter 7) and communication end points (see Chapter 6). In contrast, with a microkernel ORB each communication module and each object adapter has to have a separate table.

In general, extensibility of the microkernel ORB is limited to remote method invocations. The introduction of new communication abstractions such as data streams is not supported. Because data streams cannot be mapped to the method invocation semantics of the current CORBA specification, extensions would be required in some cases to enable the integration of data streams. The problem is that these extensions cannot be implemented as services and would therefore necessitate changes to the microkernel ORB.

Frameworks

Another approach for implementing an extensible ORB could be the provision of a *framework* [12], such as ACE [31] or the framework that originated in the ReTINA environment [36], which could be used to implement ORBs. The idea behind this approach is that specialized ORBs could be produced through the configuration and assembly of preproduced components. Unfortunately, the implementation of a CORBA system even with a powerful framework is complex, as demonstrated in the TAO example [32].

Chapter 6

INTEROPERABILITY

In many cases, an invoked object and its caller do reside in different processes, often executed on different computers connected by a network. In order to enable such invocations across process boundaries and over the network, appropriate meachanisms and protocols are needed to support interoperability of these processes.

In earlier CORBA specifications (before version 2.0), these issues were left to the vendors of CORBA products. Indeed, different CORBA products contained different, incompatible protocols for invoking methods accross process boundaries. However, in many practical settings it is desireable to use different CORBA implementations for the client(s) and object implementation(s) (e.g., supporting different programming languages). In order to enable interoperability between different CORBA implementations by different vendors, CORBA 2.0 introduced a general interoperability architecture that supports interoperability between different CORBA ORBs.

We start this chapter by looking at the model that serves as the basis for interoperability in CORBA and at the corresponding protocols specified by CORBA. We then describe how this framework has been adopted by MICO based on the microkernel ORB described in Chapter 5.

6.1 MODEL

Objects as basic units

With respect to interoperability, objects are considered an indivisible whole. Consequently, for example, all methods of an object can be invoked through the same access mechanism. Nevertheless, objects can vary considerably in terms of their interoperability characteristics. Following are some examples of such characteristics:

Interoperability characteristics of objects

- Middleware platform in which an object exists
- CORBA implementation in which an object exists
- Protocol used to access an object
- Security requirements dictating access to an object

As indicated by these examples, interoperability is not only closely linked to the protocols used for communication between objects but also to the object services utilized (such as security service).

Object domains

In our study of interoperability, objects with the same values in terms of interoperability attributes are combined into groups called *domains*. Objects are located either totally in a domain or totally outside a domain, which reflects the "indivisibility attribute" mentioned earlier. Objects can be located in one domain, in more than one domain, or not in any domain. As a result, domains can be disjoint, can overlap, or can contain one another.

Bridges

Interoperability therefore deals with the way in which objects from different domains can communicate with one another. What this requires is a bijective mapping between the different behaviors within the domains. This mapping is called a *bridge*. Mappings executed by a bridge must be bijective because each server in an object-oriented system is potentially also a client since object references (for example, callback objects) can be supplied as parameters.

There are two types of bridges (see Figure 6.1):

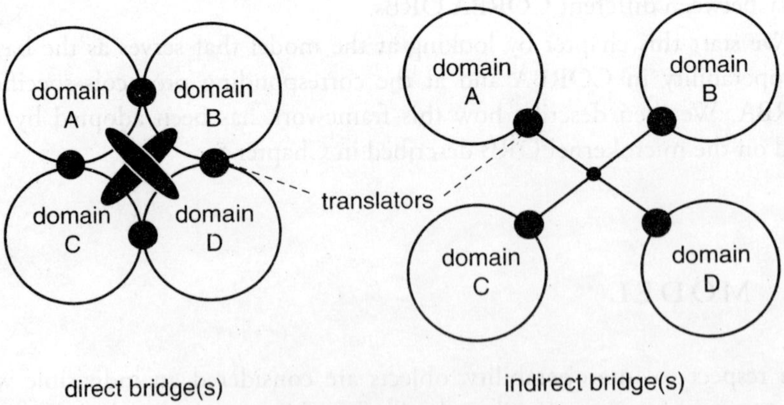

FIGURE 6.1 Direct versus indirect bridges.

- Direct bridges
- Indirect bridges

With a *direct bridge*, the behavior within a domain is translated directly into the behavior within the other domains. Therefore, for each pair of domains, a *translator* is needed that translates the behavior between the two domains. The direct bridge is characterized as follows: *Direct bridges*

⊞ One translation operation between two domains

⊟ The number of translators is squared to the number of domains

Indirect bridges use a canonical intermediate format. Each domain has exactly one translator that transfers the behavior in the domain into an intermediate format and vice versa. This approach is characterized by the following: *Indirect bridges*

⊞ The number of translators is linear to the number of domains

⊟ Two translation operations between two domains

The translators can be located at different *levels*. A distinction is made between *Implementation of bridges*

- Translators at the ORB level
- Translators at the application level

Translators at the ORB level are a part of the CORBA system and are usually provided by CORBA vendors, whereas *translators at the application level* are located outside the ORB and can be implemented by a user via DII, DSI, and interface repository. Because all calls in an application-level translator pass through DII and DSI, translators at the ORB level are considerably more efficient than those at the application level.

6.2 INTER-ORB PROTOCOLS

Based on the interoperability model described in Section 6.1, the CORBA specification defines data formats and protocols for constructing bridges be- *Interoperability levels*

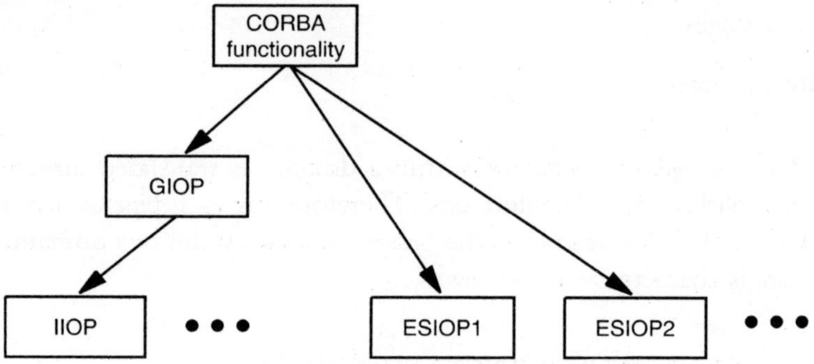

FIGURE 6.2 Interoperability support through CORBA.

tween object domains. This provides interoperability support at two levels:

- Between different CORBA ORBs over a "native" protocol
- Between different CORBA ORBs over legacy protocols

The *General Inter-ORB Protocol* (GIOP) is CORBA's native protocol to enable interoperability between CORBA ORBs. So-called *Environment-Specific Inter-ORB Protocols* (ESIOPs) also support interoperability between CORBA ORBs, but by tunneling CORBA requests over legacy protocols of other middleware systems.

GIOP and ESIOP

GIOP is not bound to any particular transport protocol and therefore cannot be implemented directly; mappings from GIOP to transport protocols first have to be defined. For example, the *Internet Inter-ORB Protocol* (IIOP) defines a mapping from GIOP to TCP/IP.

IOR

GIOP and ESIOPs use a common architecture that enables objects to be referenced across domain boundaries. These are called *Interoperable Object References* (IORs). IORs, GIOP, and ESIOPs are dealt with in detail in the following sections. Figure 6.2 shows the relationship between GIOP, IIOP, and different ESIOP.

6.2.1 Interoperable Object References

An important characteristic that distinguishes domains is the way in which they represent object references. A common intermediate format is required for object references to guarantee interoperability across domain boundaries. The specification of this intermediate format (as well as the format for the representation of IDL data types) is actually the responsibility of a protocol such as GIOP. However, CORBA provides a general framework for the representation of object references that has to be mapped to the respective protocol used. The structure of IORs is oriented to the information required by a bridge:

Information needed by bridges

- Is the object NIL?
- What is the object type?
- Which protocols can be used to access the object?
- Which object services are involved?

IORs are specified through CORBA-IDL based on this information model. Through IDL the IORs are mapped automatically to specific protocols such as GIOP based on the rules for mapping IDL data types to a transfer syntax.

Due to the potential extensibility of the usable protocols and object services, the structure of much of the information contained in an IOR (such as addresses) was unknown at the time the IOR framework was designed. An IOR therefore consists of the object's type identifier (`type_id`) and a set of `profiles`. Each profile contains all information that is necessary for access to the corresponding object through a particular access mechanism. If different mechanisms can be used to access an object, the IOR contains a profile for each mechanism. IORs without profiles represent a NIL object. A profile consists of a global identifier (`tag`) allocated by the OMG and unstructured data (`profile_data`). Each Inter-ORB protocol must specify the structure of this data.

IOR profiles

The standard specifies a mechanism for converting IORs into character strings and vice versa to enable the easy transfer of IORs (for example, via email).

6.2.2 General Inter-ORB Protocol

Interoperability between different CORBA ORBs is based on the GIOP. Note that although a CORBA ORB is not required to provide GIOP in order to be compliant with the CORBA specfication, most CORBA products do in fact implement GIOP. This often cancels out the need for a bridge when ORBs of different vendors are working together.

GIOP was designed for use over different connection-oriented protocols (such as TCP) and consists of three components:

GIOP specification

- *Common Data Representation* (CDR) defines a mapping of IDL data types to a byte stream.

- *GIOP-message formats* map ORB functionality (such as method invocations) to protocol messages.
- *Protocol state machine* defines sequences of possible messages exchanges (e.g., a reply message must be preceded by a request message).

The protocol messages themselves are specified by CORBA IDL and are also mapped through CDR to a byte stream that is to be transmitted. GIOP is abstract because it is not bound to any particular transport protocol. The specification merely contains some assumptions about the characteristics of usable transport protocols:

Requirements of transport layer

- *Connection-oriented:* The connection must be open before messages are transmitted and then closed afterwards.
- *Reliable:* Messages are not reordered and are only sent once.
- *Byte-stream-oriented:* There are no length restrictions for messages being transmitted and no packet boundaries.
- *Failure notification:* The user is informed in the case of failure.

Before GIOP can be used over a transport protocol that incorporates these characteristics, a definition of the mapping of GIOP to the respective protocol is required. IIOP is a mapping of GIOP to TCP/IP that each standard-compliant ORB must provide. Aside from IIOP, the CORBA standard does not currently define any other GIOP mappings. However, some products use special mappings. For example, the *Realtime Inter-ORB Protocol* (RIOP) used in TAO [32] is a mapping of GIOP to ATM. In addition to specifying the transport protocol to be used, each GIOP mapping defines the structure of the protocol profiles used in IORs (see Section 6.2.1). For example, an IIOP protocol profile contains the Internet address and the TCP port number of the communication end point where the object belonging to the IOR is located.

6.2.3 Environment-Specific Inter-ORB Protocols

While GIOP is CORBA's native interoperability protocol between ORBs (also of different vendors), ESIOPs enable the interoperation of ORBs using existing legacy protocols of other middleware systems (e.g., DCE). ESIOPs therefore enable the intergration of other middleware platforms with CORBA at the protocol level. The provision of ESIOPs by CORBA vendors is optional.

Each ESIOP defines the mapping of IDL data types to the data types of the middleware being linked. The mapping of ORB functionality to the communication mechanisms of the other platform is also defined. Lastly, each ESIOP specifies the format of the IOR protocol profiles. *ESIOP specification*

The first ESIOP defined by the OMG was the *DCE Common Inter-ORB Protocol* (DCE-CIOP), introduced with CORBA 2.0. This protocol enables a simple integration of CORBA and OSF-DCE applications. *DCE-CIOP*

6.3 DESIGN OF MICO'S INTEROPERABILITY

As an extendible CORBA platform, MICO offers a general framework for the implementation of interoperability mechanisms. Based on this framework, we will present a design for the support of GIOP in MICO. Use of the framework not only enables the implementation of a certain GIOP mapping such as IIOP but also the provision of GIOP as a general mechanism. *GIOP framework*

6.3.1 Framework

Along with some general tools, the interoperability framework provides mechanisms on the OSI model's transport, presentation, and application layers. Most of these mechanisms are abstract in the sense that they are not linked to any particular protocol or data format. They are not linked to a concrete protocol or data format except through inheritance (derivation) from the framework classes and the implementation of additional methods. Figure 6.3 shows a UML diagram of the abstract components in the framework.

STORAGE MANAGEMENT

Efficient storage management is the key to an effective CORBA system. It is particularly important to avoid data copying as much as possible. The following is a list of some important locations where data potentially has to be copied:

Data copying

- Between network hardware and interoperability modules
- Between interoperability modules and ORB kernel
- Between ORB kernel and object adapters

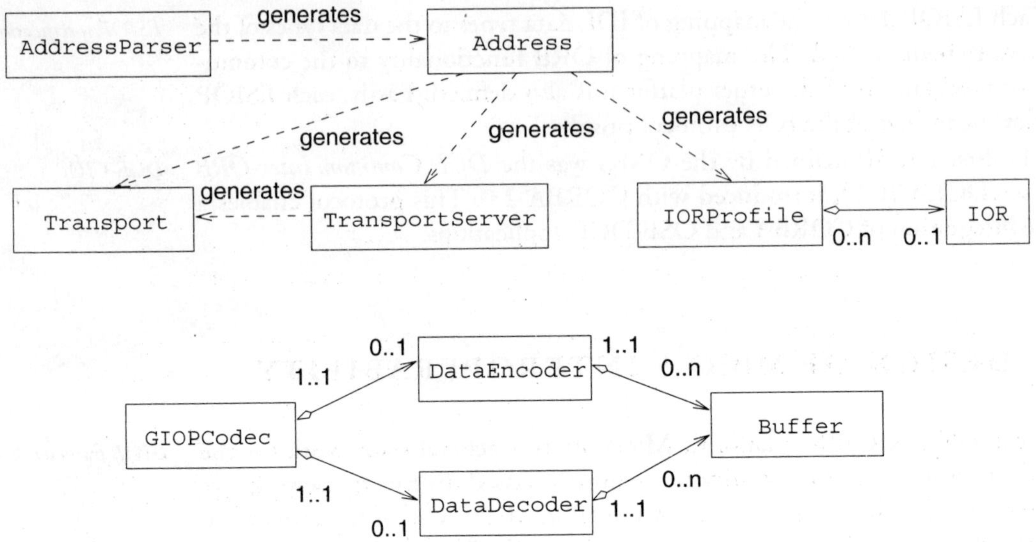

FIGURE 6.3 UML diagram of interoperability framework.

- Between object adapters and object implementations
- With data marshalling

An important element of an interoperability framework is the ability to transform data items (e.g., an integer value) into a sequence of bytes that can be sent to a remote program as part of a network message. The process of converting a data item to such a byte sequence is commonly referred to as *marshalling*, and the reverse process of reconstructing a data item from a byte sequence is called *demarshalling*. The amount of storage space that will be required for data marshalling (i.e., the size of the resulting byte sequence) is often not known in advance. Therefore, in some cases data that has already been marshalled has to be copied into a larger storage area during marshalling.

Marshalling

Demarshalling

Buffer

The framework offers `Buffer` objects that manage contiguous storage areas, thereby limiting the amount of data that requires copying. These storage areas can be increased without copying through a close cooperation with dynamic storage management. Moreover, each `Buffer` has a *reference counter*. Thus the reference counter can simply be increased anywhere that stored data potentially has to be copied. If the `Buffer` is no longer required, the reference counter is decremented. If the reference counter reaches zero, the `Buffer` is deleted.

TRANSPORT LAYER

The framework offers suitable abstractions on the transport layer for connection-oriented transport protocols. `Transport` and `TransportServer` objects model the semantics of a connection-oriented protocol just as the GIOP expects. Just like GIOP, these objects are abstract in the sense that they are not linked to any specific protocol. Through inheritance these abstract objects can be bound to a specific protocol, such as TCP.

Transport

`Transport` objects model a communication end point using the following operations:

- Establish/terminate a connection to a remote `TransportServer`
- Transmit data from a buffer
- Receive data in a buffer

TransportServer

Invisibly to the user, the `Transport` objects work closely with the scheduler described in Section 5.3.4 to send and receive data. `TransportServer` objects model special communication end points that are used to set up new connections on the server side. If a remote `Transport` object sets up a connection to a `TransportServer` object, then the `TransportServer` object generates a new `Transport` object that can be used in exchanging data with the remote `Transport` object.

Address

`Address` objects are used to address communication end points. They offer the following functions:

- Conversion of an address into a character string
- Conversion of a character string into an address
- Factory for `Transport`, `TransportServer`, and `IORProfile` objects

AddressParser

`AddressParser` objects are used for reconverting character strings into `Address` objects. A class derived from `AddressParser` must be provided for each address type.

`Address` objects are used as a factory [13] for creating `Transport`, `TransportServer`, and `IORProfile` objects. (Note that `IORProfile` objects model the protocol profiles for the interoperable object references described in Section 6.2.1 and are provided by the framework as a mechanism for the application layer.)

For example, if an address exists in the form of a character string entered by the user, it can be converted into an `Address` object through the use of an `AddressParser`. Without the knowledge of which specific protocol the address belongs to, the `Address` object can create a `Transport` object that implements the protocol matching the address. Lastly, a connection can be established to the communication end point with this address and data exchanged without knowledge of which protocol was used.

`Address` and `AddressParser` objects are also abstract and must be linked to a particular protocol through inheritance.

PRESENTATION LAYER

Encoder and decoder

The framework offers support on the presentation layer for marshalling and demarshalling IDL data types. `DataEncoder` objects convert IDL data types into a byte stream that is filed in a `Buffer` object. `DataDecoder` objects read a byte stream from the `Buffer` object and convert it into IDL data types. `DataEncoder` and `DataDecoder` objects are also abstract and have to be linked to a specific marshalling format such as CDR through inheritance.

APPLICATION LAYER

IOP codec

The application layer of the framework offers support in the creation and the decoding of the messages of an inter-ORB protocol, such as GIOP. Among other things, `GIOPCodec` objects provide operations for creating and decoding the following messages:

1. Invocation request
2. Invocation response
3. Cancel request

These messages are used to carry out method invocations (1, 2) and to cancel method invocations currently being processed (3). A `DataEncoder` object is used to generate a message that it then files as a byte stream in a `Buffer` object. When a message is received, the byte stream read from a `Buffer` object is decoded via an `DataDecoder` object.

Another component of the application layer consists of `IOR` objects that model the interoperable object references described in Section 6.2.1. Along with the type and the identification of a CORBA object, each `IOR` object contains a set of protocol profiles. The latter are modeled by `IORProfile` objects in the framework and have to be bound to a particular protocol through inheritance. At a minimum, protocol profiles contain the address where the corresponding CORBA object can be found. Consequently, `Address` objects can be used as a factory for creating the appropriate `IORProfile` objects.

IORProfile

6.3.2 GIOP

The abstract framework described in the preceding subsection enables GIOP to be implemented as an abstract mechanism independent of a particular transport protocol such as TCP. For a specific GIOP mapping such as IIOP, the corresponding abstract components of the framework have to be linked to concrete protocols through inheritance. For example, Table 6.1 lists the components used for IIOP.

Figure 6.4 shows how the two components *GIOP client* and *GIOP server* support GIOP in MICO. From the view of the ORB, the GIOP client is an invocation-executing component that—like an object adapter—accepts method invocations from the ORB but then converts them into GIOP messages and sends them to a GIOP server. The GIOP server is an invocation-generating component that receives messages, converts them into method invocations, and then sends them to the local ORB. The two subsections that follow take a closer look at the structure of GIOP clients and servers.

GIOP client and GIOP server

GIOP CLIENT

Figure 6.5 shows how components of the framework are used to implement the GIOP client. A `GIOPCodec` converts a method invocation arriving from the

TABLE 6.1 IIOP components

Components	Inherits from	Description
`TCPTransport`	`Transport`	TCP communication end point
`TCPTransportServer`	`TransportServer`	TCP communication end point for establishing new connections
`InetAddress`	`Address`	Internet address, contains IP address and port number
`InetAddressParser`	`AddressParser`	Parser for Internet addresses
`CDREncoder`	`DataEncoder`	Components for marshalling IDL data types in accordance with CDR
`CDRDecoder`	`DataDecoder`	Components for demarshalling IDL data types in accordance with CDR
`IIOPProfile`	`IORProfile`	IIOP protocol profile, contains IP address, port number, IIOP version, and object ID
`GIOPCodec`		Components for creation and decoding of GIOP message

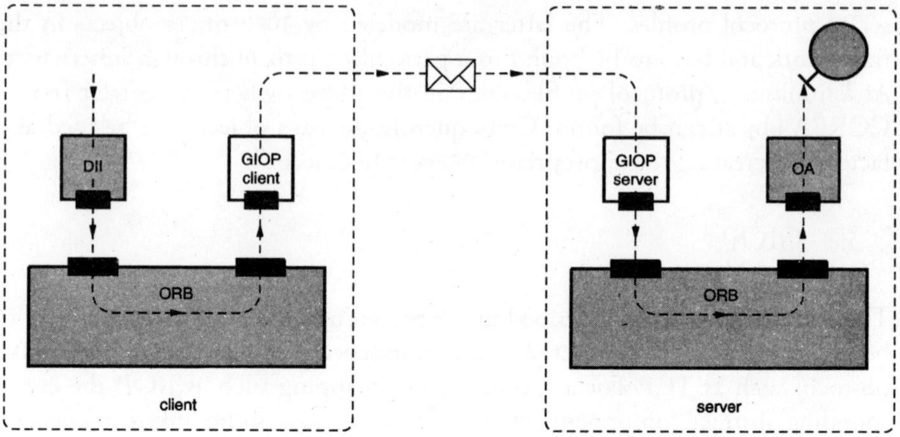

FIGURE 6.4 GIOP support in MICO.

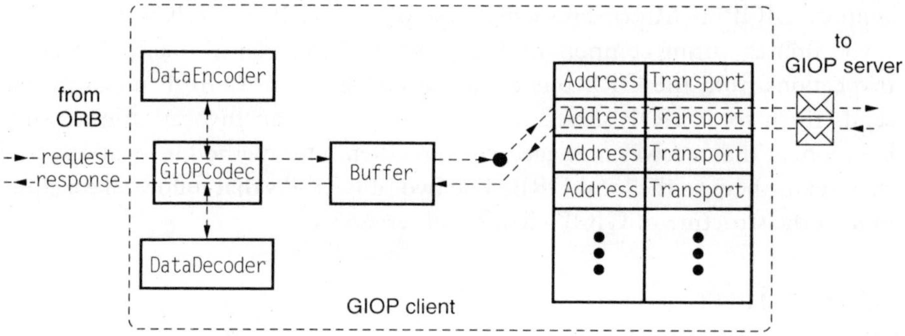

FIGURE 6.5 GIOP client.

ORB (`request` in Figure 6.5) into a protocol message and files it as a byte stream in a `Buffer`. The `GIOPCodec` uses a suitable `DataEncoder` to marshal the data types. Connections to GIOP servers are represented in the client by `Transport` objects. For reasons of efficiency, a connection to a GIOP server exists beyond the duration of a method invocation so that later method invocations to the same GIOP server can use the same connection. Consequently, the GIOP client uses a table to keep a record of existing connections and the addresses of the corresponding servers. When it sends a message, the GIOP client extracts the address of the appropriate GIOP server from the object reference of the target object of the method invocation and consults its table. If the address is not listed in the table, it sets up a new connection and enters it into the table. The message is then sent via the `Transport` object.

Connection table

The results of the method invocation are filed in a `Buffer` and decoded by the `GIOPCodec` with the help of a `DataDecoder`. The result (`response` in Figure 6.5) is made known to the ORB.

GIOP SERVER

The GIOP server is the counterpart of the GIOP client. It also has to use a table to keep a record of the connections that exist to the GIOP client. If a GIOP client wants to send a message to a GIOP server, it first has to establish a connection to the server. As shown in Figure 6.6, it sends a connection request to the server that arrives at the `TransportServer` object in the GIOP server (`connect` in Figure 6.6). A `Transport` object for the new connection is then created in the server and entered into the connection table. The GIOP client is now able to exchange messages with the GIOP server. *Connection table*

If a message arrives at the server, it is decoded by the `GIOPCodec` using a `DataDecoder`. The resulting method invocation (`request` in Figure 6.6) is sent to the ORB for execution. If the ORB later notifies the GIOP server of the result of the method invocation (`response` in Figure 6.6), the `GIOPCodec` then uses `DataEncoder` to marshal the result into a `Buffer`. Lastly, the server consults its connection table to find the `Transport` object over which the message is to be sent to the GIOP client. In contrast to the client, the GIOP server can assume that a corresponding entry already exists in the table, since the client had already opened the connection to receive the method invocation message.

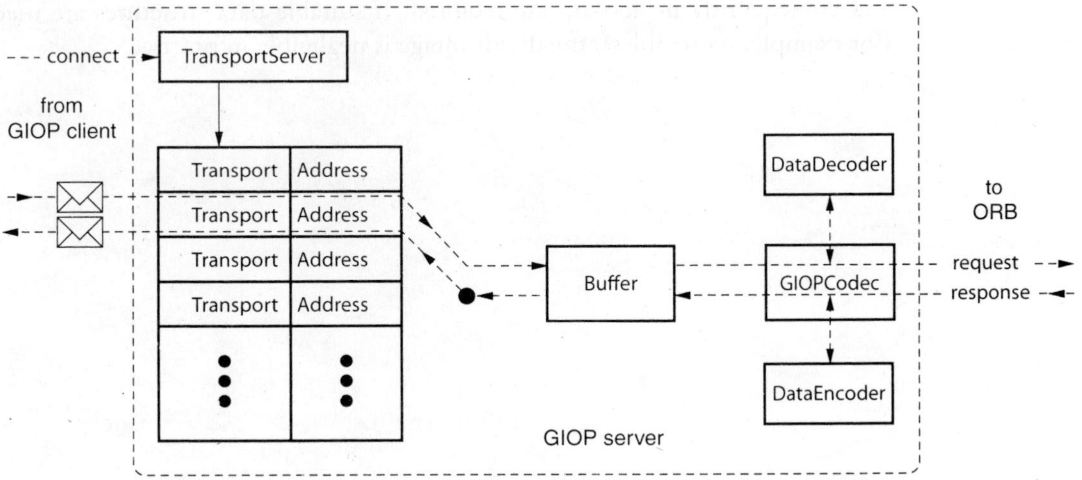

FIGURE 6.6 GIOP server.

6.4 SUMMARY, EVALUATION, AND ALTERNATIVES

The construction of interoperability components is supported in MICO by an abstract framework that is not bound to any particular protocol. On the basis of this framework, GIOP in MICO can be implemented without being bound to specific transport protocols such as TCP. For the support of certain GIOP mappings such as IIOP, the abstract components of the framework merely have to be linked to concrete protocols through inheritance.

GIOP support is implemented through two services outside the microkernel ORB presented in Chapter 5: the *GIOP client* transforms the method invocations received from the ORB into network packets; the *GIOP server* receives these network packets and converts them into method invocations on the ORB. This approach is characterized as follows:

Advantages and disadvantages

- ⊞ Simple integration of new GIOP mappings
- ⊞ Simple integration of new inter-ORB protocols (e.g., ESIOPs)
- ⊟ Additional overhead

The additional overhead means that a lookup is required in the connection table for each method invocation. With a conventional ORB implementation in which the interoperability modules are part of the ORB, the allocation to the `Transport` objects can be stored directly in stub objects. In this case, no table and consequently no lookup are required. If suitable data structures are used (for example, hash tables), the disadvantage is negligible in practice.

Chapter 7

OBJECT ADAPTERS

Object adapters separate object-specific behavior from the ORB kernel. This additional layer exists to allow for different object adapters to support the numerous functionality requirements that exist in a server. For example, the needs of a server representing an object database—which may provide numerous individual objects that cannot all exist in memory at the same time—are very different from a server that provides a printing service.

This chapter begins with an overview of the functionality of object adapters. The overview is followed by some examples of object adapters, including the *Portable Object Adapter* (POA) that must be supplied by all standard-conformant CORBA implementations. The chapter concludes with a discussion of the object adapters implemented by MICO based on the mechanisms presented in Chapter 5.

7.1 TERMINOLOGY

Object ID: Part of the identity of a CORBA object; assigned either by the object adapter or by the user. Object IDs are unique within an object adapter.

Object key: Identifies a CORBA object within an ORB. It includes the object ID and an identifier that uniquely identifies the object adapter that the object is active in. The ORB uses this identifier to determine the object adapter responsible for the associated object; then the object adapter separates the object ID from the object key to select the target object of a method invocation.

Object reference = global address of an object

Object reference: Sometimes also called "interoperable object reference" (IOR). The object reference represents the globally unique identity of a CORBA object. It includes the object key as well as address information that identifies the ORB that the object is collocated with (the "IOR template"). The object reference can be used to access a CORBA object remotely. To applications, an object reference is opaque, only to be interpreted by an ORB. Object references can be "stringified" to be stored in a file or for display.

Servant = object implementation

Servants: Programming-language constructs that incorporate the state and the behavior (implementation) that is associated with a CORBA object. Servants are activated with an object adapter and are the target of CORBA invocations. In procedural languages such as C, a servant is a collection of functions (behavior) and data fields (state); in object-oriented languages such as C++ or Java, servants are instances of a class.

Object = identity + state + behavior

CORBA object: Defined by its identity, state, and behavior. Based on the terminology introduced so far, a CORBA object is represented by an object reference and a servant. In many cases, there is a one-to-one mapping between object references and servants; in many applications, there is one servant per object reference and vice versa. However, object adapters allow different usage patterns to exist.

Skeleton = linking servant to object adapter

Skeletons: Programming-language constructs that enable object adapters to execute methods on servants. Skeletons present a known (private) interface to the object adapter and delegate invocations to the servant. "Static" skeletons are usually generated according to an interface by the IDL compiler; however, there is also a special "dynamic" skeleton interface (DSI) that can be used to execute invocations on objects for which no IDL compiler-generated skeletons exist. In C++, servants inherit skeletons.

Creation: The onset of the existence of a CORBA object.

Activation: Brings a CORBA object into a state in which it is able to receive method invocations. Activation may or may not include incarnation.

Incarnation: The act of associating a CORBA object with a servant.

Etherealization: Releases the connection between a CORBA object and the associated servant.

Deactivation: Brings a CORBA object into a state in which it is not able to execute method invocations. An object may be inactive temporarily; that is, it is possible to reactivate an object after deactivation.

Destruction: Irrevocably ends the existence of a CORBA object.

Active Object Map: A per-object adapter map that records the current mapping between CORBA objects (in the form of object IDs, which, as seen above, completely identify a CORBA object within an object adapter) and servants.

7.2 FUNCTIONALITY

Gamma et al. [13] define an object adapter as a design pattern to achieve a "reusable class that cooperates with unrelated or unforeseen classes." According to their definition, an object adapter receives a client's request and translates it into a request that is understood by the "adaptee."

This definition matches object adapters in a CORBA system quite well. An object adapter's primary task is a simple one of dispatching incoming client's requests—that the object adapter is handed by its client, the ORB kernel—to the adaptee, a servant. In the process, the request must be translated; the object request, which arrives from the Object Request Broker as a blob of binary data, must be demarshalled into the method parameters that the servant expects.

The premise of request unmarshalling and dispatching must be supplemented with some associated functionality. An object adapter's functionality can be segmented into five categories:

- *Management of servants:* An object adapter must provide a user—the implementer of a service—with an interface to register request recipients, servants. The user must then be able to selectively activate and deactivate servants on a per-object basis.
- *Management of objects:* The object adapter must provide an interface to manage objects throughout their life cycle. This involves associating a state of the object life cycle with the object identities that an object adapter manages.
- *Generation and interpretation of object references:* The object adapter must be able to create and interpret object references that encapsulate a certain object identity.
- *Mapping objects to servants:* For incoming requests, an object adapter must be able to map the object identity requested by the client to a particular servant as a target for the method invocation.

- *Method invocation:* After interpreting an object reference, and identifying the target servant, the object adapter must be able to execute the method invocation.

7.2.1 Object Management

When seen from the client side, an object is in either of two states: requests can be processed, or they can't. In the former case, the client will receive the expected result; in the latter case, it gets an `OBJ_NOT_EXIST` exception.

Object life cycle

On the server side, an object's state is more fine-grained. There is a total of four states that an object adapter can associate with a CORBA object, as shown in Figure 7.1.

An object begins and ends its life cycle in the nonexistent state. In this state, an object adapter has no information about an object. This state is left during object creation and reentered by object destruction.

During creation, the object adapter is made aware of an object's identity, and the object enters the inactive state. Once an object is created, the object

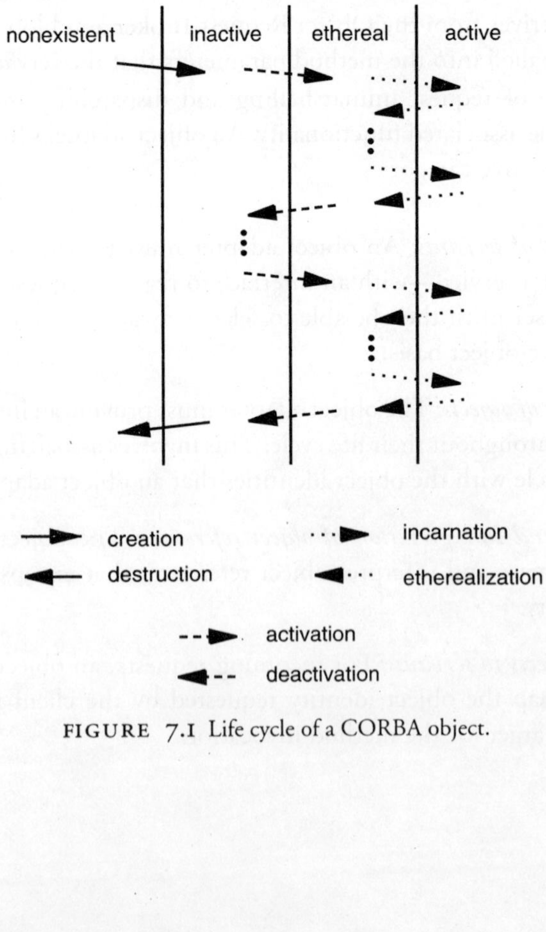

FIGURE 7.1 Life cycle of a CORBA object.

adapter is able to generate and export object references. However, clients are unable to distinguish between inactive and nonexistent objects, as the object is still unable to receive method invocations.

Activation makes an object accessible by clients. In the ethereal state, an object is ready to receive requests, but there is yet no servant associated with the object. In the case of incoming method invocations, object adapters have different options for treating the request:

- *Rejection:* The invocation is rejected with an error message.
- *Holding:* The invocation is deferred. If the object becomes active, the invocation is executed; if the object becomes inactive, it is rejected.
- *On-demand activation:* An object adapter could actively invoke some user callback code to incarnate a servant for activation.

Incarnation associates an ethereal object with a servant. Method invocations can now be executed.

Note that transitions between these states need not be distinct. In fact, this is the more common case. Usually, creation, activation, and incarnation happen at the same time, and later, objects are usually etherealized and deactivated simultaneously. Frequently, the ethereal state is not considered, and in many terminologies, "activation" implicitly includes incarnation, and "deactivation" implicitly includes etherealization.

Common difference in "activation" terminology

As another dimension of object state, objects can be characterized as being *transient* or *persistent.* Even though this distinction is made at the object adapter level, it is more commonly associated with the object itself. An object is called persistent if and only if the object adapter is persistent—and likewise for transience.

Transient versus persistent objects

The life cycle of transient object adapters and of the transient objects it holds is bounded by the life cycle of the server process they were created by. If the server process is terminated, all its transient object adapters and transient objects are implicitly destroyed. Persistent objects, however, are implicitly deactivated when the server process is terminated, but not destructed. Therefore, it is possible to reactivate persistent objects when the server restarts.

Persistent objects allow a servant to evolve or migrate, ideally without interruption in service.

7.2.2 Servant Management

While an object adapter has to provide an interface to associate servants with active objects as part of object incarnation, a servant's life cycle is usually handled by the application.

Servant life cycle != Object life cycle

Note that the life cycle of servants may be entirely independent of the life cycle of any objects it may be associated with. Object creation may be disassociated from servant creation—a servant need not exist until object incarnation. Also, a servant can be destructed when an object is etherealized, and a different servant could be created for its next incarnation.

An object adapter must notify servants of incarnation and etherealization, that is, of an association that is made between the servant and an active object. This is especially important for persistent objects, so that the servant may have a chance to store or load its state in or from persistent storage.

Another complication in servant management is introduced by multithreading. In a multithreaded server, a servant might still be processing requests upon etherealization. In that case, an object adapter must provide hooks that allow a servant to be destructed after all invocations have completed, to avoid race conditions.

7.2.3 Generation of Object References

An object reference is the global address of an object; clients can use the object reference to send requests to an object.

In order to generate an object reference, the object adapter retrieves the *object reference template* from the ORB (see Section 5.3.5). The template contains addressing information for the ORB only. The object adapter then complements that information with an *object key* that uniquely identifies an object within an ORB.

An object key contains or implies two separate pieces of information: a unique identifier for the object adapter that created this object, and the *object ID* that identifies an object within the object adapter. Within a specific object adapter, the object ID represents the full object identity.

Object IDs can be assigned to objects implicitly by the object adapter or explicitly by the user.

The ORB receives the object key as part of an incoming request and uses it to determine the object adapter to delegate the request to. The object adapter then extracts the object ID and uses it as an identifier to locate a servant.

7.2.4 Mapping Objects to Servants

For incoming requests, an object adapter must be able to identify a specific servant that is able to process the request. The user must thus be able to create associations between objects and servants.

An easy way to accomplish the mapping would be an active object map and an interface to create and remove entries from the map. The object adapter could then consult the map to find a servant or to reject the request if no entry exists for an object.

However, this approach by itself is not scalable because the number of objects that a server can handle would be limited by the size of the active object map. In addition to the active object map, object adapters can support various patterns to allow for the handling of an arbitrary number of objects, such as on-demand incarnation of servants or default servants.

The common case for mapping objects to servants is a 1-to-1 mapping, that is, there is exactly one servant that is associated with an object. However, other cardinalities are possible:

Object-to-servant mapping cardinalities

- 1-to-1: The common case—an object is associated with a single servant and vice versa.
- 1-to-0: If there is no servant that is associated with an object, the object is ethereal or inactive.
- N-to-1: One servant can be associated with many objects. In this case, the servant needs information to identify the object that it implements for each invocation.
- 1-to-N: There can be more than one servant per object (for example, to support load balancing).

7.2.5 Execution of Method Invocations

Methods can be executed if an object is in the active state. As Figure 7.2 illustrates, a method invocation passes through several dispatching stages before it is finally executed. First the object adapter uses the object reference to determine the target object for the method invocation and the servant attached to it; this may require on-demand incarnation if the object is currently ethereal.

Dispatching a method invocation

Associated with each servant is a skeleton. In step 2, the servant selects a skeleton that matches the servant type. The skeleton decodes (unmarshals) the method's input parameters (see Section 5.3.1), and in step 3 hands over control

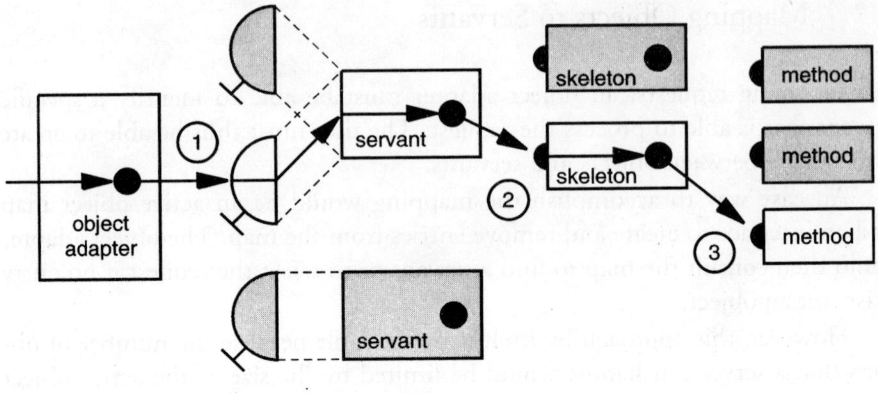

FIGURE 7.2 Dispatching a method invocation.

to the user implementation, according to the method name that is passed along as part of the client request.

Skeletons establish the connection between object adapter and the method implementation. Their structure therefore depends on the object adapter as well as on the language mapping used. For example, there is a considerable difference between skeletons in procedural programming languages such as C and those in object-oriented programming languages. In C++, skeletons are associated with servants by inheritance.

Static versus dynamic skeletons

Skeletons are usually *static:* generated by the IDL compiler according to an interface definition, static skeletons are specific to that interface. Here, "static" refers to the fact that a static skeleton can make use of the programming language's static typing, as the types of parameters are known a priori, at compile time.

There are also *dynamic* skeletons, which are implemented by the applications programmer. Since CORBA requests do not contain type information, a dynamic skeleton needs to supply that information in order to interpret incoming requests. However, unlike a static skeleton, type information is not required at compile time. For example, a dynamic skeleton could access an interface repository to dynamically find out about a method's parameter types.

Static skeletons are much easier to use. In C++, a static skeleton hands over control to an implementation using pure virtual operations that are overloaded in a user-implemented class that inherits the skeleton, so the implementation is not concerned with request processing, type information, or the unmarshalling of parameters. Also, static skeletons perform better than dynamic skeletons because compile time type knowledge allows for numerous optimizations. For both reasons, static skeletons are used almost exclusively.

Dynamic skeletons are useful in two niches. One is in applications where advance type information is not available—for example, in a bridge between CORBA and Web services. Such a bridge should be able to handle any requests; it should not be limited to a narrow set of types for which compile time knowledge is available. The bridge could therefore use a dynamic skeleton, and retrieve the required type information from a type repository at runtime. The other niche for dynamic skeletons is in footprint constrained environments. Each static skeleton requires some amount of object code, while a dynamic skeleton may even support multiple object types simultaneously.

7.3 THE PORTABLE OBJECT ADAPTER

The *Portable Object Adapter* (POA) was introduced in CORBA 2.2, published in 1998, and it became the only object adapter defined by CORBA. It replaced the *Basic Object Adapter* (BOA), which was introduced by the first version of CORBA and largely unchanged since 1991.

The BOA was to be a "simple and generic" type of object adapter to be used, as its name suggests, for basic purposes. It was never designed to be a general-purpose object adapter. The OMG expected more sophisticated object adapters to be specified over time, which never happened. Instead, ORBs implemented vendor-specific extensions on top of the deficient BOA specification, rendering the idea of portable server code impossible.

With the introduction of the Portable Object Adapter, the BOA was removed from the CORBA specification.

Over the years, other object adapters like a "Library Object Adapter" or an "Object-Oriented Database Adapter" were suggested, but never realized.

Today, most ORBs implement the Portable Object Adapter only, and the rest of this chapter details the POA's functionality and describes its implementation in Mico.

CORBA 3.0 introduces the CORBA Component Model (CCM), which includes the "Container Programming Model," in which a container takes on the role of an object adapter for its components.

7.3.1 Overview

The Portable Object Adapter is the result of the experience gathered from coping with the inadequacies of the BOA and its vendor-specific extensions. The foremost design goals for the POA were

- *Portability:* By defining comprehensive interfaces and their semantics for the POA, it should be possible to port source code between different vendors' ORB without changes.
- *Configurability:* Configuration options allow the selective enabling or disabling of certain standard POA features, influencing its behavior.
- *Flexibility:* By providing hooks to control a servant's life cycle and readiness to receive requests, the POA should be usable even for servers with exotic requirements. Sensible defaults exist to make the programming of simple servers as easy as possible.

Many POA instances can exist in a server, organized in a hierarchical structure. The *Root POA* is created by the ORB; more POA instances can then be created by the user as children of existing ones.

Each POA maintains its own *Active Object Map*, a table mapping currently active objects to servants. Objects are activated with a particular POA instance and henceforth associated with "their" POA, identified by a unique *Object ID* within its namespace.

Synchronization between POAs is achieved by *POA Managers*, which control the readiness of one or more POAs to receive requests. Figure 7.3 shows an example of using many POAs: in this diagram, the Root POA has two children, and the POA named ABC has another child, with which it shares a separate POA Manager. Servants can be registered with any of the four POA instances.

Apart from providing control over synchronization, the POA provides many hooks that enable a user to influence request processing:

- Many POA features are controlled via configurable *policies*.

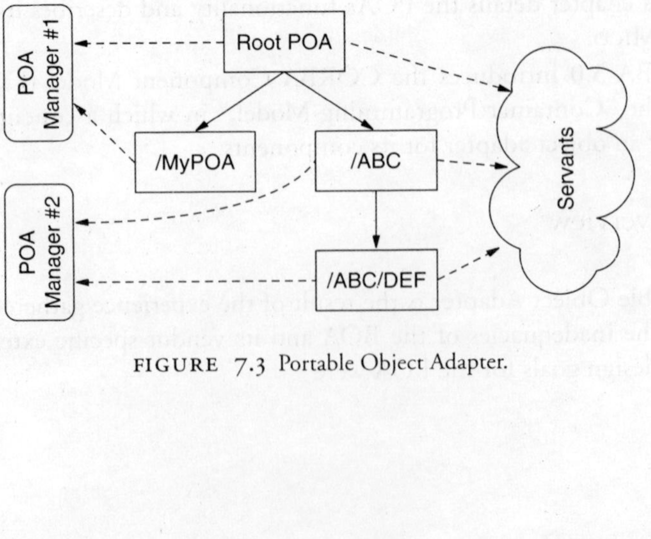

FIGURE 7.3 Portable Object Adapter.

- The life cycle of servants can be controlled and monitored by *servant managers*.
- *Default servants* can service many objects at once.
- *Adapter activators* can be used to create new POAs on demand, if necessary.

The following sections will examine these concepts more closely.

7.3.2 Policies

Each POA has its own separate set of *policies*, which adjust different aspects of a POA's behavior. Policies are configured by the user upon POA creation and cannot be changed over its lifetime. Since objects are associated with a fixed POA instance, some policies can also be said to be that of an object's—most obvious with the lifespan policy.

Thread policy: Addresses multithreading issues. Can be set to either "Single Thread" (`SINGLE_THREAD_MODEL`) if the servants are not thread-aware and requests must be serialized, or to "ORB controlled" (`ORB_CTRL_MODEL`) if servants are reentrant and requests can be processed regardless of ongoing invocations. While the "Single Thread" option allows reentrant calls that an implementation makes to itself (including, for example, callbacks during a remote invocation), a third "Main Thread" (`MAIN_THREAD_MODEL`) option does not.

Lifespan policy: Can be either "transient" or "persistent." The lifespan of transient objects (i.e., objects that are registered in a POA with the transient lifespan policy) is limited by the lifespan of the POA instance they were activated in. Once a POA with the transient lifespan policy is destroyed (for example, as part of server shutdown), all objects that were activated with that POA are destructed, and their object references become permanently invalid. Objects that are activated in a POA with the persistent lifespan policy ("persistent objects") can outlive their POA and even their server. Missing POAs for persistent objects can be recreated, and if their server is shut down, it may be restarted at a later time and continue serving the object.

Object ID uniqueness policy: Slightly misnamed, "Servant Uniqueness" might be more appropriate, as it controls whether a single servant can be registered (activated) with the POA more than once to serve more than one object (`MULTIPLE_ID`) or not (`UNIQUE_ID`).

TABLE 7.1 POA policy defaults for the root POA and other POAs

Policy	Root POA	Default
Thread policy	ORB_CTRL_MODEL	ORB_CTRL_MODEL
Lifespan policy	TRANSIENT	TRANSIENT
Object ID uniqueness	UNIQUE_ID	UNIQUE_ID
ID assignment	SYSTEM_ID	SYSTEM_ID
Servant retention	RETAIN	RETAIN
Request processing	USE_ACTIVE_OBJECT_MAP_ONLY	USE_ACTIVE_OBJECT_MAP_ONLY
Implicit activation	IMPLICIT_ACTIVATION	NO_IMPLICIT_ACTIVATION

ID assignment policy: Selects whether Object IDs are generated by the POA (SYSTEM_ID) or are selected by the user (USER_ID)—for example, to associate objects with application-specific identity information, such as a database table key. If a single servant is registered more than once to serve multiple objects, it could use a user-selected Object ID (which would be different for multiple activations) at runtime to discriminate between them.

Servant retention policy: Normally, when an object is activated, the association between the object (or rather, its Object ID) and the servant is stored in the Active Object Map (RETAIN). This behavior can be changed if desired (NON_RETAIN). A user might not want to store active objects in the Active Object Map if the POA is expected to handle a large or even unbounded number of objects that would inflate the Active Object Map. If the POA does not maintain a list of active objects, the user must provide either a servant manager or a default servant to aid the POA in selecting servants for incoming invocations.

Request processing policy: Specifies if the POA will consult its Active Object Map only when looking for a servant to serve a request (USE_ACTIVE_OBJECT_MAP_ONLY), or whether the POA should also consider using a servant manager (USE_SERVANT_MANAGER) or a default servant (USE_DEFAULT_SERVANT).

Implicit activation policy: Whether servants can be activated implicitly (IMPLICIT_ACTIVATION *versus* NO_IMPLICIT_ACTIVATION). Some operations on a servant require its activation—for example, the request to generate an object reference. The most popular application for implicit activation is a servant's _this() operation, which implicitly activates a servant as a side effect of generating an object reference. This operation would fail if implicit activation was disabled in a POA instance.

Some of these policies are of more interest than others. The implicit activation policy or the Object ID uniqueness policy can be considered sweeteners; they have no effect on request processing but are mere safeguards to protect the careless developer. Implicit activation saves but a line of code that would be necessary with the enforcement of explicit activation.

The ID assignment policy can relieve the developer of the need to generate unique names. While this feature is also redundant, it is nonetheless useful. In most scenarios, the Object ID is of no interest to the application, so that system-provided Object IDs are convenient.

The other policies are more crucial and will be referred to again in later sections.

If some policies are not set upon POA creation, they are set to their respective defaults as shown in Figure 7.1. Note that the Root POA has an implicit activation policy that differs from the default.

7.3.3 POA Manager

One problem with the BOA was that no mechanism existed to synchronize servants, or to control a servant's readiness to receive requests: as soon as an object was activated, invocations were processed and delivered, and as soon as it was deactivated, a new server would be started by the BOA.

The POA offers "POA Managers" for this purpose. A POA Manager is a finite-state machine associated with one or more POA instances that can enter one of four states, with state transitions as shown in Figure 7.4.

Active: This state indicates normal processing; incoming requests are dispatched to their respective servants.

Holding: Incoming requests are not processed immediately but queued. When the holding state is left, queued requests are handled according to the new state: if the active state is entered, deferred requests are processed. If the

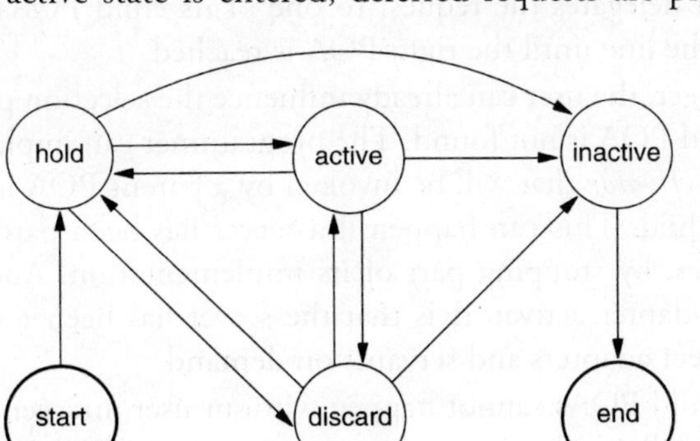

FIGURE 7.4 POA Manager state diagram.

inactive state is entered, deferred requests are rejected, and if the discarding state is entered, all requests in the queue are discarded.

Discarding: Requests are discarded, and the client receives a "transient" exception, indicating temporary failure. Useful, for example, in real-time environments instead of the holding state, when the queuing of requests and their delayed handling is not sensible.

Inactive: This state is entered prior to the destruction of associated POAs and cannot be left. Incoming requests are rejected, indicating permanent failure. With the POA Manager in the inactive state, a server can perform cleanup work, such as storing objects' persistent state.

For simplicity, it can be said that a POA is active if the POA Manager associated with that particular POA is in the active state.

By using one POA Manager for more than one POA (for example, only one POA Manager for the complete server), it is possible to control more than one group of objects with a single call, thus working around possible race conditions if each POA had to switch state individually.

7.3.4 Request Processing

When a request is received by the ORB, it must locate an appropriate object adapter to find the responsible servant. POAs are identified by name within the namespace of their parent POA; like in a file system, the full "path name" is needed to locate an object's POA—obviously, it must be possible to derive this information from the object reference. One implementation option is that the request is delivered to the Root POA, which then scans the first part of the path name and then delegates the request to one of its child POAs. The request is handed down the line until the right POA is reached.

In this respect, the user can already influence the selection process whenever a necessary child POA is not found. The programmer can implement and register an *adapter activator* that will be invoked by a parent POA in order to create a nonexisting child. This can happen if a server has been partially deactivated to save resources, by stopping part of its implementation. Another possibility for the use of adapter activators is that the server has been restarted and now reinitializes object adapters and servants on demand.

Creating child POAs cannot happen without user intervention because the programmer usually wishes to assign a custom set of policies: if a new POA has to be created but no adapter activator has been registered with its parent, requests fail.

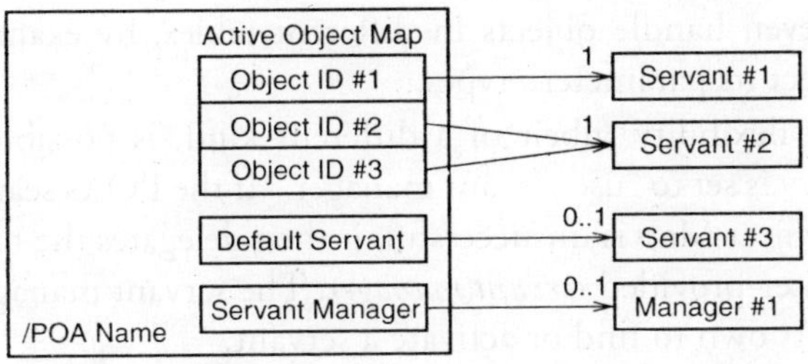

FIGURE 7.5 A POA with its own Active Object Map.

Within the adapter activator, the user not only can create further child POAs, but also can activate objects within, possibly by reading state information from disk. This process is transparent to the client, which does not notice any of this server-side activity.

Once the target POA has been found, further processing depends on the POA's servant retention policy and its request processing policy. The POA uses the Object ID—which is again part of the object reference—to locate the servant.

Figure 7.5 shows the three options that a POA uses to find the responsible servant for an incoming request. The simple case is that servants are activated explicitly and then entered into the Active Object Map. If a POA has a servant retention policy of "retain," this table is consulted first. If an appropriate entry is found, the request is handed to the registered servant.

If the servant retention policy is "nonretain," or if the Object ID in question is not found in the Active Object Map, the request processing policy is considered. If its value is "use default servant," the user can provide a single *default servant* that will be used regardless of the request's Object ID. This allows a single servant implementation to handle a group of objects with a single servant; usually, all these objects are of the same type. This default servant can use the POA's context-sensitive introspection methods to query the Object ID of the current request and behave accordingly.

Default servants provide scalability using the flyweight pattern: the server does not grow with the number of objects. Rather, the server can produce arbitrary numbers of object references while the number of active servants is constant.

A database server is an example for the usage of a default servant. Each table would be represented using a different POA with the table's same name, and the table's key value is used as Object ID. This way, all table rows are objects with their own object reference. Only a single default servant is needed per table; in an invocation, this default servant would query the request's Object ID and use it as table index to query the database. By using the DSI, the same default servant could even handle objects in different tables, by examining the table structure to select its parameter's types.

Even more flexibility, albeit of a different kind, is possible if the request processing policy is set to "use servant manager." If the POA's search for a servant in the Active Object Map is unsuccessful, it then delegates the task of locating a servant to the user-provided *servant manager*. The servant manager can then use intelligence of its own to find or activate a servant.

Like adapter activators for POAs, a servant manager can be used to activate servants on demand after a partial shutdown or after server restart. The servant manager receives the request's Object ID and could, for example, use that information to read back the object's state from persistent storage.

Another interesting pattern that can be implemented with servant managers are *ethereal objects*—objects that are able to receive requests even when no servant is associated with them. Implementations can create object references to ethereal objects and pass them to clients; on the server side, a servant manager is then registered with the POA to incarnate a servant on demand.

An example for this mechanism is a file service. A "directory" object might provide an operation to return the directory's contents—a list of files—as a sequence of object references to "file" objects. It would be inefficient to activate all file objects just for the purpose of returning their object references because only a small part of these files are going to be actually read in the future. Instead, the directory implementation would create ethereal object references, encoding the file name in the Object ID, using user-assigned Object IDs. Once a file is opened, the file object would be activated on demand by a servant manager.

Servant managers come in two different flavors with slightly different behavior and terminology, depending on the servant retention policy. If this policy's value is "retain," a servant *activator* is asked to *incarnate* a new servant, which will, after the invocation, be entered into the Active Object Map itself; this would be sensible in the sketched file service example, since the newly incarnated file object will receive more than just this one request in the future. If an object is deactivated, either explicitly or because of server shutdown, the servant activator's *etherealize* method is called to get rid of the servant—at which point the object's state could be written to persistent storage.

If, on the other hand, the servant retention policy is "nonretain," the servant manager is a servant *locator*, tasked to locate a servant suitable for only a single invocation. A servant locator supplements the default servant mechanism in providing a pool of default servants; it is the flyweight factory according to the flyweight pattern. It can also be used for load balancing, for example, for a printing service, in which the `print` operation would be directed to the printer with the shortest queue.

TABLE 7.2 Design patterns and different types of servants

	Servant	Default servant	Servant activator	Servant locator
Object state	yes	no	yes	no
Scalability	no	yes	no	yes
Ethereal objects	no	no	yes	yes
Life cycle	no	no	yes	no

Both kinds of a servant manager can also throw a special "forward exception" instead of returning a servant. This exception contains a new object reference to forward the request to—possibly to an object realized in a different server—employing the GIOP location forwarding mechanism. Forwarding allows, for example, the implementation of load balancing or redundant services: the servant manager would check its replicated servers and forward the request to an available one.

The flowchart in Figure 7.6 shows in detail how a POA tries to locate a servant according to its policies. To summarize a developer's choices, Table 7.2 shows a matrix of the different types of servants and their possible design patterns:

Object state: Explicitly activated servants and servants managed by a servant activator encapsulate their own state, whereas default servants must be stateless or store an object's state externally.

Scalability: For stateless objects, default servants can serve many objects without the overhead of having numerous (C++) objects in memory, and servant locators can dispatch requests to a small pool of servants.

Ethereal objects: The idea of ethereal objects that are activated and etherealized on demand can be realized by either kind of servant manager.

Life cycle: An object's life cycle can be monitored by a servant activator; that is, the activator is notified by the POA upon servant activation and etherealization, and can, for example, store a persistent servant's state in a database.

7.3.5 Persistence

The life cycle of POA-based objects depends on the POA's life span policy, which can be "transient" or "persistent." The lifetime of a transient object—an object activated in a POA with the transient life span policy—is bounded by the lifetime of its POA instance: once the POA is destroyed, either explicitly or as part of server shutdown, all objects within that POA are destructed, and their object references become invalid.

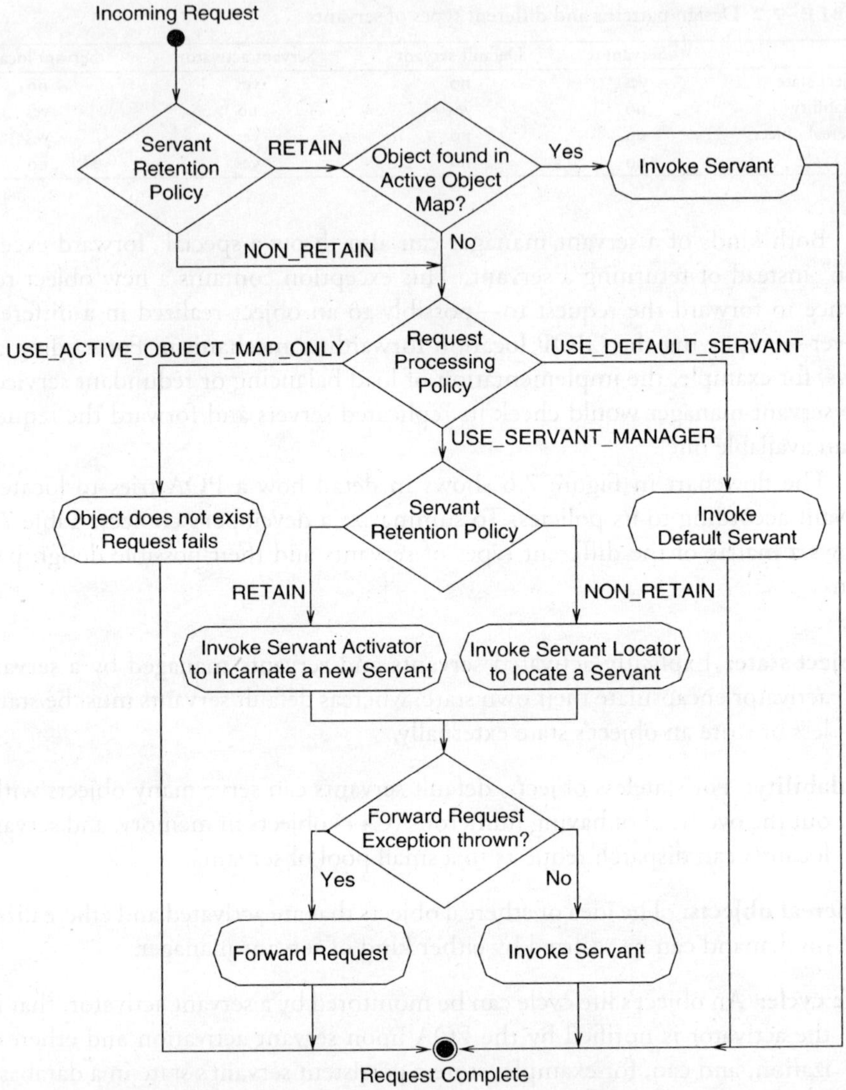

FIGURE 7.6 Request processing within the POA.

Persistent objects can, according to the definition of the "persistent" life span policy, outlive their server. In a server, it is possible to reactivate persistent objects that correspond to the same object identity that was created by a prior server instance.

With persistent objects have several advantages over transient objects. It is possible

- to shut down a server to save resources
- to update an implementation transparently by stopping the old server and starting the new version
- to recover from a server or system crash

Unfortunately, the POA specification does not address some issues that must be solved when servers are restarted. In a process-oriented environment, such as UNIX or Windows, requests might fail while the process containing the server is stopped. An external component, such as a "daemon," is required to receive requests while the actual server is not running. This daemon can then start servers on demand or hold requests while a server is (re-)starting. Implementing such a "POA daemon" is a vendor-specific issue.

7.4 DESIGN OF MICO'S POA

Of the multiple POA instances that can exist in a server, only the Root POA is registered with the ORB. It is responsible for receiving requests for any POA, inspecting the request's target object, and then dispatching the request to child POAs as necessary. Mico allows for multiple object adapters, so another possible design would have been to register each POA instance directly with the ORB. However, that would have posed a problem with nonexistent adapters: because of adapter activators, a nonexisting POA instance does not mean that a request is undeliverable. Rather, if a POA does not exist, the request must be delivered to the parent POA, which can then invoke its adapter activator to recreate the missing POA on demand. Only the Root POA is guaranteed to exist throughout the server's lifetime. By handing requests from the Root POA down along the line of descendants, adapter activators can be invoked at each step if necessary.

As a minor optimization in configurations with deeply nested child POAs, the Root POA keeps a map of all existing POAs. If a request targets an existing POA instance, the request can be dispatched directly to the responsible POA. Otherwise, the Root POA locates the most specific "ancestor" that currently exists, which will then either re-create the missing POA instances, or fail the request if no adapter activator is registered.

Once the target POA is found, it proceeds as shown in Figure 7.6 to find a servant. First, if the servant retention policy is `RETAIN`, the Active Object Map is consulted. If the servant retention policy is `NON_RETAIN`, or if the target object is not found in the Active Object Map, a servant manager is asked to incarnate or locate a servant, if configured and registered.

The following sections present details about the implementation of the Portable Object Adapter in MICO.

7.4.1 Object Key Generation

One central part of an object adapter's functionality is the generation and interpretation of object references. Object references must be created in a way so that incoming requests can be dispatched to the proper servant.

As mentioned in Section 7.2.3, the POA cooperates with the ORB to generate object references. The ORB provides an *object reference template* containing addressing information (e.g., a TCP/IP address).

The POA then constructs the *object key* in a way that allows

- identification of the object adapter
- identification of the POA instance
- identification of the servant

The servant can be identified within a POA using its Object ID, and the POA instance can be identified using the POA's "full path name," that is, the name of the POA and all of its ancestors, up to the Root POA.

That leaves the identification of the object adapter. In MICO, object adapters need an identifier that must be globally unique. In a transient POA, this GUID is composed of the server's host name, the process's PID, and a numerical timestamp. Host name and PID are included in this GUID because the object adapters' location mechanism is also used to disambiguate between local and remote objects.

In a persistent POA, a user-provided identifier, the "implementation name," is used as GUID. The following section deals with persistent objects in more detail.

The server-specific object adapter identification, the POA instance-specific "full path name," and the object-specific Object ID are then concatenated, with "slash" characters in between, to form the full object key, as shown in Figure 7.7.

This process results in a well-defined, printable object key. This enables users to publish `corbaloc:`-style object references as defined by the Interoperable Naming Service (INS) specification. The idea is to have Uniform Resource Identifier (URI)-style object references that can easily be exchanged by email. Using

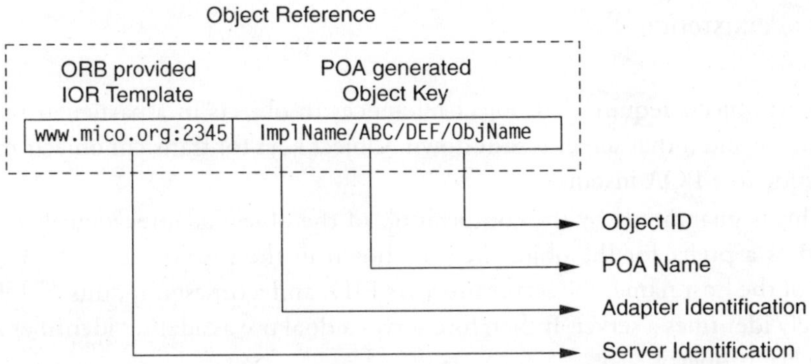

FIGURE 7.7 Dissecting a POA-generated object reference.

this notation, an object reference looks like `corbaloc::`*`hostname`*`:`*`portno/object key`*.

To achieve even shorter object keys, a special rule of encoding the object key is implemented. If the object adapter identification and the POA's full path name are identical, they are "collapsed" into a single string. If, in addition, the Object ID is the same, it is collapsed as well, resulting in an object key with a single component only.

Therefore, to enable using a shortest possible `corbaloc:` object reference, an application should

- set the implementation name, using the `-POAImplName` command line option
- create a POA with the same name as the implementation name, the "persistent" life span policy, and the `USER_ID` ID assignment policy
- activate an object within that POA using the same Object ID as the implementation name

This is done, for example, by the Naming Service implementation in MICO, which sets all three strings to "`NameService`." Therefore, if the Naming Service were started on `www.mico.org:2809`, it could be accessed using the object reference `corbaloc::www.mico.org:2809/NameService`.

7.4.2 Persistence

Transient objects require that object references to objects in a particular server become invalid if that server is shut down. Object keys for transient objects must be unique to a POA instance.

This is guaranteed by the composition of the object adapter identifier that is used as a prefix for the object key, as shown in the previous chapter. Composed of the host name, the server process's PID, and a timestamp, this "GUID" uniquely identifies a server. It therefore serves a dual use as adapter identifier and transience property.

For persistent servers, however, the object adapter identifier must be chosen so that it *is* reusable across server instances. The CORBA specification does not define how to assign such an identifier in a portable manner.

MICO's POA implementation provides the `-POAImplName` command line option to set an *implementation name*. Such an implementation name must be provided whenever persistent objects are to be activated—that is, when a POA with the `PERSISTENT` life span policy is created, and objects are activated with that POA instance. This identifier is then used as the adapter identifier in the object key. It is then the user's responsibility for keeping the implementation name unique.

7.4.3 POA Mediator

For transient objects, there is no distinction between the termination of a server and the destruction of its POA instances and objects; the one implies the other.

This is not true with persistent objects. When a server process is restarted, it may continue serving the same persistent objects as before.

There are several reasons to temporarily shut down a server—for example, to save resources while a server is not in use, or to update a server's implementation with a later and hopefully less buggy implementation. However, while a server is down, any client trying to contact the server would fail. This situation is unacceptable in high-availability scenarios.

The POA Mediator, also known as the "MICO Daemon," exists to remedy this situation. MICO's POA implementation cooperates with the POA Mediator to allow for uninterrupted service. The MICO Daemon supports

- transparently starting servers on demand
- holding client requests while a server is down for maintenance

- restarting servers in case of failure
- server migration

The MICO Daemon cooperates with MICO's POA implementation to provide these services, exploiting a GIOP feature known as "location forwarding." The GIOP protocol includes a special exception that may be thrown by a server. This exception includes an object reference and instructs clients to redirect their request to a different address.

When a server is configured to use the POA Mediator, its persistent POA instances generate object references pointing to the POA mediator rather than to itself.

Clients will thus send requests to the POA Mediator, also known as the MICO Daemon, which then replies with a location forward exception, pointing the client to the current server address as shown in Figure 7.8. The POA Mediator can also be configured to hold requests for a while—for example, in the case of a server restart, and to start a server if it is not running. MICO's `imr` program is used to administer the MICO Daemon.

A client contacts the POA Mediator only once, and then continues to use the new address for all requests as long as it remains valid. This way, the overhead of sending a request twice (first to the POA Mediator, then to the "real" server) is limited to the first request.

However, according to the semantics of location forwarding, clients remember the original address, the one pointing to the POA Mediator, as a fallback. If

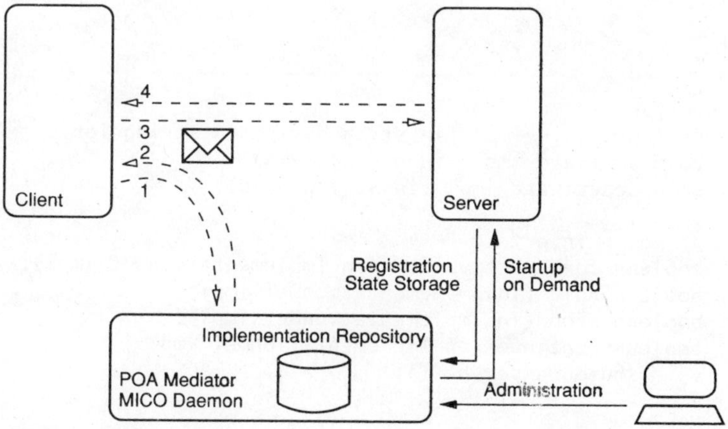

FIGURE 7.8 The POA Mediator redirecting requests to the current server instance.

the server instance that a client was redirected to disappears, the client will again send requests to the POA Mediator to be redirected to the new server instance.

While the setup of location forwarding requires some MICO-specific magic on the server side, it is transparent to the client program. Because it is part of the GIOP protocol, this feature will work regardless of the ORB used on the client side.

When a server is configured to use the POA Mediator by using the `-POARemoteIOR` command line option, POA instances use the interface shown in Figure 7.9 to register and communicate with the POA Mediator.

Upon startup, the Root POA will call the POA Mediator's `create_impl` operation, passing the server's implementation name (as shown in Section 7.4.1) as the first parameter and its object reference template, which contains the server's addressing information (as seen in Section 5.3.5), as the second parameter. In return, it receives the POA Mediator's own object reference template.

From then on, persistent POA instances in the server will use the POA Mediator's object reference template to compose references to active objects, resulting in object references pointing to the POA Mediator.

The POA Mediator does not need to store any per-object state. It only keeps a table mapping implementation names to the object reference template of the currently running server instance. This keeps the amount of data exchanged by the server and the POA Mediator to a minimum.

When the POA Mediator receives a request, all it has to do is to extract the implementation name from the incoming object reference, as described in Section 7.4.1, use the implementation name as an index to look up the current server's object reference template, and then compose a new object reference using that template and the incoming request's object key.

```
interface POAMediator {
  string create_impl (in string svid, in string ior);
  void activate_impl (in string svid);
  void deactivate_impl (in string svid);

  // admin interface
  boolean force_activation (in ImplementationDef impl);
  boolean hold (in ImplementationDef impl);
  boolean stop (in ImplementationDef impl);
  boolean continue (in ImplementationDef impl);
  void shutdown_server ();
};
```

FIGURE 7.9 IDL for the POA Mediator.

Note that the GIOP protocol mandates requests to be resent if a server closes a connection without acknowledging a request (i.e., by either sending back a reply or an exception). This solves a race condition upon shutdown, in case a server receives a request during shutdown. Thanks to this protocol feature, a client will then retry sending a request to the server, once it is fully shut down (and the connection is broken). It then notices that the server is gone and sends the request to the POA Mediator again.

One bootstrapping problem remains: while the POA Mediator can be configured to start a server that is not running at the moment (using the `imr` utility), a server must run at least once so that an object reference to the service can be exported—for example, to the Naming Service. Possible solutions include a manual first start with a special command line option so that the server exports an object reference and then shuts down again, or using `imr` to force the activation of a server the first time around.

7.4.4 Collocation

Location transparency is one of the cornerstones of CORBA. The client is not aware of a servant's location; the ORB alone is responsible for reading an object reference and contacting the respective server. Generated stub classes package their parameters in a CORBA request, which is then transported by the ORB and decoded by the skeleton on the server side.

This is fine for remote invocations, but suboptimal for local invocations, when the servant happens to be in the same process as the client, be it by coincidence or by design. While performance optimizations might not be necessary for the random case, inefficient handling is annoying if a server knowingly manipulates local objects through CORBA calls.

An example is the Naming Service, which maintains a tree of "Naming Context" objects. These must be CORBA objects, since they must be accessible from remote. But if the root context is asked to locate a node, it needs to traverse the tree, resulting in unsatisfactory performance if each step required a CORBA invocation to occur. In the local case, marshalling and unmarshalling parameters to and from a request seems overly complicated when the data could be used directly.

Effort to circumvent the "inherent remoteness" of ORB request handling is well spent and allows for more scalability because the user can easily migrate between efficient local invocations and ORB-mediated remote invocations.

A naive collocation optimization could exploit that stubs and skeletons both implement the same interface. If there was a common base class for that interface, stubs and skeletons could be used interchangeably. Clients within the same process could just be given a pointer to the skeleton, instead of a stub object. In the C++ language, the expense of an invocation would be no more than a virtual method call. The ORB wouldn't be involved at all.

While many early ORBs implemented the above behavior, it has some problems:

- The lifetimes of stubs and servants are independent of each other. A servant can be replaced, and stubs must reflect that change. This is not possible if "stubs" are actually pointers to the servant.
- Invocations must honor the POA's threading policy and the state of the POA Manager. It may be necessary to defer or to fail the request. With the above approach, invocations would always be "delivered" immediately.
- The POA must be involved; for example, the `POACurrent` object must reflect the invocation, and the `_this` member must return the correct value.
- Parameters of type `valuetype` may need to be copied to preserve their semantics; so that the callee can not affect the value of a shared parameter in the caller.

As a solution, a proxy is introduced to control access to the servant. For each interface, the IDL compiler creates a *collocation proxy* (e.g., `Account_stub_clp` in Figure 7.10). This class is a stub that specializes the normal stub class in the case of a collocated servant. Whenever the client acquires an object reference (as the result of a method invocation or ORB operation), the ORB checks if that object reference points to an object that is served by a local servant. If yes, it produces a collocation proxy.

The collocation proxy uses delegation instead of inheritance to invoke the servant. Before an invocation is actually performed, the proxy has to cooperate with the servant's POA to find out if a direct procedure call can proceed:

1. Make sure the servant's POA that we refer to has not been destroyed.
2. Check that the POA is in the active state.
3. Ask the POA to retrieve the servant from its Active Object Map.
4. Verify that the servant is implemented through a static skeleton and not using the DSI.
5. Update the `POACurrent` settings to reflect the invocation in progress.

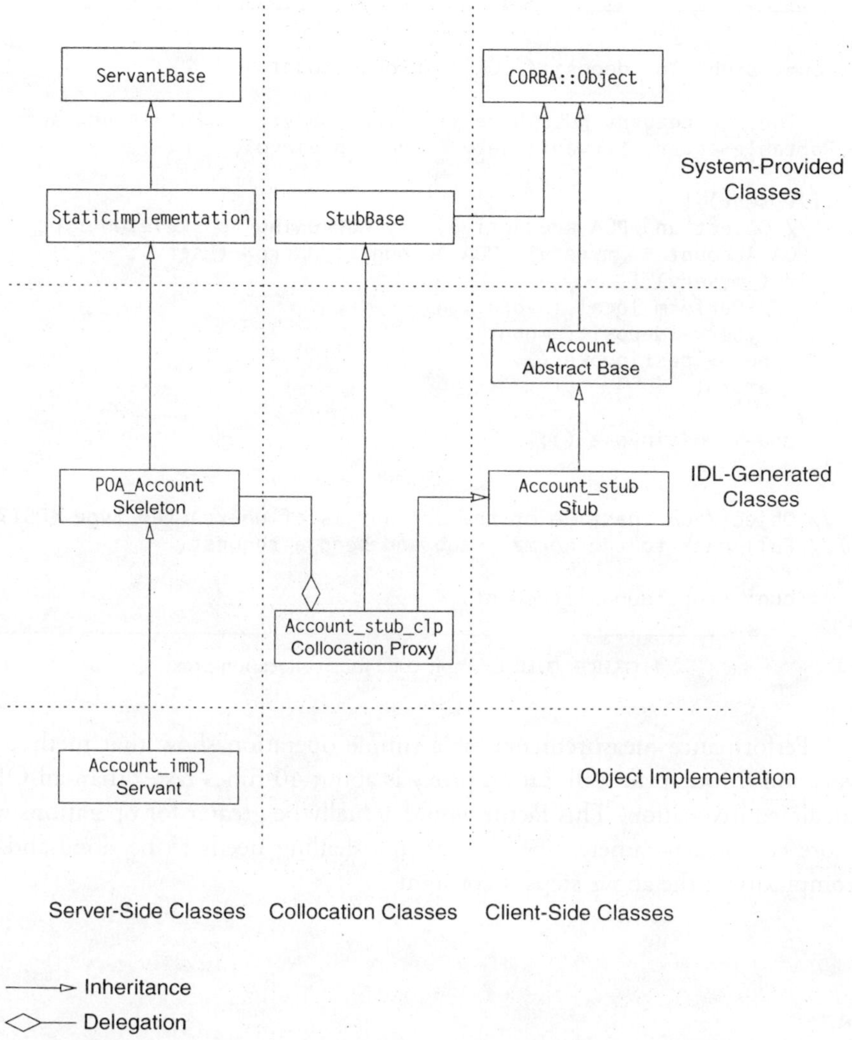

FIGURE 7.10 Using a proxy to mediate between the stub and the servant.

Only after this checklist is complete, the proxy can delegate the invocation to the servant by invoking the skeleton's virtual methods. If any of the above steps fails, the collection proxy falls back to the default stub's behavior by calling its parent class, where the parameters are marshalled into a CORBA request and fed to the ORB as usual, guaranteeing correct behavior in all circumstances. An example of the code generated by the IDL compiler is shown in Figure 7.11 (abbreviated by the removal of failure handling for presentation purposes).

```
void
Account_stub_clp::deposit( CORBA::ULong amount )
{
  // The POA returns NULL here if either object or POA is not active
  PortableServer::Servant _serv = _poa->preinvoke (this);

  if (_serv) {
    // Object and POA are active, try narrowing to skeleton type
    POA_Account * _myserv = POA_Account::_narrow (_serv);
    if (_myserv) {
      // Perform local invocation
      _myserv->deposit(amount);
      _poa->_postinvoke ();
      return;
    }
    _poa->_postinvoke ();
  }

  // Object/POA Inactive or the servant is of unexpected type (DSI?)
  // Fall back to the normal stub and send a request.

  Account_stub::deposit(amount);
}
```

FIGURE 7.11 Example code for a collocation proxy.

Performance measurements for a simple operation show that method invocation through the collocation proxy is about 40 times faster than an ORB-mediated invocation. This factor would actually be greater for operations with more complex parameters because no marshalling needs to be done and the complexity of the above steps is constant.

CHAPTER 8

INVOCATION ADAPTERS

Invocation adapters form the connection between a caller (of a method) and an ORB similar to the way in which object adapters establish a connection between an ORB and object implementations. Invocation adapters in a microkernel ORB are separate services from the ORB core. Similar to object adapters, they conceal different types of callers from the ORB, thereby making it possible for the ORB kernel to be small and flexible.

This chapter will first introduce some of the fundamental concepts concerning invocation adapters. It will then look at two special adapters—the *Dynamic Invocation Interface* (DII) and the *Static Invocation Interface* (SII)—and how they are implemented in MICO.

8.1 FUNCTIONALITY

Invocation adapters are components of the CORBA system that enable clients to execute method invocations. They are used by stub objects but can also be used directly by a user to invoke methods on objects for which no stubs exist.

To carry out a method invocation, invocation adapters require the object reference of the target object, the method name, and the values of the input parameters. A successful method invocation produces a result value and the values of the output parameters. If an error occurs, an exception is returned instead.

Invocation adapters can support one of several CORBA invocation semantics (also see Section 3.1):

Invocation semantics

- *synchronous* with *at-most-once* semantics

TABLE 8.1 Orthogonal characteristics of dynamic and static invocation adapters

Characteristic	Static	Dynamic
Performance	good	poor
Handling	easy	complicated
Type information at compilation	required	not required

- *asynchronous* with *at-most-once* semantics
- *one-way* with *best-effort* semantics

Static versus dynamic invocation adapters

CORBA differentiates between *static* and *dynamic* invocation adapters. Stub objects generated by the IDL compiler use static invocation adapters. Because users usually do not employ static invocation adapters directly but only indirectly through stub objects, the CORBA specification does not cover the design of static invocation adapters. Dynamic invocation adapters and specifically the Dynamic Invocation Interface (DII) specified by CORBA enable methods to be invoked for objects for which no stubs are available.

Table 8.1 presents a comparison of the characteristics of static and dynamic invocation adapters. Static invocation adapters are easier to deal with because they are not used directly but only through stub objects. One reason for the difference in performance between the two adapters is the fact that the lack of a prescribed design for static invocation adapters allows generous scope for optimization. The IDL compiler can already start carrying out tasks during the translation phase, whereas in the case of dynamic invocation adapters this has to be done at runtime (also see Section 7.2.5).

At the heart of each invocation adapter is a mechanism for the representation of the value and the type of arbitrary IDL data types. Compound data types such as structures and unions determine the complexity of such a mechanism. Another important function of invocation adapters is type checking. This topic is dealt with in detail in the following two subsections.

8.1.1 Representation of IDL Data Types

Representation of types using TypeCode

CORBA specifies a standard mechanism for the representation of the type and the value of arbitrary IDL data types as part of the DII. `TypeCodes` are used to represent two levels of types: `TypeCode` constants exist for basic data types such as `long`. For example, in the C++ mapping the type `long` is represented by the constant `_tc_long`. `TypeCodes` containing `TypeCodes` of their constituent data types and other type-determining data (such as index limits of arrays) can be generated for compound data types. CORBA also provides a mechanism for checking different `TypeCodes` for type equality.

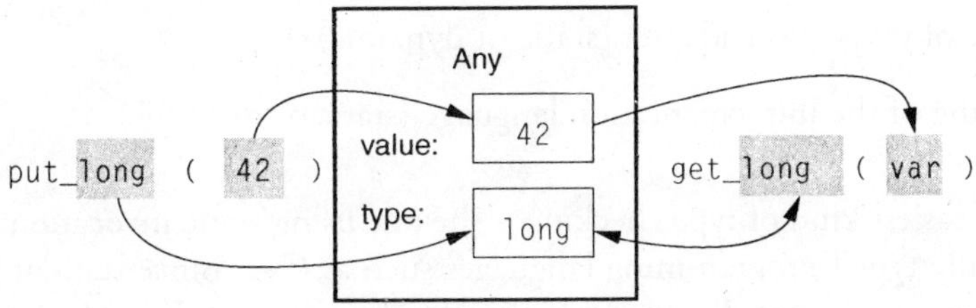

FIGURE 8.1 Insertion and extraction of data in or out of Any.

Representation of values using Any

CORBA uses Any objects to represent values. In addition to a TypeCode that represents the type of an IDL data type currently contained in an Any, Any objects contain a nonspecified internal (in-memory) representation of the values of this particular type. Operations for the type-safe insertion and extraction of all basic data types are provided by Any at its interface:

```
// IDL
interface Any {
    // Insertion operations
    void put_long (in long l);
    void put_short (in short s);
    ...

    // Extraction operations
    boolean get_long (out long l);
    boolean get_short (out short s);
    ...
};
```

In this context "type-safe" means that the insertion operations automatically set the TypeCode contained in Any and that the extraction operations compare the type of the value stored in the Any with the type of the variable in which the value is to be stored. As shown in Figure 8.1, the type information is implicitly contained in the insertion or extraction operation used.

8.1.2 Type Checking

Type checking ensures that the number, the type, and the value of the parameters of a method invocation are compatible with the signature of the method invoked. The overhead for a type check depends heavily on the following:

- Type of invocation adapter (static or dynamic)
- Typing of the implementation language (static or dynamic)

Using compilers for type checking

The easiest kind of type checking is the one using static invocation adapters in statically typed programming languages such as C++. Since static invocation adapters are never used directly and instead only indirectly through stub objects, the type checking is carried out completely by the compiler or by the interpreter of the implementation language.

Using the interface repository for type checking

In contrast, when nonstatically typed implementation languages are used, dynamic invocation adapters and static invocation adapters have to handle the type checking themselves. In this case use is made of an interface repository in which the signatures of the methods in the form of a sequence of `TypeCodes` are filed. The object reference of the target object and the method name enable the invocation adapter to call up these `TypeCodes` and to compare them with the types of the parameters supplied.

Some type violations are not detectable at all. For example, when using a dynamic invocation adapter, wrong parameter types may be passed to a method. A server that receives these wrong parameters has no way to detect this problem.

8.2 DYNAMIC INVOCATION INTERFACE

The Dynamic Invocation Interface is the interface of the dynamic invocation adapter specified by CORBA. It is used to invoke methods on objects for which no stubs are available in the application (e.g., to implement a bridge that works for all object types).

The main components of a DII are `Request` objects that represent a method invocation, the name of the method being invoked, the object reference of the target object, and the parameters.

When a method invocation is executed over the DII, all parameters of the method invocation are packaged into `Anys` and conveyed along with the object reference of the target object and the method name to the DII. An example of this is the interface `Account`, which models a bank account and includes deposit, withdrawal, and balance display operations:

```
// IDL
interface Account {
    void deposit (in long amount);
    void withdraw (in long amount);
```

```
    long balance ();
};
```

The following C++ code piece shows the invocation of the method `deposit (100)` using DII:

```
// C++
// Provide object reference for account object
CORBA::Object_var account_obj = ...;

// Generate DII request
CORBA::Request_var dii_request =
    account_obj->_request ("deposit");

// Provide argument 'amount'
dii_request->add_in_arg ("amount") <<= (CORBA::Long)100;

// Invoke method
dii_request->invoke ();
```

The invocation of `_request()` on the target object of the method invocation with the name of the method being invoked used as the parameter produces a new `Request` object. This `Request` object represents the DII method invocation. The input parameter `amount` is added to the list of parameters through the use of `add_in_arg()`. The invocation returns a reference to an `Any` object in which the value 100 is inserted via the overloaded operator `<<=`. (Note: In the C++ mapping, insertion and extraction operations to `Any` objects are mapped to `<<=` or `>>=` operators.) The invocation of `invoke()` transfers the method invocation to the ORB and then blocks until the method invocation has been processed.

8.3 STATIC INVOCATION INTERFACE

Although the DII is primarily provided for direct use, as shown in Figure 8.2, it can also be used to connect stubs to the ORB, somewhat like a substitute for a separate SII. The only disadvantage to this solution is the low level of performance that results for the reasons explained in the preceding sections:

Reasons for poor performance of DII

- Type checking (for example, when extracting a value from an `Any`).

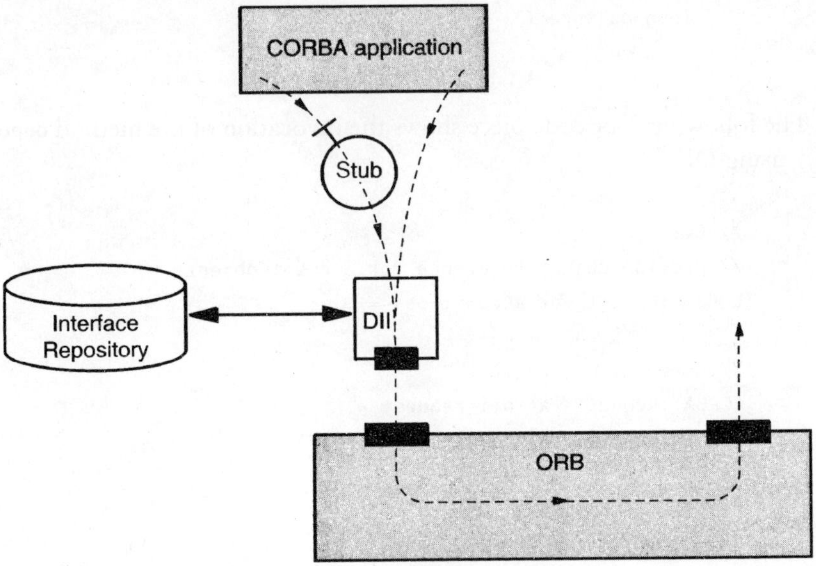

FIGURE 8.2 Linking of DII.

- Data must be copied many times (for example, when a value is inserted into an Any).
- No benefit can be derived from known type information.
- Detailed specification of the DII allows no scope for optimization.

No type checking required

The SII allows optimization in all four points mentioned. Type checking is practically not required because the stubs and skeletons generated from the IDL compiler ensure that only correct parameter values are provided.

No copying of data

The main reason why data has to be copied at the DII is because it cannot be assumed that the parameters provided exist for the duration of the entire method invocation. On the other hand, due to the synchronous invocation semantics with the SII, it can be assumed that the parameter values exist during the entire method invocation. Therefore, a reference to the data suffices rather than an actual copy.

Using known type information

The code for marshalling and demarshalling an Any must be generic because it has to be able to deal with all conceivable types of data. However, special marshalling and demarshalling code can be generated if the IDL compiler uses an SII because the type information is already available at the time of translation.

Because CORBA does not specify an SII (since it is used only indirectly through stubs), the SII can deliberately be kept simple to keep the number of dynamic storage allocations and releases to a minimum. This is a big factor in the efficiency of an SII.

Minimization of dynamic storage allocation

8.4 DESIGN OF MICO'S DII

`Any` objects representing arbitrary IDL data types form the core of the DII. Although the interface of these objects incorporates operations for the insertion and extraction of simple data types, corresponding operations for compound data types such as structures and unions are not specified.

Except for this missing interface, the DII specification is so detailed that there is little scope for flexibility in implementation. Therefore, the following discussion focuses only on the design of interfaces for inserting and extracting compound data types into or from `Any` objects.

As already described in Section 8.1.1, the operations for the insertion and extraction of simple data types into or from `Any` objects are type-safe. Therefore, programmers find it easy to use `Any` objects because they are not prone to errors.

For the insertion and extraction of compound data types, a sequence of insertion/extraction operations must be performed for the constituent data types. It would be desirable if such insertion/extraction of compound types could also be made type-safe as for simple data types. However, from a sequence of insertion operations of simple data types alone, the type of the compound object cannot be automatically decoded. The programmer must therefore first indicate the type in the form of a `TypeCode` before inserting a compound data type. When the data is inserted, `Any` then checks whether the inserted values conform to the indicated type.

Type-safe `Any` interface for compound data types

The CORBA `Any` interface was extended to include the following additional operations (in fragments):

```
// IDL
interface MICOAny {
    // Insertion operations
    void type (in TypeCode type);

    boolean struct_put_begin ();
    boolean struct_put_end ();
```

```
      boolean union_put_begin ();
      boolean union_put_selection (in long index);
      boolean union_put_end ();

      boolean any_put (in any a);
      ...

      // Extraction operations
      boolean struct_get_begin ();
      boolean struct_get_end ();

      boolean union_get_begin ();
      boolean union_get_selection (in long index);
      boolean union_get_end ();

      boolean any_get (out any a);
      ...
  };
```

type()is used to indicate the type before the insertion of data. Operations that indicate the start and the end of a data structure exist for each compound data type. Consequently, the insertion of a structure looks like the following [extraction is similar except type() is not invoked beforehand]:

```
// Pseudo-code
MICOAny mico_any;

mico_any.type (<TypeCode for structure>);
mico_any.struct_put_begin ();

// insert elements of structure
...

mico_any.struct_put_end ();
```

Depending on the type of elements, insertion and extraction take place either through the operations for simple data types or through a nested use of the operations for compound data types.

Operations are also available so that a value contained in an Any can be inserted into or extracted from another Any. These operations behave as if the data from one Any were manually being extracted from one Any and immediately being inserted into the other one.

Despite its usefulness, the direct use of MICOAny in CORBA applications results in a loss of portability to other CORBA products that do not provide this interface. As part of CORBA 2.2, *Dynamic Any* has been introduced to overcome this limitation. Dynamic Any is not an extension to the Any interface, but instead defines a set of IDL interfaces that are independent of it.

Dynamic Any

Along with enabling the insertion and extraction of compound data types into or from Any objects, Dynamic Any offers extensive functionality for traversing and manipulating the contained compound data types, which has a negative effect on efficiency. Dynamic Any is therefore not a substitute for MICOAny but an addition to it that provides the functionality of MICOAny over a standardized but less efficient interface.

8.5 DESIGN OF MICO'S SII

The basic structure of the SII is similar to that of the DII: objects of the StaticRequest type represent a method invocation. A StaticRequest has a list of StaticAny objects that contain the values of the parameters. These StaticAny objects—and, consequently, the representation of the parameter values—are what actually make the SII special. We will look at this in detail below.

Representation of values using StaticAny

Basically, StaticAny contains a pointer to a parameter and not a copy. In the C++ implementation an untyped void pointer is used. In addition to this pointer, StaticAny contains a reference to an object of the type StaticTypeInfo that supplies methods for copying, releasing, marshalling, and demarshalling the parameters pointed to by the void pointer.

StaticTypeInfo *provides type-specific operations*

Compiled versus interpreted (de)marshalling code

For basic types such as long, the appropriate StaticTypeInfo objects are contained in the Mico library; for compound IDL data types, the IDL compiler generates the appropriate classes. An important advantage of this procedure is that the code for (de)marshalling the data types exists in a *compiled* form, whereas with the DII the Any (de)marshalling methods *interpret* the type information in TypeCode in order to (de)marshall the parameter contained in Any. See Section 9.1 for a detailed description of the SII.

8.6 SUMMARY

MICO provides two invocation adapters: the Dynamic Invocation Interface and a Static Invocation Interface. The DII is mostly compatible with the CORBA specification, but Any has been extended to support the insertion and extraction of compound data types. The SII is a proprietary but more efficient invocation adapter that is used by stubs generated by the IDL compiler.

Chapter 9

IDL COMPILER

The Interface Definition Language (IDL) of CORBA represents a powerful tool for the development of distributed applications. It enables a separation of the interface and the implementation of objects. The CORBA standard contains a description of the syntax and the semantics of the IDL. Applications programmers use IDL compilers to generate type-safe access to CORBA objects from interface specifications. This chapter is devoted to the design of MICO's IDL compiler. The proxy objects generated by IDL are based on an ORB API that is described in Section 9.1. Section 9.2 follows with general principles relating to compiler construction. Sections 9.3 and 9.4 offer a detailed presentation of the design of MICO's IDL compiler.

9.1 INVOCATION ADAPTERS

One of the tasks of an ORB consists of preparing and processing remote operation invocations. The initiator and the receiver of such operation invocations is an application based on CORBA. To execute an operation invocation, an application requires an invocation adapter, which is also used for the proxy objects generated by the IDL compiler. The invocation adapter allows the delivery of information associated with a remote operation invocation. This includes information about the target object, the operation name, and the actual parameters. This section focuses on the different alternatives for the design of invocation adapters.

IDL compiler creates proxy objects

9.1.1 Dynamic versus Static Invocation Adapters

An application uses an invocation adapter to send operation invocations (also see Section 5.3.1). The Dynamic Invocation Interface (DII) is an example of an invocation adapter. The DII defines an API with which operations including their parameters can be built at runtime and transferred to the ORB for further processing. Since the interfaces, which are based on the DII, do not have to be known at the compile time of an application, they are an example of a dynamic invocation adapter.

The specification of object interfaces is an important step in the design of an application. The interfaces are therefore already established at the time of the compilation of an application. With its IDL the CORBA specification offers a tool for the specification of such interfaces. A static invocation adapter converts object interfaces that are already known at the time of translation of an application.

Advantages and disadvantages of static interface adapters

Static invocation adapters incorporate the following benefits and disadvantages:

- ⊞ Documented interface is part of the design of an application.
- ⊞ Allows type-safe handling of objects; errors are often detected before translation.
- ⊞ Easy to handle.
- ⊟ Interface can no longer be modified at runtime.
- ⊟ Special tools required for working with IDL specifications.

In contrast, dynamic invocation adapters incorporate the following benefits and disadvantages:

Advantages and disadvantages of dynamic interface adapters

- ⊞ Interface can be modified during runtime.
- ⊞ Flexible; allows applications that are not possible with static interfaces.
- ⊟ Not type-safe.
- ⊟ Error prone; not easy to handle.

9.1.2 Support of Static Invocation Adapters

Proxy objects that guarantee type-safe access to object interfaces are a component of static invocation adapters. The proxy objects, which include stubs and skeletons, are derived from IDL specifications. Because proxy objects are linked to an application, they must exist in the same programming language as the application. Consequently, standard IDL language mappings are specified in CORBA for different programming languages.

According to the CORBA standard, a compliant ORB implementation must support an IDL language mapping for at least one programming language. The mapping is supported by a tool that can be implemented in various ways. For example, a C++ compiler could be extended to support the IDL directly. However, this would imply a close coupling between C++ compilers and special ORB implementations, which is not practical in reality.

CORBA defines IDL language mapping

Another approach can be taken to avoid the close coupling. A special tool translates IDL specifications into stubs and skeletons as the source code for a higher programming language taking into account the IDL language mapping rules. This source code must be compiled and linked with the rest of the application. Because of its task, this tool is called an *IDL compiler*. A CORBA application therefore consists of several components that exist in a specific dependency relationship to one another.

Components of a CORBA application

ORB library: The ORB library contains CORBA-specific functions that are required by all CORBA applications (such as implementation of the IIOP protocol).

Proxies: The proxy objects that the stubs and skeletons belong to are generated automatically by an IDL compiler from IDL specifications.

Application: The semantics of the actual application that is contributed by the programmer.

Figure 9.1 shows the dependencies between the three components in the form of layering. The ORB library provides the basic functionality of a CORBA application and is self-sufficient in terms of the other two components. The proxies have recourse to the functionality of the ORB library. For their part the proxies offer applications type-safe access to CORBA objects. The application itself uses the proxies as well as the functionality of the underlying ORB library.

Different interfaces exist between the three layers:

Interfaces between components

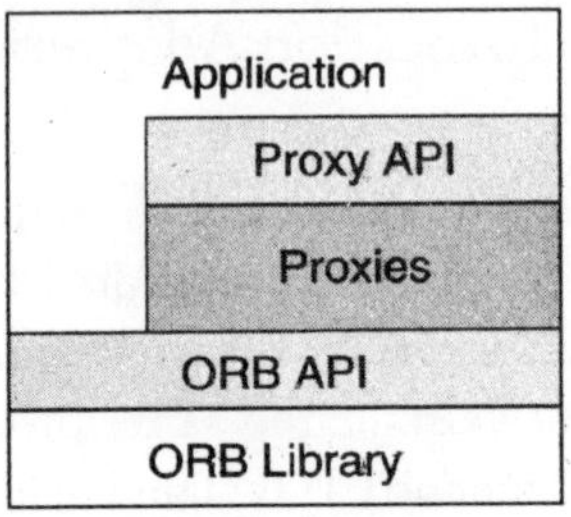

FIGURE 9.1 CORBA application consisting of the application itself, the generated code, and the ORB library.

- *ORB library ↔ Application:* The application can access ORB-specific functions. These include initialization of the ORB or general functions for the management of object references.
- *Application ↔ Proxies:* The proxies generated from an IDL specification are used by an application for type-safe access to remote objects.
- *Proxies ↔ ORB library:* Proxies for their part need the support of the ORB to convert the parameters of a remote operation invocation into a byte sequence, for example.

Two of the three interfaces between the layers are prescribed by the CORBA standard and therefore offer no freedom for design decisions. However, the CORBA standard makes no statements about the interface between the proxies and the ORB library. From the standpoint of its functionality, this interface must provide support for remote operation invocations. This task corresponds to that of the dynamic invocation adapter already discussed. So it is possible that the proxies access the DII and the DSI. The advantage of such a procedure is that it makes maximum use of the components of the ORB, and this is what earlier versions of MICO did. However, the DII and the DSI are not runtime efficient, which indicates a weakness in the CORBA standard. Later versions of MICO therefore use the MICO-specific interface that is described in the following subsection.

9.1.3 MICO's Static Invocation Adapter

Figure 9.2 shows the class diagram for the static invocation adapter under MICO. Functionally, the static invocation adapter is identical to the DII and the DSI. However, this is a MICO-specific interface that should never be used directly by applications to guarantee portability. Unlike the DII and the DSI, the static

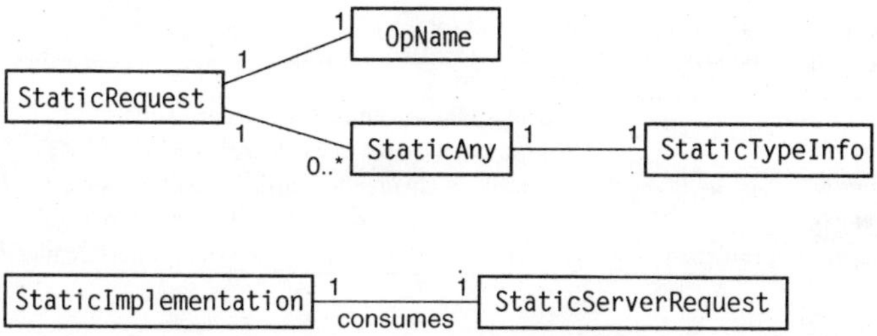

FIGURE 9.2 Static invocation adapter.

invocation adapter avoids the process of copying parameters as much as possible because of its focus on increasing runtime efficiency.

Classes of MICO's *static interface adapters*

The class `StaticAny` is the counterpart of the static invocation adapter to the type `Any` defined in CORBA, which is used as a generic data container. An instance of the class `StaticAny` manages a typed data instance. Access to a `StaticAny` is via the class `StaticTypeInfo`. The class `StaticTypeInfo` takes on the role of a *marshaller*, which packs and unpacks user-defined data into and from a `StaticAny` instance. The class `StaticTypeInfo` is abstract. A class that can marshall the instances of this type must be derived for each user-defined type in an IDL specification. The following code fragment shows an extract from the declaration for the class `StaticTypeInfo`:

```
 1: class StaticTypeInfo {
 2: public:
 3:   virtual StaticValueType create () const = 0;
 4:   virtual void free (StaticValueType) const = 0;
 5:   virtual CORBA::Boolean demarshal (CORBA::DataDecoder &,
 6:                                     StaticValueType) const = 0;
 7:   virtual void marshal (CORBA::DataEncoder &,
 8:                         StaticValueType) const = 0;
 9:   // ...
10: };
```

Along with other declarations, pure virtual methods for the storage management of data (lines 3 and 4) as well as the packing and unpacking of data (lines 5 and 7) are found in the abstract class `StaticTypeInfo`. An instance of the type `StaticValueType` represents a raw byte sequence managed by the class `StaticAny` together with the type information. The IDL data marshallers `DataDecoder` and `DataEncoder` are used to pack or unpack these byte sequences.

The class `StaticRequest` allows the client access to the functionality of the static invocation adapter. An instance of this class represents an operation in-

TABLE 9.1 Classes of static invocation adapters

Class	Description
`StaticAny`	Manages a datum and its type information
`StaticTypeInfo`	Defines interface for marshaller
`StaticRequest`	Encapsulates client-side information of an operation invocation
`StaticServerRequest`	Encapsulates server-side information of an operation invocation
`StaticImplementation`	Base class of the implementation of an interface hierarchy

vocation and manages all information associated with the operation invocation, including the operation name and the list of actual parameters. The class `StaticServerRequest` reflects the same behavior on the server side. An incoming operation invocation is delivered to the object implementation through the class `StaticImplementation` at the server. The skeleton generated by the IDL compiler is derived from this class. An instance of the class `StaticServerRequest` is passed to the class `StaticImplementation` for each incoming operation invocation. Table 9.1 summarizes the individual classes of static invocation adapter.

9.2 COMPILER FUNDAMENTALS

The task of a compiler is to translate a word of the language L_1 into a word of the language L_2 (see Figure 9.3). Compilers are typically used for the translation of higher programming languages such as C++, Fortran, and Pascal to assembly language. In the context of CORBA, the compiler translates IDL specifications into proxy objects. The source language is IDL, and the target language is a higher programming language—in our case, C++. The IDL compiler has to obey the IDL language-mapping rules for C++ at the time of translation. Before we look at IDL compilers in detail, we first want to start with a brief overview of the fundamentals of compiler construction.

9.2.1 Formal Languages and Grammars

The concept of formal language is central to the understanding of compilers. A *formal language* is based on an *alphabet* from which *words* are formed. For example, the alphabet $\Sigma = \{a, b\}$ enables the forming of words such as a, aa, ab, and $abba$. The set of all words that can be created from an alphabet is represented by Σ^+. In addition to all words from Σ^+, the set Σ^* also contains the empty word ϵ.

Formal language

Based on the alphabet Σ, the language L is a subset of all words: $L \subseteq \Sigma^*$. If $\Sigma = \{a, b\}$, then a possible language L_P is the one of the palindrome, that is,

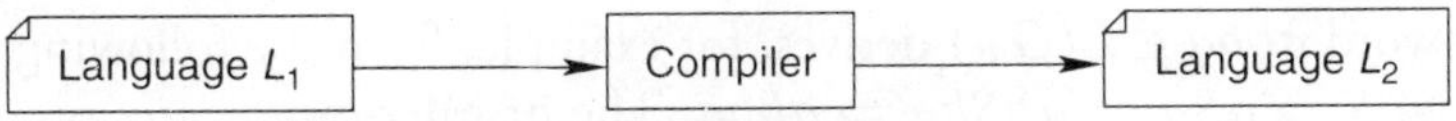

FIGURE 9.3 Compiler concept.

words that are the same read forwards and backwards. Some valid words in this language are $L_P = \{a, bb, bab, abba, \ldots\}$.

Nonterminal symbols

First we will look at how a language is represented by a finite description. This requires the helper alphabet N, which is also called a set of *nonterminal symbols*. The name originates from the fact that the symbols of the alphabet do not appear in the words of a language. Therefore, $N \cap \Sigma = \emptyset$. In the discussion below, nonterminal symbols are characterized by capital letters: $N = \{Q, R, S, \ldots\}$.

Production

A *production* is the mapping of a nonterminal symbol to a word that consists of a union of the alphabets Σ and N. For the production $u \to v$, the symbols $u \in N$ and $v \in (\Sigma \cup N)^*$ are valid. The set of all productions is defined by $P = \{u \to v | u \in N, v \in (\Sigma \cup N)^*\}$. For example, if $\Sigma = \{a, b\}$ and $N = \{S, R\}$, then $R \to a$, $R \to bS$, $S \to aSa$, and $S \to aSaR$ are possible productions.

Derivation

A *derivation* is the transformation of a word into another one according to a production. If $w, w' \in (\Sigma \cup N)^*$ are two words, the derivation is $w \Rightarrow w'$ if when the production is $u \to v \in P$, so that w' derives from w, whereby all occurrences of u in w are replaced by v. For example, $bSb \Rightarrow baSab$ with the productions of the last paragraph because $baSab$ is derived from bSb when the production $S \to aSa$ is used to exchange the S in bSb with aSa. A *derivation sequence* $w_0 \Rightarrow w_1 \Rightarrow \ldots \Rightarrow w_n$ is abbreviated as $w_0 \overset{*}{\Rightarrow} w_n$.

Grammar

A grammar G is a quadruple $G = (\Sigma, N, P, S)$ with the alphabet Σ, the nonterminal symbol N, a set of productions P, and a start symbol $S \in N$. A grammar is a finite representation of a formal language. The language $L(G)$ induced by the grammar G is defined as $L(G) = \{w \in \Sigma^* | S \overset{*}{\Rightarrow} w\}$. This means $L(G)$ contains all words resulting from a finite derivation sequence from the start symbol S of the grammar G. For example, the grammar $G_P = (\Sigma_P, N_P, P_P, S)$ creates the language of the palindrome, with $L(G_P) = L_P . \Sigma_P = \{a, b\}$, $N = \{S\}$ and the set of the productions P_P:

$$S \to \epsilon \tag{9.1}$$

$$S \to a \tag{9.2}$$

$$S \to b \tag{9.3}$$

$$S \to aSa \tag{9.4}$$

$$S \to bSb \tag{9.5}$$

The word $abba \in L(G_P)$ derives, for example, from the following derivation string: $S \Rightarrow aSa \Rightarrow abSba \Rightarrow abba$. The first derivation uses production 9.4; the second one, production 9.5; and the third one, production 9.1 from P_P.

9.2.2 Parse Trees

Parse tree

An analogous graphic representation exists for the derivations presented in the last subsection. This structure is called a *parse tree* and is a tree in the mathematical sense: its inner nodes consist of nonterminal symbols and its leaves consist of words of the alphabet. Figure 9.4 shows the parse tree for the derivation $S \Rightarrow aSa \Rightarrow abSba \Rightarrow abba$ based on the grammar G_P presented in the last section.

The use of a production is represented in the parse tree by an inner node. The node corresponds to the left side of the production and its successor node to the right side of the production. The children of a node therefore represent the substitutions undertaken during a derivation. A traversing of the parse tree in in-order traversal visits the terminal symbols (i.e., leaves) in the sequence in which they appear from left to right in the word.

One of the tasks of a compiler is to find a suitable derivation, which is the generation of a parse tree. Tools are available that take the description of a grammar to generate programs that create parse trees from input words. The CORBA standard specifies the IDL through a grammar so that when these tools are used the conversion of an IDL specification (i.e., word of the input language) into a parse tree is for the most part automated.

CORBA uses a grammar to define the IDL

9.2.3 Structure of a Compiler

The creation of a parse tree is the first step in the translation of one language into another one. It normally makes sense to translate a language into more than

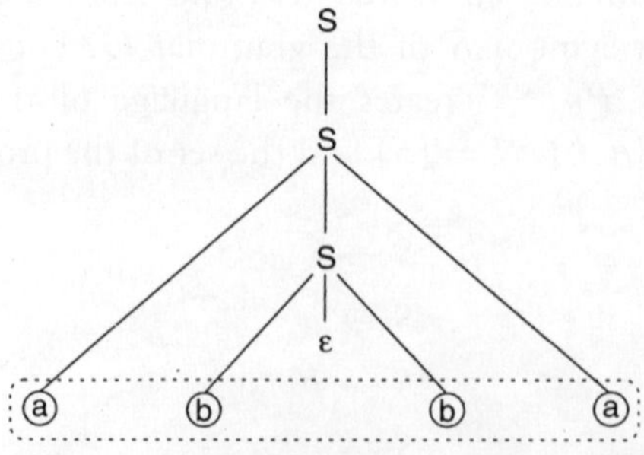

FIGURE 9.4 Parse tree of word abba.

one target language instead of only into one. In the context of an IDL compiler, for example, there are various target languages for which CORBA has specified IDL language mappings. This requires breaking down the translation process for the generation of a parse tree and the subsequent code generation into the target language. The parse tree is used as a link that separates the two phases of the translation.

As we illustrated in the preceding subsection, the structure of the parse tree is oriented toward the productions of the grammar of the input language. If this grammar contains numerous productions, as is the rule with complicated languages, the parse tree will become fairly complex. Therefore, it is useful first to convert the parse tree into a more compact representation. The more compact form, also called the *abstract syntax tree* (AST), serves as the starting point for code generation. *Abstract syntax tree*

The phases passed through by the translation process are called *parsing* and *code generation* (see Figure 9.5). The task of a parser consists of converting a word from the source language into an abstract syntax tree. The syntax and the semantics are checked during this process. Only correct input words (in our context this means correct IDL specifications) are represented as abstract syntax trees. The components of a compiler that implement the first phase of the translation process are referred to as the *front end* in the literature. *Front end*

The second phase of the translation process is code generation. The components of a compiler that have this responsibility are accordingly referred to as the *back end*. The back end traverses the abstract syntax tree that was constructed beforehand by the front end and produces code in the target language. The back end implements the rules of IDL language mapping for the target language and generates the necessary proxy objects. Figure 9.5 shows two different back ends *Back end*

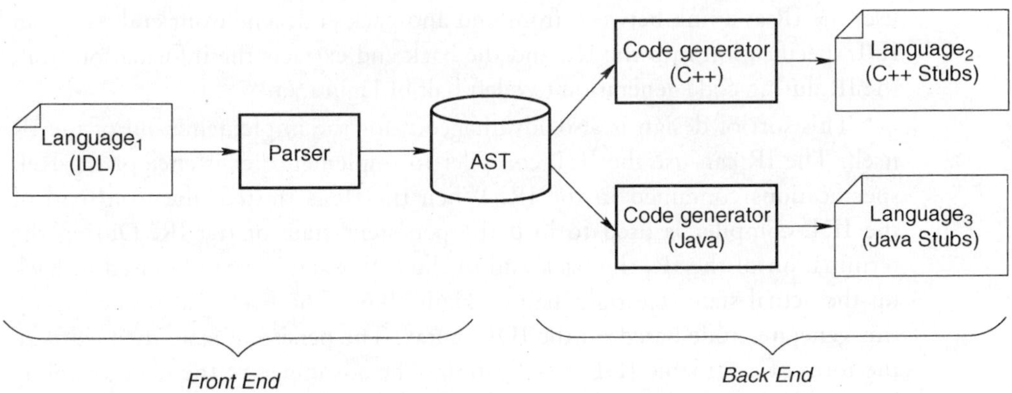

FIGURE 9.5 Compiler structure.

that are creating these proxy objects in both the programming languages C++ and Java.

9.3 ABSTRACT SYNTAX TREE FOR IDL SPECIFICATIONS

An abstract syntax tree is the link between the front end and the back end. In the context of IDL compilers, there is the issue of the structure of the abstract syntax tree for IDL specifications. The abstract syntax tree of an IDL specification must be able to represent all information necessary for the back end, including the IDL specification itself as well as information about file structures in which the IDL specification is filed. For example, the latter is important in order to establish in which file each part of the IDL specification is defined (such as through the use of the preprocessor instruction `#include`).

For the purposes of object-oriented modeling, a separate class can be introduced for each IDL construct (for example, `typedef`, `struct`, `interface`, ...) in order to represent the complex information contained in an IDL specification. Each class then manages information that exists for this IDL construct. For example, the class that represents `interface` definitions would contain a list of nested objects that represent the IDL constructs defined locally in an interface.

IR can store an abstract syntax tree

A closer examination reveals that a similar modeling already exists in the CORBA standard. The interface for the interface repository (IR) mirrors the language constructs contained in the IDL exactly. The actual task of the IR is to store IDL specifications. Therefore, it is possible for an IR to be used as an abstract syntax tree for an IDL compiler. The resulting design of the IDL compiler uses the IR as a link between front end and back end: The front end writes an IDL specification into the IR, and the back end extracts the information from the IR during code generation (see left half of Figure 9.6).

Advantages

This sort of design is also advantageous for the implementation of the IR itself. The IR can use the IDL compiler to implement persistence of the IDL specifications contained in the IR. When the IR is started, the front end of the IDL compiler is used to load the persistent state of the IR. During the termination of the IR, the back end of the IDL compiler can be used to back up the actual state (see right half of Figure 9.6). The back end needed to do this generates code based on the IDL syntax. The persistent state then exists in the form of a readable IDL specification. The advantage of the close coupling between IDL compiler and IR is the reusability of the components required for their conversion.

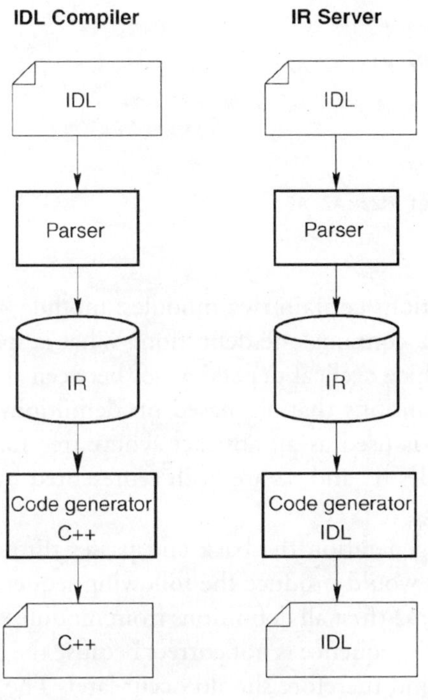

FIGURE 9.6 Structure of IDL compiler and interface repository.

Another benefit of this design is that different configurations are possible. Because the abstract syntax tree is represented by an IR, the IDL compiler can access a remote IR. Because the IR is a regular CORBA object, it can be reached with normal remote operation invocations. This also applies to IRs of other ORB vendors, so long as the implementation conforms to the CORBA standard. The IDL compiler can therefore "feed" a remote IR (using the front end) as well as implement code generation in the back end using the information of a remote IR.

Disadvantages

These advantages are also offset by some disadvantages. One disadvantage is the result of a peculiarity of the CORBA IDL that allows the reopening of module specifications. The following IDL specification is used to elucidate this point:

```
// IDL
module M1 {
  typedef char A1;
};

```

```
module M2 {
  typedef M1::A1 A2;
};

module M1 {
  typedef M2::A2 A3;
};
```

The above specifications contain two modules: module `M1` contains two definitions and module `M2` contains one definition. What is special about this is that the definitions produce cyclical dependencies between the two modules. Module `M1` contains definitions that are based on definitions from module `M2` and vice versa. If an IR is used as an abstract syntax tree for representing an IDL specification, modules `M1` and `M2` are both represented by an object within the IR.

If during code generation the back end passes through the content of the IR sequentially, this would produce the following sequence of IDL definitions: `M1::A1`, `M1::A3`, `M2::A2` (first all definitions from module `M1` and then from module `M2`). However, this sequence is not correct because the definition from `M1::A3` is based on `M2::A2` and therefore should occur later. The more serious problem here is that some of the information contained in the IDL specification is lost in the IR. This includes the sequence in which IDL specifications occur in a specification and the mapping of IDL definitions to source files in which they are defined. We will deal with these problems later.

Another disadvantage of using an IR as a link between the front end and the back end of an IDL compiler is the conversion of this design during implementation. The CORBA standard defines the interface of the IR through an IDL specification. This means that the front and back ends of the IDL compiler access the IR over a CORBA interface. A typical "chicken-and-egg" problem occurs during the development of the IDL compiler and the IR: An implementation of the IDL compiler requires the availability of an IR and vice versa. The reason is that, as a regular CORBA object, the IR requires proxies, but these first have to be created by a working IDL compiler.

This problem can be solved through a bootstrap procedure: The required stubs and skeletons for the IR are first developed manually and later replaced by ones generated by the IDL compiler as soon as the compiler has sufficient functionality. The result is that automatically generated code, produced during the bootstrap procedure, is also contained in the MICO source code. Because the generated code is part of the MICO source code, this also means that the code generated by the IDL compiler must be translatable with all supported C++ compilers.

In summary, the use of an IR to represent an abstract syntax tree produces the following advantages and disadvantages:

IR as an AST container

- ⊞ Simple design; interfaces specified by CORBA
- ⊞ Reuse of components of the CORBA architecture
- ⊞ Support for basic persistence of the IR
- ⊞ Code generation from a remote IR possible
- ⊟ Persistence of IR not scalable or failsafe
- ⊟ Some information from IDL specifications not representable in the IR
- ⊟ Bootstrap procedure required during development of IDL compiler

9.4 MICO'S IDL COMPILER

The following sections examine the design of Mico's IDL compiler. We start by looking at the general class structure of an IDL compiler in Section 9.4.1. A more detailed discussion about the structure of the front end follows in Section 9.4.2 and about the C++ back end in Section 9.4.3.

9.4.1 Class Structure

Figure 9.7 shows the complete class structure of an IDL compiler in the UML-based notation. Brief descriptions of the individual classes in Figure 9.7 are found in Table 9.2.

The arrangement of the classes among themselves reflects the division into the front end and the back end of the IDL compiler linked together over an abstract syntax tree (based on the IR). The class `IR` forms the separation between the front and back ends. The classes `Parser`, `ParseNode`, and `IDLParser` represent the front end, and the other classes the back end.

In Figure 9.7 the IR is only represented by one class, but in reality it is based on a set of classes. The design of the IR will not be discussed further. The CORBA standard already suggests a design through its abstractions for the interface of the IR. The implementation of the IR in Mico relies closely on the interface structure defined by the CORBA standard.

IR separates front and back ends

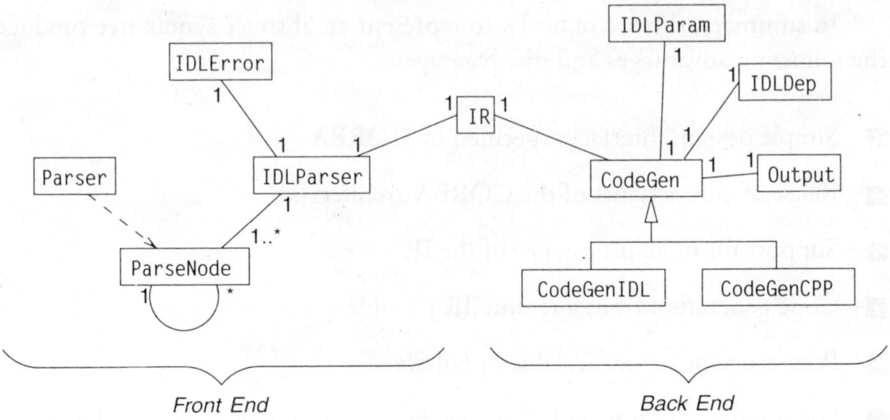

FIGURE 9.7 Design of the IDL compiler.

TABLE 9.2 Classes of IDL compiler and their function

Class	Description
`CodeGen`	Abstract base class for all back ends
`CodeGenCPP`	Code generation for C++
`CodeGenIDL`	Code generation for IDL
`IDLDep`	Computes dependencies between IDL definitions
`IDLError`	Output of detailed error messages
`IDLParam`	Command line parameters of IDL compiler
`IDLParser`	Traverses parse tree and fills IR
`IR`	Interface repository
`Output`	Supports structured output
`ParseNode`	Parse tree
`Parser`	Encapsulates parser generated by YACC

In Section 9.3 we explained that the IR is not able to store all information that exists in an IDL specification. For example, it is not possible from the IDL definitions contained in an IR to extract the source code file from which they originated. This could be seen as a weakness in the CORBA specification. On the other hand, the standard does not make it mandatory for the IR to be used for the IDL compiler. In Section 9.3 we also explained that the sequence of IDL definitions, as they occur in a source code file, is lost in an IR. The back end has a class `IDLDep` (standing for dependency) that computes the correct sequence for the code generation. This information can be calculated by `IDLDep` based on the dependencies between IDL definitions contained in the IR.

9.4.2 Front End

The task of the front end is to input source code files that contain IDL specifications and to store their content in an IR. The CORBA standard defines the syntax of the IDL through a grammar. As already explained in Section 9.2.2, tools are available that automatically generate parsers from grammars. The output of a parser is a parse tree, the information of which is filed in a compact form in an IR.

MICO uses YACC

MICO uses the parser generator YACC (Yet Another Compiler Compiler). The class `Parser` in Figure 9.7 encapsulates the code generated by YACC. The parser converts input streams with valid IDL specifications into parse trees. A parse tree is represented by a set of instances of the class `ParseNode`. The tree that is created is processed by the class `IDLParser` and stored in a compact form in the IR.

The class `Parser` checks the syntax of an IDL specification, whereas the class `IDLParser` tests the semantics of the input. This includes the reference to a user-defined IDL type that was not defined before its use. If such an error occurs, the class `IDLError` is used to give an informative error message. If the input is error free, the first phase of the translation of an IDL specification is completed when the IR contains the complete specification.

Example

The following example clarifies the front-end procedure. The IDL specifications that appear serve as the input of the IDL compiler.

```
// IDL
struct Person {
  string   name, surname;
  short    age;
};
```

The IDL specification is syntactically and semantically correct and defines a user-specific data type `Person`. The following extract from a CORBA specification shows the part of the IDL grammar that provides the syntax of the above IDL specification:

struct_type	→ '`struct`' IDENTIFIER '{' member_list '}'
member_list	→ member
	→ member member_list
member	→ type_spec declarators ';'
type_spec	→ base_type_spec

```
                         → scoped_name
                         ...
base_type_spec           → 'string'
                         → 'short'
                         ...
declarators              → declarator
                         → declarators ',' declarator
declarator               → IDENTIFIER
                         ...
```

The parser generator YACC is used to generate a parser from the grammar. Using the above IDL specification as input, the parser generated by the YACC creates the parse tree shown in Figure 9.8. Each node in the parse tree in Figure 9.8 corresponds to an instance of the class `ParseNode`. Once the parse tree is constructed (and consequently the input recognized as syntactically correct), the class `IDLParser` collects the information contained in the parser tree and represents it as an object within the IR. This object is created with the name `create_struct()` through an operation of the IR. The input parameters of `create_struct()` correspond to the information contained in the parse tree.

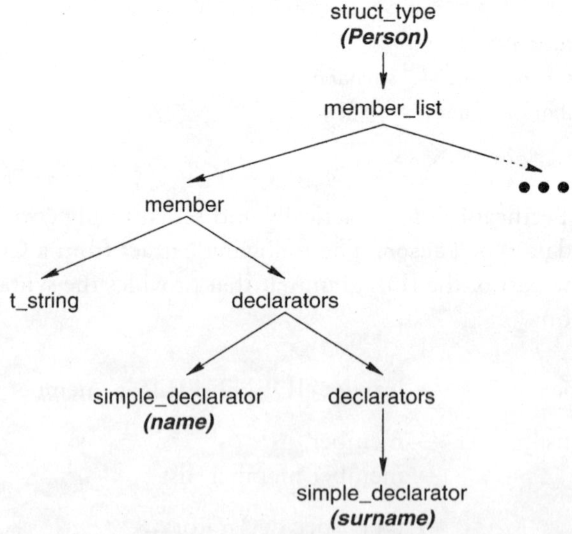

FIGURE 9.8 Section of parse tree for the IDL type `Person`.

9.4.3 Back End

Mico supports different back ends

The back end is responsible for code generation. Different back ends can generate code for different target languages. For example, Figure 9.5 shows this with C++ and Java. The back end is selected on the basis of command line parameters to the IDL compiler. The back end converts the IDL language-mapping rules for a particular language. It derives the input from the content of the IR. This section focuses on the back end for the language C++.

C++ distinguishes between declarations and definitions

In C++ a distinction is made between two types of program elements: *declarations* and *definitions*. A declaration makes the definition of a program construct known to the C++ compiler without stipulating its implementation. In contrast, a definition indicates the implementation of a program construct. A declaration is more abstract than a definition in the sense that it provides a specification, whereas a definition provides an implementation.

This distinction is necessary if an application is being divided into several translation units. The dependencies between the translation units are resolved through the use of declarations. Dependencies arise, for example, between an application and the proxy objects. The application requires the declarations of the stubs and the skeletons in order to use the proxy objects. If an entire application is linked to an executable program file, the definitions of the proxies also have to be included.

Per convention, declarations and definitions are normally stored in different files. All declarations end up in a header file that is typically assigned the file name suffix `.h`. The definitions are found in an implementation file. Here different C++ compilers use different suffixes for the file names. The most common ones are `.cc`, `.cpp`, and `.cxx`. Mico's IDL compiler generates two files for C++ language mapping from one IDL specification—one each for the declarations and the definitions.

Figure 9.9 shows the design of the back end for the generation of C++ stubs and skeletons. Each back end is derived from the class `CodeGen`, which defines

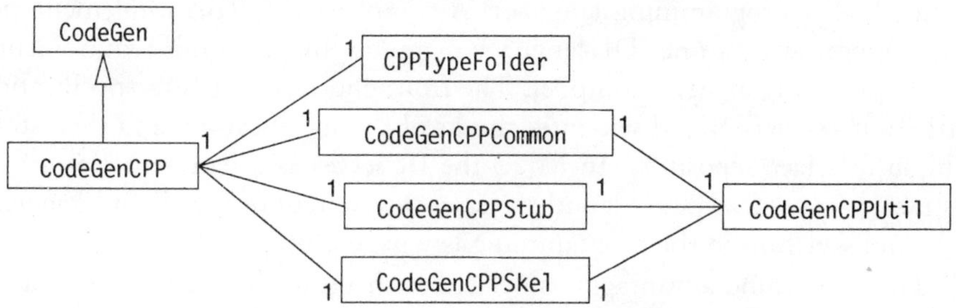

FIGURE 9.9 Design of back end for C++ code generation.

TABLE 9.3 Classes of C++ back end and their function

Class	Description
`CPPTypeFolder`	Eliminates identical C++ types
`CodeGen`	Abstract base class for all back ends
`CodeGenCPP`	Code generation for C++
`CodeGenCPPCommon`	Generates code for all declarations
`CodeGenCPPSkel`	Generates definitions belonging to skeleton
`CodeGenCPPStub`	Generates definitions belonging to stub
`CodeGenCPPUtil`	General methods

the interface to a back end. The individual rules of IDL language mapping for C++ are accommodated in different classes. Table 9.3 offers an overview of the different classes of a C++ back end, along with their functionality.

The class `CPPTypeFolder` merits special mention. Different IDL types that are all mapped to the same C++ type can occur in an IDL specification. For example, the two IDL types `string<3>` and `string<8>` (each representing length-bounded strings) are mapped to the C++ type `char*`. Because double definitions should be avoided in generated C++ code (they would cause an error when the generated C++ code is translated), the class `CPPTypeFolder` is responsible for removing duplicates.

This section has not described the structure of the generated code. The code generated by MICO's IDL compiler is based on MICO's specific static invocation adapter and therefore is not portable (and this is not something required by the CORBA standard). Section C.5 in Appendix C presents the internal implementation details of generated code for an IDL specification.

9.5 SUMMARY, EVALUATION, AND ALTERNATIVES

An IDL compiler translates an IDL specification into the proxy objects of a specific higher programming language. A compliant CORBA implementation must support at least one IDL language mapping. In MICO this requirement is met by providing an IDL compiler. The front end reads an IDL specification, carries out syntactical and semantic checks of the specification, and then stores it in an interface repository. In MICO the IR serves as a representation of the abstract syntax tree. The back end traverses the content of the IR and generates stubs and skeletons in the programming language C++.

There are some advantages associated with using the IR to represent the abstract syntax tree. An IR must exist for every compliant implementation of the CORBA standard anyway and can therefore be reused for building an IDL compiler. The disadvantage is that some of the information needed for code generation cannot be represented in an IR and therefore must be passed to the back end in different ways.

Whereas the interface between the proxy objects to be used by the IDL language mapping is defined in the CORBA specification, an ORB developer has the freedom to select how these proxies are implemented and on which ORB API they are based. From the standpoint of reusability, it would also be possible to use the DII and the DSI of the ORB API. These components are just as necessary for a compliant CORBA implementation as the IR is. This is also how earlier versions of MICO were structured. Due to deficiencies in the DII and the DSI in terms of runtime efficiency, the static invocation adapter in MICO introduced an ORB API specifically for proxies.

It is not necessarily the case that an IDL compiler is the only way that the requirement of IDL language mapping for compliant CORBA implementations can be met. With C++, IDL compilers are effective for supporting the language mapping. For programming languages that offer reflexive mechanisms, other solutions are conceivable. A reflexive language allows introspection at runtime; that is, a program based on a reflexive language is able to obtain information about itself. Therefore, generic proxy objects could be developed as part of the ORB library. The generic stub and skeleton would then use the reflexive characteristics of the language to provide the signature of an operation at runtime, for example. An IDL compiler is therefore not necessary in this case. A programming language that enables this approach is Smalltalk.

Chapter 10

CORBA AND BEYOND

The final chapter provides an overview of some advanced aspects of CORBA as well as other topics unrelated to CORBA. We first discuss the CORBA Component Model in Section 10.1. This latest addition to the CORBA specification introduces the notion of components. In Section 10.2 we give a brief overview of Web Services that have become popular in recent years. We provide a brief comparison between Web Services and CORBA. Section 10.3 gives an introduction to a whole new class of middleware technologies—middleware for ubiquitous computing. We provide an overview of this exciting area, which is still subject to active research endeavors.

10.1 CORBA COMPONENTS

CORBA 3.0 introduced the CORBA Component Model (CCM), which enables developers to implement fine-grained components, and then to assemble them into a component-based application.

This section begins with an introduction to component-based development. It then looks into the specifics of the CORBA Component Model. A brief example of using the CCM implementation in Mico is followed by an overview of the implementation's internals. The section then concludes with a discussion of CCM and future trends.

10.1.1 Component-Based Development

"Component" is a widely used and abused term not only in the world of software engineering. According to the *Merriam-Webster Dictionary*, a component is "a constituent part," and in this meaning, the term is used for almost anything that is a part of something bigger.

The Unified Modeling Language (UML) provides a more meaningful definition:

"Component" definition

> A component represents a modular part of a system that encapsulates its contents and whose manifestation is replaceable within its environment.

This definition mentions three important properties. The word "modular" indicates that a component is a building block that can potentially be used in many, as the definition puts it, systems. The component "encapsulates" its contents, meaning that it is a black box, defined not by its implementation but by its interface. Finally, it is "replaceable," so that components can be exchanged with a different implementation, as long as the interface remains the same.

Thus far, however, a component would be no different than an object. But the definition goes on:

Components have ports

> A component defines its behavior in terms of provided and required interfaces. . . . Conformance is defined by these provided and required interfaces.

This extends the component model beyond the object model. Where an object has a single interface that consists of operations and attributes, a component's interface is characterized by offered and required *ports*. For example, a coffeemaker component could provide a user interface (an offered port) and require a socket interface (a used port), which would have to be provided by your power company.

The idea of component-based programming then is to create applications *by assembly* (i.e., by instantiating a number of components) and then interconnecting matching provided and required ports according to an *assembly specification*. The execution of a component-based application is called *deployment*.

The vision is greater component reusability and to mature from application *engineering* to *manufacturing:* after all, a car is manufactured from numerous standard components rather than by reinventing the wheel for each new make and model.

In a way, client/server programming is a relic from the 1960s, when terminals acted as clients to monolithic, mainframe-based databases. Such an architecture can be described as egocentric: it is all about the server. Clients contact the server, which is responsible for handling requests. Delegation—servers acting as clients to other servers as part of handling requests—is possible, but has to be modeled explicitly, and in fact, many real-life servers do not delegate any functionality at all.

A popular program paradigm of the 1990s was the three-tier, or more generally the *n*-tier, architecture, where (Web) clients interacted with front-end services (e.g., a CGI script executed by the Web server) that then delegated requests to their (database) back ends. This is but an extension of the client/server architecture, where the middle tiers delegate everything, and the back ends delegate nothing.

Components are peers

In contrast, components are building blocks in a peer-to-peer architecture. Their paradigm is to implement a self-contained task as a reusable component, which in turn delegates tasks that are not related to its core functionality.

Component-based programming anticipates the cooperation of components in order to achieve a common task. The feature of required ports invites developers to design components with dependencies, to delegate tasks to a specialized external component to be connected at assembly time, rather than implementing all functionality within, which would then have to be maintained as a monolithic piece.

For example, a coffeemaker's core functionality is to brew coffee. It offers an interface to brew a couple of cups, but requires connections to a wall socket for power, to a faucet for water, and to a filter with coffee. With these standard interfaces, it is possible to brew different kinds of coffee (by substituting the filter), to use either tap or purified water (by substituting the faucet), and the coffeemaker interface can be used to brew at the touch of a button or at a specified time. Keeping the pieces of functionality separate allows for any amount of flexibility.

10.1.2 The CORBA Component Model

The CORBA Component Model allows for component-based development, using CORBA as the glue and means of communication between components. The CCM specification can be separated into three major parts. The *component model* defines components and ports using extensions to the IDL language. The *container programming model* defines the implementation of components and a component implementation's interaction with its runtime environment, the "container." Finally, *packaging and deployment* defines how to package component-based applications (assemblies), composed of component implementations and metadata, and their deployment (execution).

COMPONENT MODEL

Components

CORBA's component model follows the ideas outlined earlier. A CORBA component, defined with the `component` keyword, may have the following features:

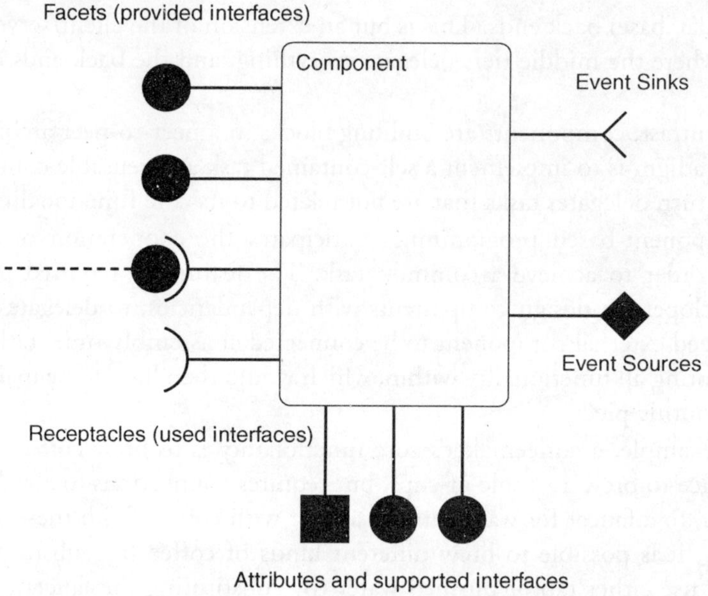

FIGURE 10.1 Features of a CORBA component.

1. Zero or one base components (inheritance)
2. Supported interfaces
3. Attributes
4. Ports

Interface and event ports

There are two classes of ports, *interface* and *event* ports. Interface ports can be *provided* or *required*, and event ports are either *event sources* or *event sinks*. For event source ports, the CORBA component model further distinguishes between unicast, where an event is delivered to a single event sink, and broadcast, where an event is broadcast to any number of peers.

Figure 10.1 illustrates a possible visualization of a CORBA component with its features.

New IDL keywords

New keywords are introduced into the IDL language for each kind of port:

provides: A provided interface port, also called a *facet*. The component implements this interface, with is declared as a regular IDL interface, having operations and attributes.

`uses:` A required interface port, also called a *receptacle*. This implies a dependency on another component. In an assembly, a facet must be connected to the receptacle, so that this component can access its functionality. A receptacle can be *simplex*, to be connected to a single facet, or *multiplex*, which can be connected to multiple facets simultaneously.

`publishes:` An event source port for broadcast.

`emits:` An event source port for unicast.

`consumes:` An event sink port.

While components in the abstract model do not have operations of their own—their functionality is rather advertised via its facets—the CORBA component model also allows components to *support* one or more interfaces. This feature exists largely for the use case of legacy components, that is, where an existing service shall be made available as a component. However, it is debatable whether the code changes to port a service to a component supporting the service's interface are less invasive than the changes necessary to port the service to a component that offers the service's interface as a facet.

Note that the CORBA specification makes a distinction between what it calls *basic* and *extended* components. Basic components may have attributes and supported interfaces, but no ports. Basic components exist solely to provide a concept equivalent to Enterprise Java Beans, because the original specification tried to provide full source compatibility, to be able to run Java Beans in a CORBA Components container. For the purposes of component-based development, basic components are, with their lack of ports, useless. The text above thus describes "extended" components.

Homes

Components are *managed* by *homes*. A home is a singleton that acts as a factory for a specific type of component. When a component implementation is executed in its container, a home is created as part of the bootstrapping process; in C++, there is a well-defined, user-provided entry point that creates the home. The deployment software can then interact with the home to create the desired number of components.

The CORBA component model distinguishes *keyless* and *keyed* homes. In a keyed home, each component instance is identified by a specific key value. Keyed homes are used with persistent components, to associate a component with a specific entry in a database. Nonpersistent components (i.e., components that do not exist across restarts) always use keyless homes.

Homes may have a base home and attributes may support interfaces, and can have special operations called *factories* or *finders*.

Factories and finders may have a parameter list, and their return type is, implicitly, the managed component type. While factories create new component instances, finders locate and return existing component instances. However, user-defined factories and finders are of questionable value in a component-based application because generic deployment software is not able to use them. In the metadata that is associated with component instantiation, there is no information about which factory to use or what parameters to pass.

Equivalent IDL

At runtime, although it is not visible to component implementations, an ORB is used to invoke operations on facets and to transport events between components. For interoperability, the ORB is also used during setup (i.e., at deployment time) to interconnect ports. For this purpose, the CORBA component model uses *equivalent IDL*.

Equivalent IDL for noncomponent clients

A set of rules exists to define *equivalent interfaces* for components and homes. A component's equivalent interface contains all component attributes and "equivalent operations" for each of its ports. For example, if a component has a facet called `foo`, this interface will contain a `provide_foo` operation that returns an object reference of the appropriate type. A `bar` receptacle is translated into a `connect_bar` operation. The equivalent interface also inherits all of its supported interfaces, and the base component's equivalent interface, if it is a derived component.

At deployment time, software can use a component's equivalent interface to access object references for facets and event sinks, and pass them on to other components' receptacles and event sources.

The equivalent interfaces can also be used by *component-unaware* clients—software that is not a CORBA component itself, but wants to interoperate with components using regular remote invocations.

Component implementations need not be concerned with their equivalent interface. At runtime, the "container" is responsible for implementing this *client-side view* of a component. It is also the container that generates CORBA object references that can be used by the deployment software or by other clients.

CONTAINER PROGRAMMING MODEL

The second concept introduced by CCM is the container programming model, which describes component implementations and the interaction with their runtime, the *container*. Containers act as the component's object adapter. Like the Portable Object Adapter (see Section 7.3.1), it adapts component implementations to the ORB; it mediates requests from and to a component instance.

The POA suffered from the complexity that comes with its flexibility as a "one size fits all" object adapter. There was only one kind of POA, and implementations had to program POA instances to fit their needs.

Containers provide runtime services

In contrast, CORBA envisions containers as an extensible concept and anticipates a set of different containers. Containers may offer various services to an implementation, such as automated persistence or security. An implementation can then choose the container that matches its runtime requirements.

A side effect is that the amount of repetitive code in each server is reduced. Many POA-based servers face the same startup and shutdown tasks: create a POA instance with the desired set of policies, activate a servant instance, load persistent state from a database, then register the object in the Naming Service, and so on. A component developer need not be concerned with these details, but will just select the appropriate container type.

Component Implementations

As mentioned in the section about equivalent IDL, every container must implement a component's client-side view. This includes the generation of object references for a component and its facets, connection management such as storing a receptacle's peer, and the setup of appropriate event channels to facilitate event delivery.

Server-side equivalent IDL

Operations on facets or supported interfaces must eventually be delivered to the component implementation. Again, the concept of equivalent IDL is used to define a callback interface that the container can use for this purpose. In the CCM specification, this *server-side equivalent IDL* is defined as part of the language-mapping chapter—which, despite the name, is independent of a programming language. Components, homes, and facets are mapped to `local` interfaces, which are then to be implemented by the component developer. A component implementation is also called an *executor*.

For each component type, a *context interface* is also defined. This context interface is implemented by the container and provides component instances with their state, such as a receptacle's peer, and also an operation to push events to an event source port, which the container then delivers to each recipient that is connected to the port.

Container Types

The CORBA components specification defines four basic container types, called *service, session, process,* and *entity* containers, representing the possible combinations of being stateless *versus* stateful and nonpersistent *versus* persistent. Because component implementations are designed to work with a particular type of container, the same prefix can also be used for components. For example, a *session component* is a component that runs in a session container.

Predefined container types

Service: A container for stateless, nonpersistent components. Because of these properties, a container can create and destroy instances as necessary. A single instance can be shared by all clients, or a container might create an instance per connection.

Session: A container for stateful, nonpersistent components. Component instances keep a per-client state, but that state is not kept across restarts. An example is a shopping cart, which keeps its state only until checkout.

Process: A container for stateless, persistent components. This is not an oxymoron, as the "stateless" refers to a specific client. So a process component has state that is shared between all clients and that is preserved across restarts. Our coffeemaker component from above would be a good candidate: the coffee pot is shared by all users, and the amount of brewed coffee in the pot remains the same even if you unplug and "reboot" the machine.

Entity: A container for stateful, persistent components, with a client-specific state that needs to be preserved, such as an account component. This is equivalent to Entity Beans in Enterprise Java Beans (albeit with a vastly different component model, as Beans do not have ports).

CIDL and PSDL

In addition to the "language mapping" for components, CCM also defines, the *Component Implementation Definition Language* (CIDL). CIDL is based on the *Persistent State Definition Language* (PSDL) from the OMG Persistent State Service and adds some CCM-specific concepts.

CIDL deals with two orthogonal ideas. First, it allows the description of component implementation *segments* (programming language constructs that implement pieces of a component) and *compositions* (the set of segments that make up a complete component implementation). This feature of CIDL allows the automatic generation of an executor (i.e., a component implementation that can be used by a container) that delegates operations on the component or on facets to the desired segment.

Using the inherited PSDL vocabulary, CIDL then allows description of a segment's state, by identifying member variables that need to be preserved across component restarts. A process or entity container can then use this information to automate the storage and retrieval of component state.

PACKAGING AND DEPLOYMENT

Finally, this chapter in the CCM specification describes a format for packaging individual components and component-based applications, and an infrastructure to deploy components or applications.

Packages contain executables and metadata

Packages are self-contained files that include component implementations as well as metadata. CCM uses the popular ZIP file format to combine implementations and XML *descriptors* into one-file, distributable, and deployable packages.

A—somewhat misnamed—*software package*, sometimes more appropriately called *component package*, is a ZIP file containing one or more alternative implementations of the same component, and a "CORBA *software descriptor*" (`.csd`) XML file that identifies implementations, their features, and dependencies. For example, a software package might contain alternative implementations for Linux, Windows, and Java. At deployment time, the best implementation could be chosen based on available hardware.

An *assembly package* contains a component-based application consisting of one or more interconnected components. Again, it is a ZIP file and contains a set of component implementations and their matching CORBA software descriptor files. The *component assembly descriptor* (`.cad`) XML file then describes the application (i.e., its component instances and port connections).

A deployment application reads these packages in order to deploy either a single component or a full application. It contacts one or more *component server* objects to load and execute component implementations, and then uses each component's client-side equivalent interface to interconnect the application according to the assembly descriptor's plan.

The packaging and deployment chapter also defines the remaining link that is necessary to instantiate a component implementation. For the C++ and Java programming languages, a special *entry point* is defined: a global C-style function for C++, a static method for Java. An entry point must be implemented by the developer; its purpose is to create an instance of the singleton home. Its name is derived from the home's IDL name. So when a container loads a component implementation (e.g., from a shared library), it looks up the entry point and uses it to create the home.

Beyond the XML descriptors, the chapter also defines interfaces for the deployment of components. The `ServerActivator` is a daemon that needs to run on a host where components are to be deployed. It spawns servers implementing the `ComponentServer` interface. Within a component server, multiple `Container` instances can coexist, which finally support the deployment, or *installation*, of home instances. A `ComponentInstallation` interface allows the remote installation of component implementations.

10.1.3 An Example Component

This section shows the implementation of a very basic component and how to get started with using CORBA components using MICO.

COMPONENT IDL

Figure 10.2 shows the IDL file for a simple `Account` component. It offers a single `checking` facet, which implements the `CheckingAccount` interface. The

```
interface CheckingAccount {
  void deposit (in long amount);
  void withdraw (in long amount);
  long balance ();
};

component Account {
  provides CheckingAccount checking;
};

home Bank manages Account {
};
```

FIGURE 10.2 IDL for an "Account" component and its home.

`Bank` home manages the account component and will be used to create instances of the component.

CLIENT-SIDE EQUIVALENT IDL

As described in Section 10.1.2, a component's client-side interface is defined by equivalent IDL, that is, by applying a set of rules to the original component's IDL. Containers and deployment applications can use this interface to interconnect components. It can also be used by component-unaware clients (i.e., by CORBA applications that are not themselves components).

The equivalent IDL is not normally generated. However, MICO's IDL compiler can be coerced into creating an equivalent IDL file `account-eq.idl` from the `account.idl` file using

Generating an equivalent IDL file

```
idl ---idl3toidl2 --codegen-idl --no-codegen-c++ \
  --name account-eq account.idl
```

The client-side equivalent IDL for our example component is shown in Figure 10.3. The account component's equivalent interface inherits from the common base interface `Components::CCMObject`, which provides generic navigation, interconnection, and introspection features. It then contains a single operation, `provide_checking`, to access the single facet that the component offers.

```
interface Account : ::Components::CCMObject {
  CheckingAccount provide_checking();
};

interface BankExplicit : ::Components::CCMHome {
};

interface BankImplicit : ::Components::KeylessCCMHome {
  Account create();
};

interface Bank : ::BankExplicit, ::BankImplicit {
};
```

FIGURE 10.3 Client-side equivalent IDL for the "Account" component.

The "Bank" home is split into three separate interfaces. The "explicit" interface contains a home's explicit operations, including custom factories and finders. The "implicit" interface contains a single `create` operation, which can be used by clients to create instances of the "Account" component. Finally, the `Bank` interface inherits both the explicit and implicit interfaces. This separation is done in order to support inheritance. A derived home can inherit the base home's explicit interface, but will provide its own `create` operation in the implicit interface.

SERVER-SIDE EQUIVALENT IDL

Figure 10.4 shows the server-side equivalent IDL for our example, obtained with the same IDL compiler command line as above.

```
local interface CCM_CheckingAccount : ::CheckingAccount {
};

local interface CCM_Account : ::Components::EnterpriseComponent {
  CCM_CheckingAccount get_checking();
};

local interface CCM_Account_Context : ::Components::SessionContext {
};

local interface CCM_BankExplicit : ::Components::HomeExecutorBase {
};

local interface CCM_BankImplicit {
  Components::EnterpriseComponent create();
};

local interface CCM_Bank : ::CCM_BankExplicit, ::CCM_BankImplicit {
};
```

FIGURE 10.4 Server-side equivalent IDL for the "Account" component.

This file shows the `CCM_Account` local interface that a component executor must implement. In this case, there is a single `get_checking` operation to retrieve the—also local—implementation of the `checking` facet.

The equivalent IDL for the home exhibits the same separation into explicit and implicit interfaces as for the client-side equivalent IDL. The one operation that our home executor must implement is the `create` operation, returning a new `CCM_Account` instance.

COMPONENT IMPLEMENTATION

The implementation of our "Account" component and its "Bank" home is listed in Figure 10.5. Just like one would implement a servant, the `Account_impl` class derives from the `CCM_Account` base class, which can be seen in Figure 10.3. The single method that needs to be implemented is the `get_checking` operation, which returns the local implementation of the `CheckingAccount` facet.

It is easy to imagine how the implementation of a component and its facets could be composed of multiple, interdependent classes operating on a common data set.

The implementation of the home, in class `Bank_impl`, simply provides the single `create` operation, as shown in Figure 10.4. This implementation just creates a new instance of the `Account_impl` implementation of the "Account" component.

Finally, an entry point function must be defined, with the same name as the home interface and the `create_` prefix. Thus, in this case, the entry point is called `create_Bank`. The purpose of the entry point is to give containers a means of constructing home instances. In the C++ language, while objects can be used polymorphically through pointers and references, compile time knowledge is necessary to construct an object. However, a container can use system calls to look up functions in a shared object's symbol table (e.g., using the `dlopen` system call in POSIX) and then call this function, the entry point, to receive a polymorphic object. This is why the entry point must match the given signature, returning a pointer to a `Components::HomeExecutorBase_ptr` (a common base class for all homes) and using "C" linkage to avoid a C++ compiler's name mangling.

COMPILING

Compiling a component is straightforward: The IDL file is processed with the IDL compiler, and the generated C++ code is compiled and linked with the component implementation.

```
#include "account.h"

class CheckingAccount_impl : virtual public CCM_CheckingAccount {
  /* not shown */
};

class Account_impl : virtual public CCM_Account {
private:
  CheckingAccount_impl * m_checking;

public:
  Account_impl ()
  {
    m_checking = new CheckingAccount_impl;
  }

  CCM_CheckingAccount * get_checking ()
  {
    return CCM_CheckingAccount::_duplicate (m_checking);
  }
};

class Bank_impl : virtual public CCM_Bank {
public:
  Components::EnterpriseComponent_ptr create ()
  {
    return new Account_impl;
  }
};

extern "C" {
  Components::HomeExecutorBase_ptr
  create_Bank ()
  {
    return new Bank_impl;
  }
}
```

FIGURE 10.5 Implementation of the "Account" component and its home.

One added step is the generation of *component skeletons*, which will be visited in the *implementation overview* below. A separate `mico-ccm` tool is provided. It acts like the IDL compiler, reading an IDL file, generating C++ code, and adding the `_ccm` suffix into the file name before the extension. For an input file `account.idl`, it generates both the header file `account_ccm.h` and the code file `account_ccm.cc`.

The syntax of the `mico-ccm` tool is as follows:

The `mico-ccm` code generator

```
mico-ccm [<options>] idl-file
```

The following options are accepted:

`--session`: Generates code for session components. This is the default.

`--service`: Generates code for service components.

`--standalone`: Includes a `main` function in the generated code, so that the component can be built into a stand-alone executable. This will also cause the container implementation to be linked with the component.

Without the `--standalone` option, the component must be built as a shared library.

Whether built as a stand-alone executable or a shared library, the component must be linked against the `micoccm`, `micocoss` (for the Naming Service stubs), and `mico` libraries.

RUNNING

If the component was built as a stand-alone executable, it includes its container and can be run from the command line. The one mandatory command line parameter is the name of the home that shall be created. In the example above, that would be `Bank`. In addition, the following options are accepted:

Executing a stand-alone component

`--ior` *filename*: Writes the home's stringified object reference to the given file.

`--ns` *name*: Registers the home in the Naming Service, using the given name.

If the component was built as a shared library, then it needs to be loaded into a container.

The `mico-ccmd` daemon starts containers on demand

The `componentserver` application can act as a host for containers and components, implementing the `ComponentServer` and `Container` interfaces as described in Section 10.1.2. However, it is more convenient to use the MICO CCM daemon, `mico-ccmd`, which implements the `ServerActivator` interface, and which spawns `componentserver` instances on demand:

```
mico-ccmd [<options>]
```

The following options are accepted:

`--ior` ***filename*****:** Writes the daemon's stringified object reference to the given file.

`--root` ***dirname*****:** When used to remotely install components, using the daemon's `ComponentInstallation` interface, places component implementations in this directory.

`-v`**:** Prints some progress messages.

Once the MICO CCM daemon is running, the `ccmload` tool can be used to deploy a component:

Loading a component into a container

```
ccmload [<options>] <homename> <filename>
```

The `homename` is the name of the home ("Bank" in this example). The `filename` is the name of the shared library that contains the home's implementation. Note that the file name must be valid according to the MICO CCM daemon's current directory, which may be different than the directory that `ccmload` is run in.

The following options can be used with `ccmload`:

`--ccmd` ***ior*****:** The object reference of the MICO CCM daemon.

`--host` ***addr*****:** An alternate means of specifying the address of the MICO CCM daemon, using the host name and, optionally, separated by a colon, the port number. If the port number is omitted, "1234" is assumed as a default.

`--ior` ***filename*****:** Writes the deployed home's stringified object reference to the given file.

`--ns` ***name*****:** Registers the home in the Naming Service, using the given name.

`-v`**:** Prints some progress messages as the home is being deployed.

To load the example component, the following command line could be used, assuming that the shared library had the name `account.so`, the MICO CCM daemon was running on the same host on port 1234, in the same working directory:

```
ccmload --host localhost Bank ./account.so
```

This should print the home's stringified object reference, which could now be used by a client program to connect to the home, create "Account" component instances, navigate to the `checking` facet using the `get_checking` operation on the equivalent interface, and use the operations on that facet.

For simplicity, the example did not show how to remotely deploy a component, nor did it attempt to interconnect components. Given that the effort to run a single component seems overwhelming, it is hard to imagine how to deploy large applications. However, applications would not be deployed in such a piece-by-piece manner. Rather, the components in an application would be put into a *software package* as described in Section 10.1.2, so that a generic deployment application can, from the package's XML description, perform all the required steps automatically. MICO does not include such tools, but the MICO *CCM Assembly and Deployment Toolkit* is freely available.

10.1.4 Implementation Overview

As seen in Section 10.1.2, a component implementation is enveloped by its container, which adapts an executor to an ORB. This adaptation faces the same problem as the Portable Object Adapter: while an executor's interface is defined in IDL, at component development time, the container needs a static interface to communicate with. Thus, as seen above, a similar trick of using a *component skeleton* is employed. This component skeleton is generated from the IDL code that defines the component (and thus executor) interface. It implements a private, container-specific interface to receive invocations and dispatches them to the matching component or facet executor. This component skeleton is the output from the `mico-ccm` tool.

The CORBA components implementation in MICO is built on top of the Portable Object Adapter, which is used by the container to manage object references and to dispatch invocations.

MICO's containers build upon the POA

Figure 10.6 illustrates the relationship between generated component skeleton code and a component implementation. When a component's IDL file is processed by the IDL compiler, it internally generates client-side and server-side equivalent IDL. Just as for a noncomponent interface, a stub, to be used by

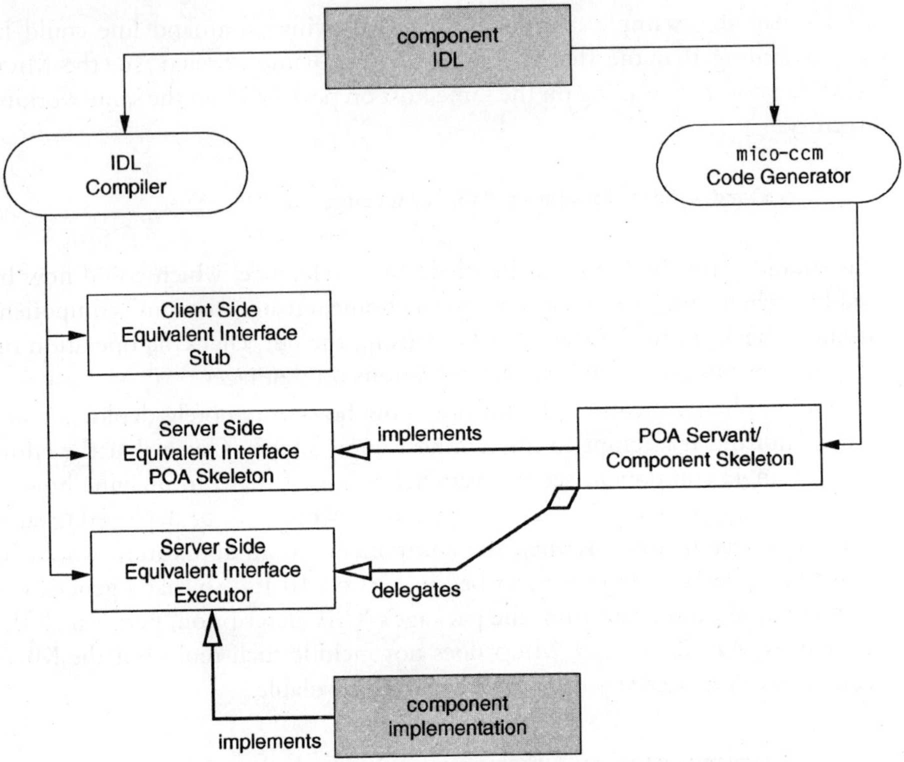

FIGURE 10.6 Relationship between generated code and implementation.

clients, and a POA skeleton are then generated for the equivalent client-side interface, as well as the equivalent server-side "local" interface that the component implementation inherits from and implements.

The component skeleton that is generated by `mico-ccm` doubles as a POA servant that implements the skeleton for the client-side equivalent interface. It is responsible for implementing this interface's behavior—that is, to delegate operations to the component implementation, the executor, and to manage interconnection requests as defined by the equivalent operations for each component feature (e.g., a `provide_foo` operation for a `foo` facet that clients can use to connect to a facet).

The component skeleton also cooperates with the container to provide container-specific behavior such as component instantiation. This way, the component skeleton can be seen as implementing part of the container itself.

Pros and cons of MICO CCM's design

The architecture of building containers on top of the POA has both benefits and drawbacks:

- ⊞ Because the POA provides the functionality for request unmarshalling and dispatching, which in a POA skeleton make up most of the code, container and component skeletons are relatively small and simple.

- ⊞ Container and component skeletons are also ORB independent, as ORB-specific hooks are hidden within the POA skeleton. Components could be ported to a different ORB by feeding the other ORB's IDL compiler with the component's equivalent IDL.

- ⊞ Container-specific information is kept out of the IDL compiler and limited to the separate `mico-ccm` code generator.

- ⊟ Processing requests by both the POA skeleton and the component skeleton before delivering it to the implementation adds an additional level of indirection and complexity. The POA skeleton is a large chunk of code that increases code size.

- ⊟ Only a fraction of the POA's functionality is used; the rest of the POA remains "added baggage," again increasing the size of executables.

An alternative architecture would recognize containers for what they are: object adapters in their own right, adapting components to the ORB. Thus containers should interface with the ORB core to act as an object adapter by themselves. By avoiding the overhead of the POA skeleton, generated code for a component would be much smaller. No skeleton code would be necessary for equivalent operations, which could be handled internally.

This architecture would require integrating the current functionality of `mico-ccm` with the IDL compiler, which would generate container-specific component skeleton code.

10.1.5 Discussion

Component model versus container programming model

The CORBA components specification is a melange of two almost orthogonal concepts, the component model and the container programming model. While the former supports component-based development, the latter is about providing components with better run-time support.

Although the combination of both ideas is more than the sum of its parts, it is somewhat unfortunate that the CCM specification does not introduce or keep them separate, as it makes the specification less accessible to both component and CCM implementors. The complexity of CCM has certainly discouraged ORB vendors from adapting components. For years after its adoption, CCM existed in the academia and Open Source implementations only.

The waters that CCM treads in are further muddied by specifications like Enterprise Java Beans (ESB)—where the CCM container model originates from—which calls itself component-based, but whose components do not support component-based development: EJB Beans do not have any ports.

Each feature is exciting in itself. While component-based development promises better software modularity and eases application manufacturing from existing components, the container programming model eases the implementation of components, especially with advanced features like container-managed persistence and transactions that are provided by the entity container.

However, in the persistence aspect, another feature mix is apparent in the design of the CIDL language, which describes both the segmentation of a component implementation into classes, and the component's persistent data. In other words, it mixes implementation details with database details. But certainly, the data that an account component maintains, such as the balance, is independent from the specifics of the component implementation.

While CCM was grown out of Enterprise Java Beans—historically, the design of CCM started as a "vendor- and language-independent" version of EJB—it is the component-based development that receives more attention today.

Skeptics argue that the step from object-oriented programming to component-based development does not provide many benefits. It is undeniable that object orientation has largely failed to deliver its promise of powerful, reusable object-oriented libraries. The number of successful reusable libraries like Qt, Swing, or MFC is small. Worse, these libraries tend to be full featured rather than modular, and do not integrate well. It remains to be seen whether components are any more successful in the area of vendor-independent, modular development.

Yet it is undeniable that components have a "harder shell" than objects, and their port-oriented interface anticipates cooperation rather than being entirely self-contained. Developers are encouraged to require a connection to a receptacle, using an external component, rather than implementing all behavior monolithically.

Also, CORBA is a much softer glue than most programming languages. In C++, it is usually impossible to interoperate with an object library that was built with a different compiler, sometimes down to the compiler's minor version. But CORBA allows components to interoperate regardless of their ORB or programming language.

The remainder of this section introduces two new component-based specifications that were recently adopted by the Object Management Group and which supplement the CCM specification with new features and possibilities. *Lightweight CCM* is a subset of the CCM specification directed at embedded systems, and *Deployment and Configuration of Component-Based Distributed Applications* improves upon CCM's Packaging and Deployment model. The final subsection details potential future ideas and research areas for CCM.

LIGHTWEIGHT CCM

Using CCM in embedded systems

It is somewhat ironic that CCM, with all its perceived complexity judged from its number of pages, is embraced in the embedded systems domain. Although embedded systems used to be monolithic, designed by a single vendor, they have become ever more heterogeneous, with one or more general purpose processors tightly integrated with, for example, DSPs, FPGAs or other special hardware. It is essential that applications, which are made up of separate components running on different pieces of equipment, integrate smoothly with any device drivers. It is not hard to imagine the benefits of component-based development in this scenario.

The full CCM specification, however, is too complex for many of such footprint-constrained environments.

Just like Minimum CORBA, *Lightweight CCM*—also called LwCCM—defines a profile of the full CCM specification.

For the purpose of embedded systems, the concept of container-managed transactions and persistence, which is most useful in three-tier business applications, is usually of less interest and is thus removed from the profile. Only the Service and the Session containers are supported.

Also disabled are introspection features that are normally part of the client-side equivalent interface, which allow a client to, for example, introspect ports and their current connections.

Because Lightweight CCM is a direct subset, a CCM implementation is automatically Lightweight CCM compliant.

DEPLOYMENT AND CONFIGURATION

Another recent addition to the canon of CCM specifications is one called *Deployment and Configuration of Component-Based Distributed Applications*, sometimes shortened to "Deployment and Configuration" or just "D+C."

This specification aims to replace CCM's Packaging and Deployment chapter and improves upon it:

Hierarchical assemblies, requirement versus resource matching

- CCM allows only a single level of hierarchy; it is not possible to reuse an assembly as a component in another assembly. In D+C, an assembly implements a specific component interface (the "encompassing component") by

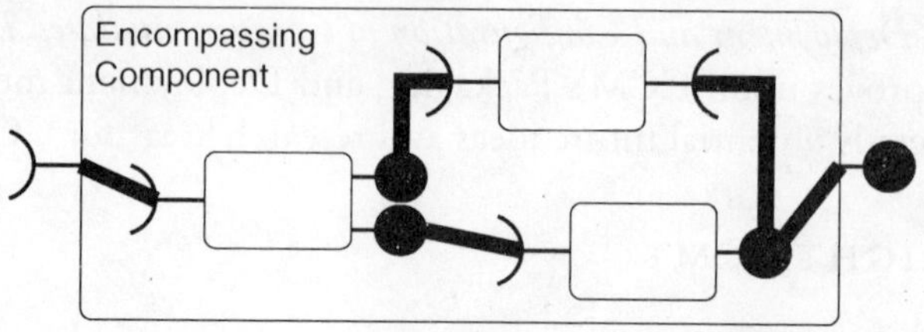

FIGURE 10.7 An assembly implements a component interface.

itself; this component's ports are then mapped to subcomponent ports, as shown in Figure 10.7.

- While CCM allowed component packages to have alternative implementations, this feature did not exist on the assembly level. D+C allows alternatives at any level of the hierarchy.
- CCM did not quite address *distributed* deployment: there was no process of matching components to nodes. D+C allows annotating implementations with their *requirements* in terms of hardware, and it adds a *target model* to describe a domain's resources.
- Available resources are tracked and may impact the deployment of other applications.

Especially the first idea of arbitrarily hierarchical assemblies is a necessity that was omitted in CCM. The idea of resource management and tracking is complex—for this to work, developers will have to add this information to their component metadata—but in the end allows for completely automatic assignment of components to nodes, including decisions about which of the alternative component implementations is better matched to the hardware.

In the face of an arbitrary hierarchy, the specification also concludes that CCM's idea of segmentation, which allowed for a total of two functional decompositions (assemblies into components and components into segments) is redundant.

The D+C specification goes into great detail of how deployment actually takes place. The Packaging and Deployment left many details undefined, with the result that the deployment infrastructure and tools were proprietary, and heterogeneity was limited to the platforms supported by those infrastructure and tools.

The infrastructure according to D+C includes, most importantly, four *managers*:

- The *Repository Manager* maintains a repository of applications that are available for deployment. New applications can be installed into the repository by passing the URL of a *component package*—a ZIP file containing component implementations and metadata in XML.
- The *Target Manager* maintains the set of available *nodes* and their resources. As resources are used up by the deployment of software, they are subtracted from the set.
- The *Execution Manager* allows the starting of applications.
- A set of *Node Managers*, one per node, is responsible for starting pieces of an application on their respective system, as directed by the Execution Manager.

All managers interact using well-defined interfaces. Adding a new kind of node to the system can be accomplished simply by registering a new Node Manager.

The remaining piece of the puzzle is the *planner*. Its responsibility is to figure out the best way of deploying an application into the local domain. The planner reads the application's metadata from the repository, and the set of available resources from the Target Manager, and matches up components with nodes, based on each component's requirements. This potentially very complex planning task ultimately results in a concrete *deployment plan* that details where to deploy pieces of the application. This plan can then be executed immediately ("online") or stored for future use ("offline").

FUTURE DEVELOPMENTS

The CORBA Component Model remains an active topic, and several new specifications are currently passing through the Object Management Group's adoption process.

One is the *Streams for CCM* specification, which aims to add support for source and sink ports, allowing the asynchronous transport data streams between components. The container will provide components with buffers to write to or read from; containers are then allowed to find the most efficient means of transferring data between them, either using a common, CORBA-based transport or using more highly efficient means—potentially supporting *zero copy*, in which only pointers to shared memory need to be exchanged between sources and sinks.

The *QoS for CCM* adds a framework for components to negotiate Quality of Service parameters among components that share a connection.

Still a research topic is *extensible containers*, which allow services to be added to containers using a plug-in architecture. This enables the implementation of *aspects* that are orthogonal to business logic, independent of any specific components, such as security or monitoring. Extensible containers would allow many of the same paradigms offered by aspect-oriented programming. The IST COMPARE (a COMPonent Approach to Real-time and Embedded systems) is one example of such a project; for more information, see their home page at *www.ist-compare.org*.

10.2 WEB SERVICES

Web Services have had a short but impressive history. In the late 1990s, Microsoft and a couple of other companies were thinking about an XML-based RPC that could work over HTTP. The term *SOAP* (Simple Object Access Protocol) was coined in 1998. The IETF published the first versions of SOAP 1.0 in December 1999. With broad support from both the commercial and Open Source community, a new version of SOAP emerged. In July 2001, the IETF published the first working draft of SOAP 1.2.

While SOAP is certainly at the very core of Web Services, there have been numerous new technologies that extend the scope of application-level interoperability. Just like SOAP, all these technologies are based on XML. Web Services are comprised of the following key technologies:

XML, SOAP, WSDL, and UDDI are the core technologies of Web Services

XML (eXtensible Markup Language) is a general markup language that can be used in a wide variety of contexts. Virtually all Web Service technologies make use of XML in one way or another.

SOAP (Simple Object Access Protocol) defines application-level interoperability. Its purpose resembles that of CORBA's GIOP/IIOP, except that the data representation is based on XML.

WSDL (Web Service Definition Language) allows the specification of service interfaces. Comparing it with CORBA again, it fulfills a similar function as IDL.

UDDI (Universal Description, Discovery and Integration) serves the role of a mediator. Service providers and service requestors use the UDDI registry to establish links between each other.

Clearly it is possible to write complete books just on Web Services. In the following, we have limited our discussion to the core technologies XML, WSDL, SOAP, and UDDI. In particular, we will compare Web Services with CORBA.

10.2.1 Overview of XML

XML (eXtensible Markup Language) allows the structured representation of arbitrary data. Based on a standard representation of arbitrary data, program libraries for parsing and generating XML files facilitate the handling of XML data. XML files are simple text files that can be edited with any editor. XML is called a markup language because the data is "marked up" through what are called *tags* in XML. Here is a simple example of an XML specification:

```
<Person>
  <FirstName>Mickey</FirstName>
  <LastName>Mouse</LastName>
  <Age>75</Age>
</Person>
```

`Person`, `FirstName`, `LastName`, and `Age` are tags. A *start tag* is surrounded by "<" and ">" while an *end tag* is surrounded by "< /" and ">". Note that the identifiers `Person`, `FirstName`, and so on are application specific and are not part of the XML standard. One way to look at XML is that XML itself provides the syntax of a language, and the applications-specific identifiers make up the vocabulary. Between the start tag and the end tag is the *content* of the tag. In our example `Mickey` is the content of the tag `FirstName`. The combination of start and end tags and the content is also referred to as an *element*.

Content is surrounded by start and end tags

Tags can be the content of other tags; for example, tag `Age` belongs to the content of tag `Person`. Tags have to be strictly nested, which results in a hierarchical or tree-like representation of the data. Tags can have one or more attributes, as illustrated by the next example:

```
<struct name="Person">
  <member type="string" name="first_name"/>
  <member type="string" name="last_name"/>
  <member type="int" name="age"/>
</struct>
```

Tags can have one or more attributes

`name` and `type` are called *attributes*. `name` is an attribute of tag `struct`. The value of an attribute is written between the double quotes. For example, `Person` is the value of attribute `name`. Technically, the values of the attributes belong to the content of a tag, but there are no absolute rules whether data should be placed as the content of a tag or as a value of an attribute of that tag. Note that if there is no content for a tag, the tag can be surrounded by "<" and "/ >" instead of an explicit end tag.

The previous example already provides a hint on how XML can be used in the context of a middleware. The previous XML could be interpreted as a type definition where `Person` is a structure with members `first_name`, `last_name`, and `age`. Each of those members has an associated type, as is common for programming languages. Note that the tags `struct` and `member` are specifically chosen for the context of representing a programming language data structure.

If the previous XML might be an example of a type definition, the first example presented in this section could be interpreted as an instance that conforms to the type definition. In this sense XML can be used to describe both the types and instances of data to be handled by a middleware.

10.2.2 Service Descriptions through WSDL

A WSDL specification is based on XML

WSDL (Web Service Definition Language) allows the specification of service interfaces. In that respect, WSDL resembles in its purpose CORBA's IDL. The main difference is that IDL is a language specifically created and tailored for the description of object interfaces, whereas WSDL builds upon XML. The technique employed by WSDL is very similar to the idea outlined in the previous subsection. WSDL introduces a specific "vocabulary" for XML tags and attributes that allows the description of interfaces. Figure 10.8 provides a top-level overview of a WSDL specification.

A `portType` is an abstract definition of an interface. It is abstract in the sense that it describes the operational interface of a service without going into the details of the data layout of the various parameters. A `portType` essentially consists of one or more `operations`, each consisting of several `messages`. By explicitly defining messages for each operation, it is possible to do interactions other than RPC-style operations. For example, a notification would only consist of one message, while an RPC-style operation would consist of two messages (request and response). The signature of a message is defined through a sequence of `part` elements, each describing one formal input/output parameter. The following XML excerpt shows the WSDL specification for our account example. Note that the XML has been simplified for readability purposes:

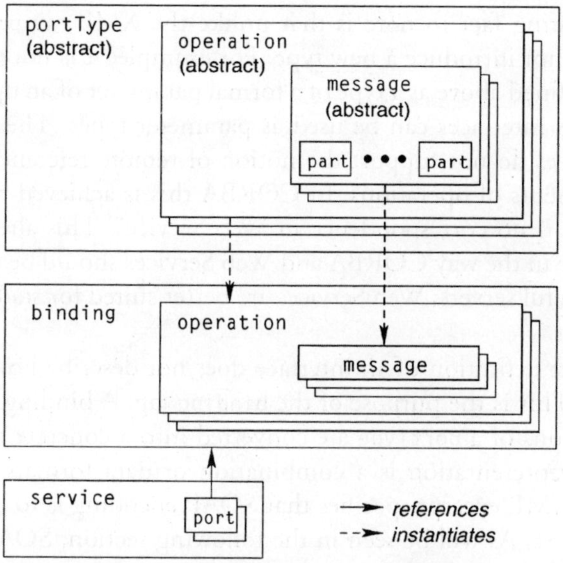

FIGURE 10.8 WSDL components.

```
<definitions name="MyAccountService">
  <types/>
  <message name="AccountIF_balance"/>
  <message name="AccountIF_balanceResponse">
    <part name="result" type="int"/>
  </message>
  <message name="AccountIF_deposit">
    <part name="amount" type="int"/>
  </message>
  <message name="AccountIF_depositResponse"/>
  <message name="AccountIF_withdraw">
    <part name="amount" type="int"/>
  </message>
  <message name="AccountIF_withdrawResponse"/>
  <portType name="AccountIF">
    <operation name="deposit" parameterOrder="amount">
      <input message="AccountIF_deposit"/>
      <output message="AccountIF_depositResponse"/>
    </operation>
    <!-- similar definitions for withdraw and balance -->
  </portType>
```

portType cannot be used as a type for formal parameters

One interesting fact to note is that unlike the XML tag portType might suggest, it does not introduce a new type. For example, it is not possible to use AccountIF as defined above as a type of a formal parameter of an operation. Note that in CORBA interfaces can be used as parameter types. The implication is that Web Services do not support the notion of remote references that can be passed as arguments of operations. In CORBA this is achieved through IORs, for which there is no correspondence in Web Services. This already hints at a major difference in the way CORBA and Web Services should be used: CORBA is better for stateful servers; Web Services are better suited for stateless, message-oriented services.

The abstract definition of an interface does not describe how the interface is represented. This is the purpose of the binding tag. A binding describes how abstract definitions of a portType are converted into a concrete representation. This concrete representation is a combination of data formats and protocol. The following XML excerpt specifies that SOAP encoding is to be used for the operation deposit. As will be seen in the following section, SOAP defines how messages look on the network.

```
<binding name="AccountIFBinding" type="AccountIF">
  <operation name="deposit">
    <input>
      <body encodingStyle="http://schemas.xmlsoap.org/soap/encoding/"
            use="encoded"/>
    </input>
    <output>
      <body encodingStyle="http://schemas.xmlsoap.org/soap/encoding/"
            use="encoded"/>
    </output>
  </operation>
  <!-- similar bindings for withdraw and balance -->
  <binding transport="http://schemas.xmlsoap.org/soap/http" style="rpc"/>
</binding>
```

The service tag describes the Web Service

The last important XML tag of a WSDL specification is the service definition. It simply is a collection of ports, detailing the location of the Web Service. The following XML excerpt specifies that the MyAccountService of type AccountIFPort with binding AccountIFBinding can be accessed at the URL mentioned in the address tag.

```
<service name="MyAccountService">
  <port name="AccountIFPort" binding="AccountIFBinding">
```

```
        <address location="http://localhost:8080/account"/>
      </port>
    </service>
  </definitions>
```

In summary, a port describes the *what* of a Web Service, the binding describes the *how*, and the service describes the *where*. Note that CORBA's IDL does not contain address information of CORBA objects. This information is only contained in the IOR of an object.

WSDL contains address information

While using XML to describe service interfaces has the benefit of not having to invent a new language, the downside is that XML specifications tend to get quite verbose. While the CORBA IDL for the Account interface only required five lines of code, it takes much more code to describe the same in XML. Web Services are promoting the idea that WSDL is generated from a programming language such as Java. These automatically generated WSDL specifications often have to be manually edited, so in most cases WSDL is not completely transparent to the applications programmer.

10.2.3 Server-Side Mapping

Services that are to be exposed as Web Services have to be implemented in a specific programming language. Just like in CORBA, the question boils down to how the server-side mapping is defined for Web Services. More specifically, given a WSDL specification, what does the server-side mapping look like for a given programming language. Recall that the CORBA specification has so-called IDL language mappings specifically for that purpose. On the basis of these language mappings, it is standardized how IDL is mapped to various high-level programming languages.

The somewhat surprising fact is that Web Services have not standardized how to map WSDL to a given programming language. The important implication is that Web Services do not support portability of applications. This means that if a programmer writes a Web Service application, that application is closely locked in with the product used.

Web Services do not support portability of applications

To demonstrate the lack of portability, we provide the implementation of the account example for two different Web Services platforms. Here is the implementation based on Sun's JDK:

```
import java.rmi.Remote;
import java.rmi.RemoteException;
```

```
public interface AccountIF extends Remote {
    public void deposit (int amount) throws RemoteException;
    public void withdraw (int amount) throws RemoteException;
    public int balance () throws RemoteException;
}
```

In Sun's version, a Web Service interface is first described by a Java interface. This Java interface has to extend the `Remote` interface, which is defined as part of the RMI (remote method invocation) package. The methods to be exposed as a Web Service have to be declared as methods in this interface. Each method has to be able to throw the exception `RemoteException`, which is also declared as part of the RMI package.

The following code excerpt demonstrates the implementation of the account interface based on BEA's WebLogic Server product:

```
public class Account implements com.bea.jws.WebService
{
    static final long serialVersionUID = 1L;

    /**
     * @common:operation
     */
    public void deposit (int amount);
    {
        ...
```

The starting point of a Web Services implementation with BEA's product is a Java class and not an interface, unlike with Sun's JDK. This class implements a BEA-specific interface. Methods to be exposed through the Web Service have to have the special comment `@common:operation`. Furthermore, the methods do not necessarily need to throw an exception.

The previous two examples show that Web Services do not support portability of applications. The question arises how important portability really is. Web Services proponents argue that interoperability is the only important aspect of a middleware platform and that portability is not. After all it is unlikely that the development environment would be switched halfway through a large project. However, it is interesting to note that early versions of CORBA also did not support portability. At some point in CORBA's history it, was decided that portability is important. Subsequently, the OMG introduced the POA in version 2.2 of the CORBA specification. It remains to be seen if the Web Ser-

CORBA supports portability through the POA

vices community will come to the same conclusion and address portability in the future or not.

10.2.4 Interoperability through SOAP

Web Services realize interoperability through SOAP. Interoperability defines the "language" that different Web Service implementations use to exchange messages. As already mentioned, Web Services use XML for this job as well. The content of the messages flowing between client and server are marked up via XML. Special tags are introduced for the purpose of marshalling actual parameters of remote operations.

SOAP is based on XML

In the following we present two SOAP messages: one request message and one response message. Just like with GIOP, the request message is sent from client to server:

```
<Envelope>
  <Body>
    <deposit>
      <amount type="int">700</amount>
    </deposit>
  </Body>
</Envelope>
```

The above XML has been simplified for the purpose of this example. The request is typically transported via HTTP from client to server. The tag `Envelope` frames the whole SOAP request message. It contains a body denoted by the XML tag with the same name. The operation is encoded as the content of the `body` tag. The operation name is represented by its own tag, as are the actual parameters that accompany the invocation. Note that the actual parameters are accompanied by type information. The PDU therefore carries more information than a corresponding GIOP request message, where it is assumed that the server knows the order and type of parameters.

SOAP request PDUs contain type information

The following XML shows a SOAP response:

```
<Envelope>
  <Body>
    <depositResponse/>
  </Body>
</Envelope>
```

This PDU will be sent by the server to the client in response to a request. Once again, the whole message is framed by the `Envelope` tag. This time, the body contains all result parameters that accompany the response. Note that there is no special message ID. This means that unlike in CORBA, there can only be one operation over a specific HTTP connection at a time; otherwise the client would not be able to associate request and response messages.

Differences between a text-based and binary protocol

Probably the biggest difference between SOAP and GIOP/IIOP is that the latter is a binary protocol, whereas the former is a text-based protocol. While the proponents of text-based protocols argue that it is a nice feature to actually see what is sent between client and server, there are also some serious drawbacks. First of all, there should not be any need to watch the wire protocol. Debugging happens on the application level, and there is no need to inspect the content of PDUs (unless one believes there is a problem with the middleware itself). Second, text-based protocols incur a high runtime overhead. They use up more bandwidth, but more importantly the stubs and skeletons have to handle XML messages. Having to parse and construct XML messages can only be done at high costs compared to a binary protocol. Therefore SOAP does not seem a good candidate for applications with high-frequency transactions.

Building bridges between CORBA and Web Services

Both CORBA and Web Services are widely used, and despite the differences between GIOP/IIOP and SOAP, it is important to build bridges between the two technologies. The OMG has published specifications that describe how to achieve interoperability between CORBA and Web Services. One standard describes a mapping from IDL to WSDL. Given an IDL specification, a WSDL specification can automatically be derived. MICO implements this standard, and MICO's IDL compiler can be invoked with the command line option `-codegen-wsdl` to create the WSDL. Another Open Source project is dedicated to building a IIOP/SOAP bridge. Details of this project can be found at *http://soap2corba.sourceforge.net/*.

10.2.5 Service Lookup through UDDI

Service lookup is an important aspect of distributed systems. The purpose of a service lookup is to provide a directory where services can be advertised. UDDI is the Web Services solution to this problem. In general, a trading cycle involves the following steps (see Figure 10.9):

1. A provider offers a service and wishes to advertise it for clients to use. In order to do so, the provider registers its service with the UDDI registry. The publication request includes information about the offered service, such as the WSDL specification.

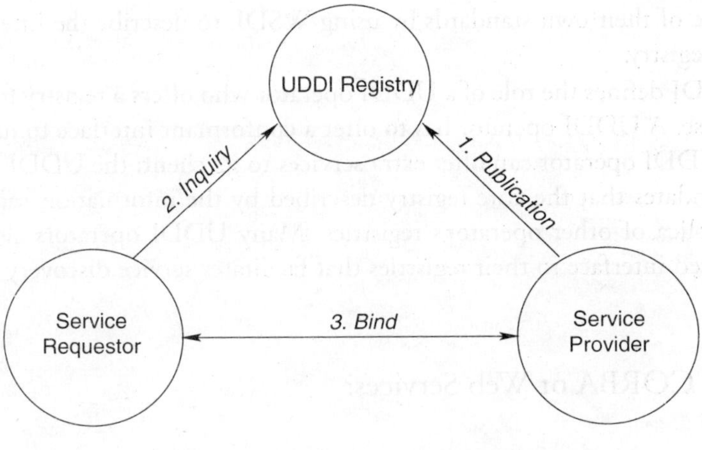

FIGURE 10.9 UDDI service trading.

2. At a later point in time, a service requestor is looking for a specific functionality. It does an inquiry to the UDDI registry, specifying what it is looking for. When there is a match, the UDDI registry responds with the information regarding a suitable service provider.
3. Once the service requestor knows the details of the service provider, it can bind to the provider. From this moment on, the requestor can interact with the provider.

Service mediation has long been a topic of research, and virtually every middleware offers a solution similar to the one outlined above. In CORBA, the combination of interface repository and the Trading Service support service mediation. The first version of UDDI was published in September 2000; it has undergone several revisions since then. The specifications as well as links to other resources are available at *http://www.uddi.org*.

The information model of UDDI

UDDI defines an information model that describes the data maintained at the registry. Conceptually this model contains business information about the entity that provides the service, the type of service being offered, and details on how to invoke the service. All the entries stored in the UDDI registry are classified according to type. For that purpose, UDDI uses several categorization schemes, such as the North American Industry Classification System (NAICS). Categorization organizes the services in a hierarchy and facilitates their discovery.

A UDDI-conformant registry has to understand about two dozen SOAP messages with which clients can interact with the registry. The SOAP interface is used for creating, updating, and querying entries in the registry. Web Services make use of their own standards by using WSDL to describe the interface of a UDDI registry.

UDDI operator

UDDI defines the role of a UDDI operator who offers a registry for general public use. A UDDI operator has to offer a conformant interface to its registry. Also a UDDI operator can offer extra services to its client; the UDDI specification mandates that the core registry described by the information model is an exact replica of other operator's registries. Many UDDI operators also offer a Web-based interface to their registries that facilitates service discovery at design time.

10.2.6 CORBA or Web Services?

CORBA and Web Services are two examples of middleware technologies. Table 10.1 summarizes the key differences presented in the previous sections. The question arises when to use which technology. There is no simple answer to that question, but rather it depends on many variables. Work on CORBA started a decade before Web Services came around. Consequently CORBA features more depth in many areas such as portability or security. The downside of this is that CORBA is difficult to master beyond the simple "Hello World" example. No doubt the perceived ease of use of Web Services will change as well once more standards and specifications have been added.

TABLE 10.1 CORBA/Web Services comparison

Criteria	Web Services	CORBA
General	Based on XML. Supports heterogeneity. Many products available. Often tight integration with development tools.	Middleware for heterogeneous, object-oriented applications. Many products available.
Interface description	Done with WSDL, an XML-based language. Specifications tend to get verbose and are not suitable for human readers.	IDL. Declarative, special-purpose language. Serves as a contract between client and server. Human readable.
Interoperability	SOAP. Text-based protocol using XML. Not suitable for high-frequency transactions due to marshalling overhead.	GIOP/IIOP. A special-purpose binary protocol.
Portability	Not supported.	Supported through IDL language mappings as well as the API defined through the ORB and POA.
Service mediation	UDDI. A general purpose service lookup allowing the publication and inquiry of services. Many UDDI operators offer Web interfaces.	Done through combination of interface repository and Trading Service.

A general guideline on where to use which technology is to look at how strongly coupled the components are that are to be connected via a middleware. CORBA is particularly well suited in tightly coupled environments that require stateful servers. Web Services, on the other hand, seem to be better suited in loosely coupled environments that are characterized by stateless services. Web Services also fare well in application-to-application integration. It has become fashionable for large online services such as Amazon.com or Google.com to make their APIs accessible through Web Services. In this case Web Services are used as wrappers around legacy applications. Internal applications within one company that rely on high performance and tight integration of its components will benefit more from CORBA's maturity.

10.3 MIDDLEWARE FOR UBIQUITOUS COMPUTING

In this section we want to discuss some issues of middleware for future computing environments known under the term "ubiquitous computing" (ubicomp). We will first introduce ubiquitous computing in Section 10.3.1, before discussing peculiarities and challenges of ubicomp with respect to middleware in Section 10.3.2. In Section 10.3.3 we want to present a study of middleware for a subdomain of ubiquitous computing known as sensor networks.

10.3.1 Ubiquitous Computing in a Nutshell

The term "ubiquitous computing" was coined by Mark Weiser in his 1991 seminal article [38]. He envisioned a world of ubiquitous computers that become invisible by being embedded into the physical environment with the goal of supporting people unobtrusively in fulfilling their tasks.

One example for an application of ubiquitous computing would be a smart room allocation system, where chairs are able to sense their occupancy status and use this information to automatically derive the occupancy level of the room, which is then displayed at the electronic door plate and by a central "room finder" in the hallway.

Networked, embedded computers equipped with sensors and actuators

This simple example already illustrates a number of technological features of the "ubiquitous computer." It consists of numerous, highly specialized wireless computing devices embedded into our physical environment. These devices can perceive and control certain parameters of their physical environment and can communicate with each other. They use ergonomic, intuitive, and unobtrusive ways of interacting with people.

Recent technological advances in six important areas enable researchers already today to construct the first prototypical ubiquitous computing systems [16–18]: processors, storage, wireless communication, sensors and actuators, energy supply, and the development of new materials. Moreover, researchers believe that the exponential rate of improvement of processing power, storage capacity, and communication bandwidth—which we observed over the last 30 years—will keep up for at least another 10–15 years. This observation is commonly known as "Moore's law," formulated by Intel founder Gordon Moore in 1965. The popular version of this rule says that the performance of computers doubles every 18 months. Traditionally, this "law" has resulted in ever faster processors, with ever increasing chip size and energy consumption. Alternatively, Moore's law can also be "exploited" to construct processors with a more moderate performance, but with ever decreasing size and energy consumption. For example, it is possible today to integrate most of the functionality of a 80286 PC (including processor, memory, analog and digital IO) on a single chip that consumes only a few milliwatts of energy. Similar trends apply to storage technologies and wireless communication technology. However, Moore's law does not apply to the capacity of batteries and other technologies for energy storage and harvesting. Although new systems allow the extraction of energy from the environment (e.g., from mechanical vibrations or temperature differences), the amount of energy stored or harvested per device volume grows only slowly over time. Hence, the construction of energy-efficient technologies is of utmost importance, since devices for ubiquitous computing often have to be wireless. New materials (e.g., flexible displays, film batteries) will allow the construction of devices with unconventional form factors.

Moore's law

Implications for computer science

Overall, the general trend towards "more, smaller, cheaper, less energy" will enable the construction of future ubiquitous computing systems from a technological perspective. From a computer science perspective, new algorithms, protocols, and architectures are needed to manage and control the expected enormous amount of networked computing devices and to make sense out of the huge amount of data collected by these sensor-equipped devices. We will discuss computer science challenges with respect to middleware architectures in Section 10.3.2.

Implications for society

The realization of Weiser's vision also heavily depends on ethical and economical questions like, Do we want to live in a world where omnipresent computing devices can easily track our daily lives? Are there value-creating applications of ubiquitous computing? Since these and other important questions are beyond the scope of this book, we refer the interested reader to [6].

10.3.2 Middleware Challenges

CONSTRAINED RESOURCES

The augmentation of artifacts with computing devices imposes constraints on the embedded devices. In order to allow an unobtrusive integration into physical objects and environments, these devices often have to be wireless and must meet certain size constraints. Limited size and energy imply that resources like computing power, memory size, communication bandwidth, and range are rather limited. Consider, for example, a matchbox-sized sensing device developed at UC Berkeley. The so-called MICA mote [4] is equipped with an 8-bit processor with 8 MIPS, provides 8 kilobytes of RAM, 128 kilobytes of program memory, and has a communication bandwidth of 40 kilobits per second over a range of up to 30 meters. This device runs for weeks or months on a pair of AA batteries. Note that further improvements in technology will likely be used to reduce size and energy consumption, such that the performance of these devices will only increase slowly as time goes by. In contrast, current PCs are equipped with processors with hundreds of MIPS, megabytes of RAM, and a communication bandwidth of tens or hundreds of megabits per second. Although there are efforts to fit traditional middleware on resource-constrained devices, middleware such as CORBA has been designed with a PC target platform in mind.

Limited size, cost, energy, and capabilities

Lightweight middleware

The limited resources must be shared among various applications executing in the network and the middleware services itself. As an immediate consequence, ubicomp middleware services must be lightweight in order to fit into the constrained resources of a MICA mote and similar devices. Additionally, ubicomp middleware should provide mechanisms that help to minimize the amount of resources that are needed to accomplish a certain application task. One particularly promising approach to achieve this is to dynamically adapt the performance of hardware, algorithms, and protocols to the varying needs of the application. Interesting examples include adaptive fidelity algorithms that can be tuned to trade off output fidelity for resource usage. Another example would be to exploit application knowledge to decide when to switch off the radio for energy efficiency reasons. More concrete examples of using application knowledge appear further below.

NETWORK DYNAMICS

A typical ubicomp application will require the collaboration of, and hence the wireless communication among, many spatially distributed devices due to the following reasons. First, ubicomp devices tend to be highly specialized: some sense environmental parameters, others extract information from the collected sensory data, and some interact with human users. A complete system often requires some or all of these functions. Second, many applications require sensory input from many spatially distributed devices (e.g., to determine the occupancy level of a room). Third, the constrained resources of individual devices often require collaboration for solving complex tasks.

Mobile ad hoc networks

Due to the limited communication range of ubicomp devices, it is unlikely that ubicomp networks would resemble mobile phone networks, where devices communicate directly with a base station, since this would require a very dense base station infrastructure. Instead, ubicomp devices will form *ad hoc networks*, where the devices act as routers, forwarding messages for their neighbors over multiple hops. More powerful devices might act as gateways that connect ad hoc network patches of ubicomp devices to an existing background infrastructure.

The topology of such ad hoc networks is subject to frequent changes due to device mobility, environmental obstructions resulting in communication failures (e.g., a truck driving by), or hardware failures (e.g., depleted batteries, stepping on a device). In sparse deployments, networks are likely to be partitioned, and devices have to operate nomadically when there are no other devices within communication range.

Ubicomp middleware has to support the robust cooperation of devices in such a highly dynamic network environment. In contrast, traditional middleware often assumes a static networking environment and considers any changes in this environment an error that is passed on to the application. CORBA, for example, throws an exception if a remote object goes temporarily offline; there are no provisions for automatically reclaiming application resources allocated for remote transactions. In the case of nomadic operation, it might be advantageous to proactively prepare for offline phases. The concept of information hoarding [20], for example, downloads data during online phases that might be needed later on.

Information hoarding

Adaptation to dynamic changes

In many scenarios, the application has to be able to adapt its behavior to the changing environment. Since this will be a common case, ubicomp middleware should provide adequate support mechanisms for application adaptation. In some cases it might be possible to provide automatic adaptation mechanisms that require no or little support by the application, as illustrated by the following example. Traditional communication is often address centric, where components are assigned identifiers (e.g., CORBA IORs), which are then used to identify communication partners. With *data-centric communication*, distributed components are identified solely based on the function or data they provide (e.g., "some device in my vicinity that can measure temperature"). The advantage of data-centric communication is, among others, that it is able to tolerate

Data-centric communication

devices going offline by transparently switching over to a device with equivalent functionality.

Dynamic resource management

A further requirement on ubicomp middleware is better support for dynamic resource management. To understand this issue, note that many distributed services maintain considerable amounts of state information for each connected client. If the client disappears without notice, the allocated resources have to be reclaimed somehow. Traditional middleware such as CORBA does not adequately support such situations, leaving the task of dynamic resource management to the application. However, in ubicomp environments this is a common case that should be supported by middleware. Jini [19], for example, provides the *lease concept*, where resources allocated for remote peers are associated with a lease, which has to be renewed regularly. If the lease expires due to a missing renewal, the system can automatically reclaim the associated resources.

SCALE OF DEPLOYMENTS

Smart Dust

Ubiquitous availability of computing resources may require a very large number of deployed computing devices. As an extreme case, consider the vision of Smart Dust [37], where millions of dust-grain-sized devices would be deployed in the environment in order to monitor various environmental phenomena. A single device consists of sensors, a processor, wireless communication, and energy supply. The devices are small enough to stay suspended in air, for example, to monitor weather phenomena or air quality. They could also be mixed into paint in order to coat buildings, which would allow monitoring the effects of seismic activity on the structural integrity of the buildings.

Supporting such large deployments of cooperating devices is a very challenging task. First, it is next to impossible to manually configure, maintain, fix, or upgrade individual devices due to their huge number. In the extreme case of Smart Dust, it might even be impossible to assign unique identifiers (e.g., similar to the unique MAC address of each Ethernet card) to individual nodes due to the involved production overhead. That is, starting from a totally symmetric situation (all devices are identical initially), the collection of devices must self-configure in order to achieve an operational state (e.g., set up a network topology, assign tasks to devices, collaboratively merge and evaluate collected data). Similarly, the network should be self-maintaining in order to fix node failures without manual intervention. Hence, ubicomp middleware should provide support mechanisms for self-configuration and self-maintenance.

REAL-WORLD INTEGRATION

By definition, ubiquitous computing devices are embedded into the physical environment, typically capturing data about their environment using attached sensors. Hence, there is a close integration of ubicomp systems with the real world. This has a number of important implications. One such implication is that physical time and location play a crucial role in ubicomp. First, it is often important to know where and when something happened. Second, time and location are crucial for correlating information from different sources. To decide whether two ubicomp devices ever met, for example, they have to share a common understanding of time and location in order to tell whether they were at the same location at the same point in time.

Time and location

Establishing such a common understanding of time (i.e., time synchronization) and location (i.e., device localization) among ubicomp devices is an important middleware service. Building on that, there is also a need for services that manage spatio-temporal data. A location service, for example, maintains an up-to-date view of the current locations of devices in the network. As an extension, a history service stores location and time of past events, providing the foundation for queries like "Where did devices X and Y meet last time?"

COLLECTION, PROCESSING, AND STORAGE OF SENSORY DATA

As a further consequence of the close integration of ubicomp systems with the real world, the collection, processing, and storage of sensory data is a core ubicomp functionality. While sensors collect rather low-level data (e.g., time series of temperature readings), applications are often interested in more high-level features (e.g., "in a conference": used to automatically switch off mobile phones), which are also known as "context." The derivation of context information often requires the evaluation of sensory data of various types (e.g., noise level, light intensity, air quality) originating from multiple sources. This functionality is provided by a *context service.*

Context information

In-network data processing

In a previous section we noted the need for energy efficiency and the high energy consumption of wireless communication. As a consequence, a trivial implementation of a context service—where large amounts of raw sensory data are transmitted to a central location for processing—is often not feasible due to the resulting high energy consumption, bandwidth limitations, and scalability issues. Instead, sensory data should be preprocessed as close to its source as possible in order to reduce the amount of data that has to be transmitted. Instead of sending all the raw data to the remote application, this *in-network data aggregation* reduces communication and saves energy by transmitting compact aggregates instead of bulky raw data.

Note that these techniques to some degree blur the clear separation of communication and data processing typically found in traditional distributed systems and respective middleware. Ubicomp middleware with support for the above data reduction techniques will require means to specify application knowledge (about how to process data) and ways to inject this knowledge into the nodes of the network.

INTEGRATION WITH BACKGROUND INFRASTRUCTURES

Although we noted in a previous section that ubicomp devices typically form infrastructureless ad hoc networks, it is quite likely that some of the devices will be connected to a background infrastructure such as the Internet. Some researchers believe that this will eventually lead to a global "Internet of Things" connecting smart artifacts all over the world.

There are several reasons for such an integration with background infrastructures. First, such infrastructures might be used to disseminate information (such as the room occupancy status in our introductory example) to remote destinations. Second, a background infrastructure may provide resources (e.g., computing power, storage) that are not available on typical ubicomp devices.

10.3.3 Case Study: Sensor Networks

After having studied general requirements on middleware for ubiquitous computing, we will take a closer look at more concrete ubicomp middleware approaches in this section. For this, we will focus on a subarea of ubicomp known under the term "wireless sensor networks" (WSN). WSN consist of *sensor nodes*—small autonomous computing devices equipped with sensors, wireless communication capabilities, a processor, and a power supply. One prominent example of such a sensor node is the MICA sensing device that we mentioned in the previous section. Large and dense networks of these untethered devices can be deployed unobtrusively in the physical environment in order to monitor a wide variety of real-world phenomena with unprecedented quality and scale while only marginally disturbing the observed physical processes.

Applications of WSN

In other words, wireless sensor networks provide the technological foundation for performing many "experiments" in their natural environment instead of using an artificial laboratory setting, thus eliminating many fundamental limitations of the latter. It is anticipated that a number of application domains can substantially benefit from such a technological foundation. Biologists, for example, want to monitor the behavior of animals in their natural habitats. Environmental research needs better means for monitoring environmental pollutions. Agriculture can profit from better means for observing soil quality and other parameters that influence plant growth. Geologists need better support for monitoring seismic activity and its influences on the structural integrity of buildings. And of course the military is interested in monitoring activities in inaccessible areas.

The typical usage model of a sensor network is a user specifying a high-level sensing task (e.g., "Report rooms where average noise level exceeds a certain threshold"). This task is split into many simple subtasks, which are distributed to the individual nodes of the network. These subtasks collect and preprocess low-level sensor readings. The resulting sensory data is then aggregated and processed to form a high-level sensing result that is reported back to the user.

While sensor networks can be realized by programming individual sensor nodes for a specific task, there is a strong need for abstractions that allow easy tasking of the network as a whole. Middleware for sensor networks should support such programming abstractions. Without such middleware and underlying abstractions, tasking and using a sensor network is a cumbersome and error-prone task reserved to specialists.

Now we will examine three middleware approaches with three different underlying programming abstractions. It should be emphasized that these are only first attempts whose appropriateness still has to be proven. Also, the presented systems are proofs of the concept, often only considering certain selected middleware aspects.

Operating systems for WSN

Likewise, operating system abstractions and concrete operating systems for sensor nodes are currently an area of active research. Hence, the functional separation and the interface between operating system and middleware is not well understood. Due to resource constraints, it is likely that operating system functionality (e.g., task and memory management) will be rather primitive compared to traditional operating systems. First operating system prototypes confirm this assumption [15].

DATABASES

A number of approaches [7,24,33] have been devised that treat the sensor network as a distributed database where users can issue SQL-like queries to have the network perform a certain sensing task. We will discuss TinyDB [24] as a representative of this class.

TinyDB

TinyDB supports a single "virtual" database table `sensors`, where each column corresponds to a specific type of sensor (e.g., temperature, light) or other source of input data (e.g., sensor node identifier, remaining battery power). Reading out the sensors at a node can be regarded as appending a new row to `sensors`. The query language is a subset of SQL with some extensions.

Consider the following query example. Several rooms are equipped with multiple sensor nodes each. Each sensor node is equipped with sensors to measure the acoustic volume. The table `sensors` contains three columns `room` (i.e., the room number the sensor is in), `floor` (i.e., the floor on which the room is located), and `volume`. We can determine rooms on the 6th floor where the average volume exceeds the threshold 10 with the following query:

```
SELECT AVG(volume), room FROM sensors
  WHERE floor = 6
  GROUP BY room
  HAVING AVG(volume) > 10
  EPOCH DURATION 30s
```

The query first selects rows from sensors at the 6th floor (`WHERE floor = 6`). The selected rows are grouped by the room number (`GROUP BY room`). Then, the average volume of each of the resulting groups is calculated (`AVG(volume)`). Only groups with an average volume above 10 (`HAVING AVG(volume) > 10`) are kept. For each of the remaining groups, a pair of average volume and the respective room number (`SELECT AVG(volume), room`) is returned. The query is reexecuted every 30 seconds (`EPOCH DURATION 30s`), resulting in a stream of query results.

TinyDB uses a decentralized approach, where each sensor node has its own query processor that preprocesses and aggregates sensor data on its way from the sensor node to the user. Executing a query involves the following steps: First, a spanning tree of the network rooted at the user device is constructed and maintained as the network topology changes, using a controlled flooding approach. The flood messages are also used to roughly synchronize time among the nodes of the network. Second, a query is broadcast to all the nodes in the network by sending it along the tree from the root toward the leaves. During this process, a time schedule is established, such that a parent and its children agree on a time interval when the parent will listen for data from its children. At the beginning of every epoch, the leaf nodes obtain a new table row by reading out their local sensors. Then, they apply the select criteria to this row. If the criteria are fulfilled, a partial state record is created that contains all the necessary data (i.e., room number, floor number, average volume in the example). The partial state record is then sent to the parent during the scheduled time interval. The parent listens for any partial state records from its children during the scheduled interval. Then, the parent proceeds like the children by reading out its sensors, applying select criteria, and generating a partial state record if need be. Then, the parent aggregates its partial state record and the records received from its children (i.e., calculates the average volume in the example), resulting in a new partial state record. The new partial state record is then sent to the parent's parent during the scheduled interval. This process iterates up to the root of the tree. At the root, the final partial state record is evaluated to obtain the query result. The whole procedure repeats every epoch.

MOBILE AGENTS

Another class of middleware approaches is inspired by mobile code and mobile agents. There, the sensor network is tasked by injecting a program into the sensor network. This program can collect local sensor data, can statefully migrate or copy itself to other nodes, and can communicate with such remote copies. We discuss SensorWare [9] as a representative of this class.

SensorWare

In SensorWare, programs are specified in Tcl [29], a dynamically typed, procedural programming language. The functionality specific to SensorWare is implemented as a set of additional procedures in the Tcl interpreter. The most notable extensions are the `query`, `send`, `wait`, and `replicate` commands. `query` takes a sensor name (e.g., `volume`) and a command as parameters. One common command is `value`, which is used to obtain a sensor reading. `send` takes a node address and a message as parameters and sends the message to the specified sensor node. Node addresses currently consist of a unique node ID, a script name, and additional identifiers to distinguish copies of the same script. The `replicate` command takes one or more sensor node addresses as parameters and spawns copies of the executing script on the specified remote sensor nodes. Node addresses are either unique node identifiers or "broadcast" (i.e., all nodes in transmission range). The `replicate` command first checks whether a remote sensor node is already executing the specified script. In this case, there are options to instruct the runtime system to do nothing, to let the existing remote script handle this additional "user," or to create another copy of the script. In SensorWare, the occurrence of an asynchronous activity (e.g., reception of a message, expiry of a timer) is represented by a specific event each. The `wait` command expects a set of such event names as parameters and suspends the execution of the script until one of the specified events occurs.

The following script is a simplified version of the TinyDB query and calculates the maximum volume over all rooms (i.e., over all sensor nodes in the network):

```
set children [replicate]
set num_children [llength $children]
```

```
set num_replies 0
set maxvolume [query volume value]
while {1} {
  wait anyRadioPck
  if {$maxvolume < $msg_body} {
    set maxvolume $msg_body }
  incr num_replies
  if {$num_replies = $num_children} {
    send $parent $maxvolume
    exit }
}
```

The script first replicates itself to all nodes in communication range. No copies are created on nodes already running the script. The `replicate` command returns a list of newly "infected" sensor nodes (`children`). Then, the number of new children (`num_children`) is calculated, the reply counter (`num_replies`) is initialized to zero, and the volume at this node is measured (`maxvolume`). In the loop, the `wait` blocks until a radio message is received. The message body is stored in the variable `msg_body`. Then, `maxvolume` is updated according to the received value, and the reply counter is incremented by one. If we received a reply from every child, then `maxvolume` is sent to the parent script and the script exits. Due to the recursive replication of the script to all nodes in the network, the user will eventually end up with a message containing the maximum volume among all nodes of the network.

EVENTS

Basic and compound events

Yet another approach to sensor network middleware is based on the notion of events. Here, the application specifies interest in certain state changes of the real world ("basic events"). Upon detecting such an event, a sensor node sends an event notification toward interested applications. The application can also specify certain patterns of events ("compound events"), such that the application is only notified if occurred events match this pattern. We discuss DSWare [23] as a representative of this class.

DSWare

DSWare supports the specification and automated detection of compound events. A compound event specification contains, among others, an event identifier, a detection range specifying the geographical area of interest, a detection duration specifying the time frame of interest, a set of sensor nodes interested in this compound event, a time window W, a confidence function f, a minimum confidence $c_{\min}$, and a set of basic events E. The confidence function f

maps E to a scalar value. The compound event is detected and delivered to the interested sensor nodes, if $f(E) \geq c_{\min}$ and all basic events occurred within time window W.

Consider the example of detecting an explosion event, which requires the occurrence of a light event (i.e., a light flash), a temperature event (i.e., high ambient temperature), and a sound event (i.e., a bang sound) within a subsecond time window W. The confidence function is defined as

$$f = 0.6 \cdot B(\text{temp}) + 0.3 \cdot B(\text{light}) + 0.3 \cdot B(\text{sound})$$

The function B maps an event ID to 1 if the respective event has been detected within the time window W, and to 0 otherwise. With $c_{\min} = 0.9$, the above confidence function would trigger the explosion event if the temperature event is detected along with one or both of the light and sound events. This confidence function expresses the fact that detection of the temperature event gives us higher confidence in an actual explosion happening than the detection of the light and sound events.

Additionally, the system includes various real-time aspects, such as deadlines for reporting events, and event validity intervals.

10.3.4 Conclusions

We discussed various challenges for ubicomp middleware, implied by resource limitations, network dynamics, close integration with the real world, handling of sensory data, and integration with background infrastructures. Some of these challenges are new problem instances in known research domains (e.g., fault tolerance, real-time aspects, embedded systems), some challenges take existing research issues to the extreme (e.g., scale of deployments), and some are new problems (e.g., energy efficiency, self-configuration).

We presented and discussed first middleware approaches for sensor networks, a subdomain of ubiquitous computing. These systems are based on known programming paradigms (i.e., databases, mobile agents, event services), adopted to the new problem domain. However, it is not yet clear which programming paradigm is best suited for programming sensor networks; it is even unlikely that there is such a single best paradigm. Though such questions are already hard to answer for a small subdomain of ubiquitous computing such as sensor networks, designing universal middleware abstractions and systems for ubicomp is an even more challenging task. Currently, a number of solutions for specific subdomains of ubiquitous computing (e.g., sensor networks) have been developed. At a later stage, it might be possible to join these efforts in order to come up with encompassing ubicomp middleware.

Designing successful middleware always requires a large body of experience with the development of real applications (i.e., not toy applications), which the prospective middleware should support. The development of middleware is an iterative process, where a middleware prototype is evaluated by reimplementing real applications. The gained experiences are then used to develop an improved middleware prototype, which again must be evaluated. The hope is that this iterative procedure will eventually arrive at a fixed point. Since we are still at an early stage of understanding ubicomp applications beyond simple toy scenarios, elaborate ubicomp middleware will remain an active research area for the next couple of years.

10.4 SUMMARY

This chapter concludes the main part of this book. We presented some advanced CORBA technologies as well as topics that go beyond CORBA. CORBA is still being actively evolved by the OMG, and with the current dissemination of CORBA platforms, this will continue for a long time. In the meantime, Web Services have gotten a strong following. As we tried to argue in this chapter, there will never be an "either or" when it comes down to choosing the right middleware technology. Rather we must think carefully about when to use CORBA or Web Services. As is generally the case, there is no silver bullet. While CORBA and Web Services will remain key technologies for many applications, new challenges arise with new kinds of network infrastructures. As shown in the last section of this chapter, we must radically redefine the notion of middleware when it comes to ubiquitous computing and sensor networks. These areas are still subject to active research, but the prospects of new technologies, new infrastructures, and new paradigms are exciting.

APPENDIX A

MICO INSTALLATION

This appendix gives an overview of how to install and use MICO on your system, including downloading the MICO source code, and compiling and installing its libraries and tools. The details of installation may differ, depending on your operating system.

Section A.1 describes MICO's installation on a UNIX system, such as Linux or BSD.

Section A.2 describes MICO's installation on Windows.

A.1 INSTALLING MICO ON UNIX

The following software packages are required to install MICO:

- An ISO C++ compiler. The GNU C Compiler *gcc* version 3.2 or later is recommended.
- GNU Make version 3.7 or later.
- Optionally, OpenSSL 0.9.7 or later.

Downloading MICO

The latest stable MICO release can be downloaded from its home page at *www.mico.org* by clicking on "Download." A few development snapshots are available, and for the cutting edge, the latest development branch can be accessed using *Arch*.

After downloading the source code in .tar.gz format, the archive needs to be unpacked using the following command, which creates a new subdirectory named `mico-`*`version`*:

```
gzip -dc mico-<version>.tar.gz | tar xf -
```

MICO can be installed using the usual GNU *autoconf* procedure:

- `configure`
- `make`
- `make install`

The first step, configuration, prepares MICO for compilation. The `configure` script checks for the availability of compilers and tools, and supports several command line options to configure MICO features and build options.

The most important command line options are

`--help`
Gives a brief overview of all supported command line options.

`--prefix=`*install-directory*
Configures the base directory into which to install MICO's executable programs, libraries, header files, and so on. Defaults to `/usr/local`. For a private installation, `-prefix=$HOME` can be used to install MICO in the user's home directory.

`--enable-csiv2`
Enables support for the Common Secure Interoperability version 2 (CSIv2) protocol for communications security. Requires OpenSSL.

`--with-ssl=`*OpenSSL-path*
This enables support for SSL. *OpenSSL-path* is the directory in which OpenSSL has been installed.

`--enable-ccm`
Enables support for the CORBA Component Model.

`--disable-threads`
By default, if supported by the operating system, the ORB is built to be multithreaded and uses a thread pool for processing requests, in turn requiring

servants to be reentrant. With this option, MICO is built single-threaded instead.

--enable-*service*

--disable-*service*
Enables or disables support for the implementations of common services. MICO includes implementations of the Naming Service (*naming*), Event Service (*events*), Property Service (*property*), Time Service (*time*), Trading Service (*trader*), and the Lifecycle Service (*life*). By default, the Naming, Event, Property, and Time services are built.

--disable-coss
Disables support for all of the aforementioned CORBA services. If this option is used, individual services can then be enabled selectively, using the above options.

--enable-compiled-headers
Uses precompiled headers, if supported by the compiler.

--disable-optimize
Disables the `-O` option when compiling C/C++ files.

--enable-debug
This enables the `-g` option when compiling C/C++ files, allowing the ORB to be debugged.

--disable-shared
By default, if supported by the operating system, MICO's libraries are built as shared libraries (usually using the ".so" extension). With this option, MICO's libraries are built as static libraries (".a").

There are a number of configuration options beyond the ones listed above—for example, for using CORBA over wireless links or Bluetooth; for integrating MICO with X11, Qt, Gtk or Tcl/Tk applications; or for tuning various aspects of the ORB.

The configuration script also looks for the `CC` and `CXX` environment variables to select the C and C++ compilers, respectively. To build MICO using a different compiler than the default (e.g., using `gcc` on a system where an incompatible compiler is available as `cc`), set `CC=gcc` and `CXX=c++`.

The `configure` script then needs to be run with the desired—possibly empty—set of command-line options, for example:

```
./configure --with-ccm
```

After completing configuration, MICO can be compiled using

```
make
```

On some systems, GNU Make is not the default, but can frequently be found as gmake.

After compilation, MICO needs to be installed. Depending on the setting of the -prefix configuration option, it may be necessary to perform installation as the superuser, root:

```
make install
```

On some systems, special action needs to be taken after installing a shared library to tell the dynamic linker about the new library. For instance, on Linux you have to run ldconfig as root:

```
/sbin/ldconfig -v
```

Also, if shared libraries are installed in a nondefault location, users may need to adjust their environment variables accordingly. For example, on Linux or Sun Solaris, the LD_LIBRARY_PATH environment variable is searched for shared libraries.

A.2 INSTALLING MICO ON WINDOWS

The following software packages are required to install MICO on Windows:

- Microsoft Visual C++ 7.0 or later, also known as Visual Studio ".NET". Other compilers may work, but are not supported out of the box.
- A program to "unzip" ZIP archives, such as *WinZip*.
- Optionally, to enable multithreading, the *Pthreads-win32* POSIX Threads adaptation layer, which is freely available at *http://sources.redhat.com/pthreads-win32/*, is required.
- Optionally, OpenSSL 0.9.7 or later.

Downloading MICO

The latest stable MICO release can be downloaded from its home page at *www.mico.org* by clicking on "Download." A few development snapshots are available, and for the cutting edge, the latest development branch can be accessed using *Arch*.

After downloading the source code in .zip format, double-clicking on the downloaded file should start your ZIP archive program. Extract all its contents into a directory of your choice.

Before compiling, some aspects of MICO can be optionally configured by editing the file `MakeVars.win32` in the MICO source directory. Here, you can configure support for multithreading, the CORBA Component Model, and for the Common Secure Interoperability (CSIv2) protocol. Follow the directions that are provided in the file.

Note that most text and source code files in the MICO distribution are in "UNIX" format, and may not open correctly in some editors, such as Notepad. All files can be opened fine in Visual Studio and many other source code editors.

TCP/IP must be configured

Another prerequisite to building MICO, and to running MICO programs, is that TCP/IP networking must be configured, even on computers that are not connected to any network. In particular, the local host name must be recognized as a network destination. This can be confirmed on the command line: the command `ping hostname`, substituting the local computer's name as *hostname*, should work.

After completing configuration, MICO can be compiled. This must be done from the command line. Start a command shell, for example, by choosing *Run* from the *Start* menu and opening `cmd`. Change to the directory that contains the MICO source code, and run

```
nmake /f Makefile.win32
```

This will compile all of MICO and place all executable files and DLL files in the `win32-bin` subdirectory. In order to run MICO programs, this directory must be added to your `$PATH` environment variable, for example, via the *System* properties in Windows' Control Panel.

A.3 ROAD MAP

For users that would like to take a look at the MICO source code, this section gives a brief overview of the subdirectories in the MICO directory:

`admin` Scripts and programs needed to build MICO

`auxdir`	ORB-related stuff (dispatchers for various GUI environments; `libmicoaux` is built in this directory)
`ccm`	File related to the CORBA Component Model (CCM)
`coss`	CORBA services (`libmicocoss` is built in this directory)
`cpp`	Preprocessor for idl files (`cpp`)
`daemon`	Object Adapter daemon (`micod`)
`demo`	Some examples
`doc`	Documentation
`idl`	IDL compiler (`idl`)
`imr`	Implementation repository and administration tool
`include`	C++ and IDL include files
`ir`	Interface repository and IR server (`ird`)
`man`	UNIX manual pages
`orb`	ORB core (`libmico` is built here)
`test`	Some test cases to check the ORB and IDL compiler
`tools`	Miscellaneous tool programs, at present only the IR browser and IOR dumper

APPENDIX **B**

MICO IMPLEMENTATION OVERVIEW

This appendix gives an overview of how MICO implements the CORBA specification, the implementation components it consists of, and how those components are used. The focus of the appendix is on details not defined by the CORBA specification such as command line option syntax and semantics.

Components of a CORBA implementation

The core of a CORBA implementation consists of the following logical components:

- The Object Request Broker (ORB) provides for object location and method invocation.
- The Interface Repository (IR) stores runtime type information.
- One or more *object adapters* form the interface between object implementations and the ORB. MICO provides the Portable Object Adapter (POA). The *implementation repository* stores information about how to activate object implementations.
- The *IDL compiler* generates client stubs, server skeletons, and marshalling code from a CORBA IDL according to the supported language mappings.

Each of these logical components has to be mapped to one or more implementation components, which are described in the next sections.

B.1 ORB

MICO library `libmico<version>.a`

The ORB is implemented as a library (`libmico<version>.a`) that is linked into each MICO application. `<version>` has to be substituted with the version of MICO installed on the system.

Every Mico application has to call the ORB initialization function `ORB_init()` before using Mico functionality:

```
int main (int argc, char *argv[])
{
    CORBA::ORB_var orb = CORBA::ORB_init (argc, argv);
    ...
}
```

That way the ORB has access to the application's command line arguments. After evaluating them, the ORB removes the command line options it understands so the application does not have to bother with them. You can also put ORB command line arguments into a file called `.micorc` in your home directory. Arguments given on the command line override settings from `.micorc`. Here is a description of all ORB-specific command line arguments:

Command line arguments understood by Mico applications

-ORBNoIIOPServer
Do not activate the IIOP server. The IIOP server enables other processes to invoke methods on objects in this process using IIOP. If for some reason you do not want other processes to be able to invoke objects in this process, use this option. The default is to activate the IIOP server.

-ORBNoIIOPProxy
Do not activate the IIOP proxy. The IIOP proxy enables this process to invoke methods on objects in other processes using IIOP. If you do not want or need this, use this option. The default is to activate the IIOP proxy.

-ORBIIOPAddr <address>
Set the address the IIOP server should run on. If you do not specify this option, the IIOP server will choose an unused address. This option can be used more than once to make the server listen on several addresses (e.g., a `unix:` and an `inet:` address).

-ORBIIOPBlocking
Make IIOP use sockets in blocking mode. This gains some extra performance, but nested method invocations do not work in this mode.

-ORBId <ORB identifier>
Specify the ORB identifier; `mico-local-orb` is currently the only supported ORB identifier. This option is intended for programs that need access to different CORBA implementations in the same process. In this case, the option `-ORBId` is used to select one of the CORBA implementations.

-ORBImplRepoIOR <impl repository IOR>

Specify a stringified object reference for the implementation repository the ORB should use.

-ORBImplRepoAddr <impl repository address>

Specify the address of a process that runs an implementation repository. The ORB will then try to bind to an implementation repository object using the given address. If the bind fails or if you specified neither `-ORBImplRepoAddr` nor `-ORBImpRepoIOR`, the ORB will run a local implementation repository.

-ORBIfaceRepoIOR <interface repository IOR>

The same as `-ORBImplRepoIOR` but for the interface repository.

-ORBIfaceRepoAddr <interface repository address>

The same as `-ORBImplRepoAddr` but for the interface repository.

-ORBNamingIOR <naming service IOR>

The same as `-ORBImplRepoIOR` but for the naming service.

-ORBNamingAddr <naming address>

The same as `-ORBImplRepoAddr` but for the naming service.

-ORBInitRef <Identifier>=<IOR>

Set the value for the initial reference by the name of `identifier` to the given object reference. This mechanism can be used both for custom and for standard initial references.

-ORBDefaultInitRef <IOR-base>

Define a location for initial references. `IOR-base` is an `iioploc-` or `iiopname-` style object reference. When a previously unknown initial reference is searched for using `resolve_ initial_references()`, the searched-for identifier is concatenated to the `IOR-base` string to produce the service's location.

-ORBNoResolve

Do not resolve given IP addresses into host names. Use dotted decimal notation instead.

-ORBDebug <level>=<file>

Instruct MICO to output debug information. `<level>` is one of `Info` (informative messages), `Warning`, `Error`, `GIOP` (network message exchanges), `IIOP` (connection handling), `Transport` (raw message contents), `Thread` (thread-related infos), `POA` (POA internals), `ORB` (ORB internals), `Support` (helper functions), `PI` (interceptors), `Security` (security service), `Exception` (exception handling), `All` (everything). `<file>` specifies the output file for this debug level (defaults to `cerr`). This option can be specified multiple times with different levels and files.

`-ORBBindAddr <address>`

Specify an address that `bind(const char *repoid)` should try to bind to. This option can be used more than once to specify multiple addresses.

`-ORBConfFile <rcfile>`

Specify the file from which to read additional command line options (defaults to `~/.micorc`).

`-ORBNoCodeSets`

Do not add code set information to object references. Since code set conversion is a CORBA 2.1 feature, this option may be needed to talk to ORBs that are not CORBA 2.1 compliant. Furthermore, it may gain some extra speed.

`-ORBNativeCS <pattern>`

Specify the code set the application uses for characters and strings. `<pattern>` is a shell-like pattern that must match the `description` field of a code set in the OSF code set registry. For example, the pattern `*8859-1*` will make the ORB use the code set ISO-8859-1 (Latin 1) as the native char code set, which is the default if you do not specify this option. The ORB uses this information to automatically convert characters and strings when talking to an application that uses a different code set.

`-ORBNativeWCS <pattern>`

Similar to `-ORBNativeCS`, but it specifies the code set the application uses for wide characters and wide strings. Defaults to UTF-16, a 16-bit encoding of Unicode.

`-ORBGIOPVersion <giop-ver>`

Specifies the GIOP version to use. The GIOP version will be included in newly generated object references to tell clients which GIOP version should be used when sending requests to the object. Currently, GIOP versions 1.0 (default), 1.1, and 1.2 are supported.

`-ORBThreadPool`

This option instructs the ORB to use the *thread pool concurrency model.* With this model, a number of threads (the thread pool) are generated a priori. Upon arrival of a new request, a thread from the pool is assigned to this request. The thread pool concurrency model is used by default. This option requires that MICO be compiled with support for multithreading enabled.

`-ORBThreadPerConnection`
: This option instructs the ORB to use the *thread per connection concurrency model*. With this model, a single thread is assigned to each network connection to serially handle all requests received from this connection. This option requires that MICO be compiled with support for multithreading enabled.

`-ORBThreadPerRequest`
: This option instructs the ORB to use the *thread per request concurrency model*. With this model, a new thread is created for every incoming request. This option requires that MICO be compiled with support for multithreading enabled.

`-ORBConnLimit <max-conn>`
: This option can be used to limit the number of network connections that can be open concurrently to the value specified. A value of 0 (the default) specifies an unlimited number of connections. This option is useful for the thread per connection concurrency model, where it limits the maximum number of threads created to serve incoming connections.

`-ORBRequestLimit <max-req>`
: This option can be used to limit the number of concurrently executed requests to the value specified, resulting in a thread pool of the requested size in case of multithreading. A value of 0 specifies an unlimited number of requests. This option defines the number of threads allocated in the thread pool when the thread pool concurrency model is used, hence defining the number of requests that will be served concurrently. The default value for this option is 4.

Security-related command line options understood by MICO

MICO features a CSIv2 level 0 compliant implementation of the CORBA Security Service. It has been written by ObjectSecurity, Ltd., and contributed to the MICO project. CSIv2 can be activated by the `-enable-csiv2` configure command line parameter, which configures all necessary options for compiling MICO with CSIv2 support. Please note that SSL/TLS support is required for building CSIv2. Since the CSIv2 specification does not specify any public API for accessing the CSIv2 implementation internals, there was a need to extend MICO by command line options required for CSIv2 configuration. In the following we briefly describe all CSIv2-related command line options. See [22] for more details.

`-ORBCSIv2`
: Activates CSIv2 support. The MICO client configured with this option will inspect the server object's IOR, and if it contains CSIv2 related information, the client will include SAS messages in GIOP request/reply. The MICO server configured with this option will search GIOP requests for included SAS messages and process them if present.

`-ORBCSIv2Realm <realm name>`
: Configures a default user realm. For example, using `-ORBCSIv2Realm objectsecurity.com` will set user realm to `objectsecurity.com`.

`-ORBGSSClientUser <user>,<passwd>`
: Sets the client user. This name will be used for GSSUP user/password login.

`-ORBGSSServerUser <user>,<passwd>`
: Adds a user to the server's user base for checking user access using the GSSUP method.

`-ORBTLSDName <TLS distinguished name>`
: Adds a distinguished user name to the server's user base. These names are checked if the client (process) does not send SAS messages along with GIOP requests but use the TLS/SSL transport layer for authentication.

`-ORBClientIdentity <identity name>`
: Adds an identity to the client process. If the client uses an attribute layer of the SAS protocol, then CSIv2 will assert this identity into SAS establish context message.

`-ORBUserIdentity <user name>,<identity name>`
: Adds a user identity into server's identity base. If the client uses an attribute layer of the SAS protocol and asserts its identity, this identity will be checked against the identity base on the server process. The user name can be a user name used for the GSSUP login or TLS distinguished user name for TLS authentication.

`-ORBTSSNoAuth`
: Turns the authentication layer off in TSS.

`-ORBTSSAuthSupported`
: Turns the authentication layer on in TSS and sets it as supported.

-ORBTSSAuthRequired
Turns the authentication layer on in TSS and sets it as required.

-ORBTSSNoAttr
Turns the attribute layer off in TSS.

-ORBTSSAttrSupported
Turns the attribute layer on in TSS and sets it as supported.

-ORBTSSAttrRequired
Turns the attribute layer on in TSS and sets it as required.

-ORBCSSNoAuth
Turns the authentication layer off in CSS.

-ORBCSSAuthSupported
Turns authentication layer on in CSS and sets it as supported.

-ORBCSSAuthRequired
Turns authentication layer on in CSS and sets it as required.

-ORBCSSNoAttr
Turns attribute layer off in CSS.

-ORBCSSAttrSupported
Turns attribute layer on in CSS and sets it as supported.

-ORBCSSAttrRequired
Turns attribute layer on in CSS and sets it as required.

B.2 INTERFACE REPOSITORY

The IR stores runtime type information

The interface repository is implemented by a separate program (`ird`). The idea is to run one instance of the program and make all MICO applications use the same interface repository. As we mentioned in Section B.1.1, the command line option `-ORBIfaceRepo Addr` can be used to tell a MICO application which interface repository to use. But where do you get the address of the `ird` program? The solution is to tell `ird` an address it should bind to by using the `-ORBIIOPAddr`. Here is an example of how to run `ird`:

```
ird -ORBIIOPAddr inet:<ird-host-name>:8888
```

where <ird-host-name> should be replaced by the name of the host executing ird. Afterward you can run Mico applications this way:

```
some_mico_application -ORBIfaceRepoAddr \
                              inet:<ird-host-name>:8888
```

To avoid typing in such long command lines, you can put the option into the file .micorc in your home directory:

```
echo -ORBIfaceRepoAddr inet:<ird-host-name>:8888 \
                               > ~/.micorc
```

Now you can just type

```
some_mico_application
```

and some_mico_application will still use the ird's interface repository.

Command line options understood by ird

The following command line arguments control ird:

--help
Shows a list of all supported command line arguments and exits.

--db <database file>
Specifies the filename where ird should save the contents of the interface repository when exiting. ird is terminated by pressing Ctrl-C or by sending it the SIGTERM signal. When ird is restarted afterward, it will read the file given by the -db option to restore the contents of the interface repository. Notice that the contents of this database file is just plain ASCII representing a CORBA IDL specification.

B.3 PORTABLE OBJECT ADAPTER

In contrast to earlier object adapters, the POA is defined in detail by the CORBA specification, so there is not much to tell about implementation-specific details of Mico's implementation of the POA.

The only enhancement of the POA as provided by Mico is better support for persistent objects, which outlive the server process they were created in.

Persistent objects outlive the server they were created in

How to implement persistent objects is almost completely described in the POA specification. However, there is one little bit of magic left to do that is specific to MICO. Persistent POAs (POAs that can host persistent objects) need a key—a unique "implementation name" with which to identify their objects. This name must be given using the -POAImplName command line option; otherwise, you will receive an "Invalid Policy" exception when trying to create a persistent POA.

Specifying the implementation name

```
./server -POAImplName Bank
```

Now the server can be shut down and restarted and objects created in the server will be available also after a restart. MICO provides an additional feature for on-demand execution of server programs. When using this feature, a server program will automatically be executed when a method is invoked on one of the objects hosted by this server.

The support for automatic server activation consists of two components, a so-called implementation repository and the MICO daemon. The former stores information on which server programs are available. The latter is a program running in the background. If a persistent POA is in contact with the MICO daemon, object references to a persistent object, when exported from the server process, will not point directly to the server but to the MICO daemon. Whenever a request is received by the daemon, it checks if your server is running. If it is, the request is simply forwarded; otherwise, a new server is started using information from the implementation repository.

B.3.1 MICO Daemon

The MICO daemon (micod) is the part of the POA that activates object implementations when their service is requested. micod also contains the implementation repository. To make all MICO applications use a single implementation repository, take similar actions as for the interface repository described in Section B.2. That is, tell micod an address to bind to using the -ORBIIOPAddr option and tell all MICO applications this address by using the option -ORBImplRepoAddr. For example:

```
micod -ORBIIOPAddr inet:<micod-host-name>:9999
```

Now you can run all MICO applications like this:

```
some_mico_application -ORBImplRepoAddr \
                        inet:<micod-host-name>:9999
```

or put the option into `.micorc` and run `some_mico_application` without arguments.

Command line options understood by `micod`

`micod` understands the following command line arguments:

`--help`

Shows a list of all supported command line arguments and exits.

`--dont-forward`

By default `micod` makes use of GIOP location forwarding, which results in much better performance (almost no overhead compared to not using `micod` at all). Unfortunately, this requires some client-side GIOP features that some ORBs do not support properly although prescribed in the CORBA specification. Use this option to turn off GIOP location forwarding when using clients implemented with such broken ORBs.

`--db <database file>`

Specifies the file name where `micod` should save the contents of the implementation repository when exiting. `micod` is terminated by pressing `Ctrl-C` or by sending it the `SIGTERM` signal. When `micod` is restarted afterward, it will read the file given by the `-db` option to restore the contents of the implementation repository.

B.3.2 Implementation Repository

The implementation repository (IMR) is the place where information about an object implementation (also known as a server) is stored. The CORBA specification only gives you an idea of what the implementation repository is for and does not specify the interface to it. Mico's implementation of the IMR simply contains a set of entries—one for each available server program. Each such entry contains the

Information maintained for each server by IMR

- name
- activation mode
- shell command

Activation modes

for the server. The name uniquely identifies the server and is the same as would be used as an argument to `-POAImplName`. The activation mode tells the Mico daemon how and when to activate a server. Currently, only one such mode (called poa) is supported. The shell command is executed by the MICO daemon whenever the server has to be (re)started.

If you have written a server that should be activated by the MICO daemon when its service is requested, you have to create an entry for that server. This can be accomplished by using the program `imr`. `imr` can be used to list all entries in the implementation repository, to show detailed information for one entry, to create a new entry, or to delete an entry. The implementation repository is selected by the options `-ORBImplRepoAddr` or `-ORBImplRepoIOR`, which you usually put into your `.micorc` file.

LISTING ALL ENTRIES

Just issue the command `imr list` to get a listing of the names of all entries in the implementation repository.

DETAILS FOR ONE ENTRY

`imr info <name>` shows detailed information for the entry named <name>.

CREATING NEW ENTRIES

The command

```
imr create <name> <mode> <command>
```

creates a new entry with name <name>. <mode> has to be poa.

<command> is the shell command that should be used to start the server. Note that all paths have to be absolute since `micod`'s current directory is probably different from your current directory. Furthermore, make sure that the server is located on the same machine as `micod`; otherwise you should use `rsh`.

DELETING ENTRIES

`imr delete <name>` deletes the entry named <name>.

FORCING ACTIVATION OF AN IMPLEMENTATION

Usually, the first instance of your server must be started manually for bootstrapping so that you have a chance to export object references to your persistent objects. `imr activate <name> [<micod-address>]` activates the implementation named `<name>`. To do so, however, `imr` needs to know the address of the MICO daemon. Usually, this is the same address as for the implementation repository, and you do not need to specify `<micod-address>`. Only if the MICO daemon is bound to an address different from the implementation repository address must you specify `<micod-address>` as a command line option to `imr`.

EXAMPLE

This section demonstrates how to use the MICO daemon and the `imr` tool to implement a persistent server. The descriptions in this section are based on a demo that is shipped with the MICO source code in directory `mico/demo/poa/account-3`. The first step consists in running the MICO daemon:

```
# run micod in the background
micod --ior /tmp/micod.ior &
```

The command line option `-ior` of the MICO daemon tells `micod` to store the IOR of `micod` in a file called `/tmp/micod.ior`. Once the MICO daemon is up and running, we use the `imr` tool to create an entry in the implementation repository for the bank server:

```
imr -ORBImplRepoIOR file:///tmp/micod.ior create \
          Bank poa <path-to-executable>/bank-server
```

The `imr` tool is told via the `-ORBImplRepoIOR` command line option about the IOR of `micod`. This implies that the `imr` tool can be run on any host, as long as you have the IOR of `micod`. The command line argument `Bank` assigns a symbolic name to the bank server, which will create an entry in the implementation repository under this name. The following argument `poa` specifies the activation mode. The final argument is the absolute path to the executable of the bank server. Note that the bank server is not running at this point in time; we have merely created an entry in the implementation repository. The following command will run the bank server:

```
imr -ORBImplRepoIOR file:///tmp/micod.ior activate Bank
```

Once the bank server is up and running, it will create the IOR using the usual ORB primitives such as `ORB::object_to_string()`. Note, however, that the IOR that the bank server creates actually points to `micod`. This means that a client using that IOR actually talks to the bank server via `micod`. To make the communication more efficient, `micod` will inform the client of the actual address of the bank server after it is launched. This happens transparently to the client via location forwarding as explained in Section 7.6. The bank server is free to terminate itself at any time. Whenever the client invokes a method on the bank server, `micod` will automatically relaunch it.

B.4 IDL COMPILER

MICO has an IDL compiler called `idl`, which is briefly described in this section. The `idl` tool is used for translating IDL specifications to C++ as well as feeding IDL specifications into the interface repository. The tool takes its input from either a file or an interface repository and generates code for C++ or CORBA IDL. If the input is taken from a file, the `idl` tool can additionally feed the specification into the interface repository.

MICO's IDL compiler translates IDL specifications to C++ stubs and skeletons

The following gives a detailed description of all the options:

Command line options understood by the IDL compiler

`--help`
Gives an overview of all supported command line options.

`--version`
Prints the version of MICO.

`--config`
Prints some important configuration information.

`-D<define>`
Defines a preprocessor macro. This option is equivalent to the `-D` switch of most C compilers.

`-I<path>`
Defines a search path for `#include` directives. This option is equivalent to the `-I` switch of most C compilers.

`--no-exceptions`
Tells `idl` to disable exception handling in the generated code. Code for the exception classes is still generated, but throwing exceptions will result in an error message and abort the program. This option can only be used in conjunction with `-codegen-c++`. This option is off by default.

--codegen-c++

Tells `idl` to generate code for C++ as defined by the IDL-to-C++ language mapping. The `idl` tool will generate two files, one ending in `.h` and one ending in `.cc` with the same base names. This option is the default.

--no-codegen-c++

Turns off the code generation for C++.

--codegen-idl

Turns on the code generation for CORBA IDL. The `idl` tool will generate a file that contains the IDL specification, which can again be fed into the `idl` tool. The base name of the file is specified with the `-name` option.

--no-codegen-idl

Turns off the code generation of CORBA IDL. This option is the default.

--c++-impl

Causes the generation of some default C++ implementation classes for all interfaces contained in the IDL specification. This option requires `-codegen-c++`.

--c++-suffix=<suffix>

If `-codegen-c++` is selected, this option determines the suffix for the C++ implementation file. The default is "`cc`".

--hh-suffix=<suffix>

If `-codegen-c++` is selected, this option determines the suffix for the C++ header file. The default is "`h`".

--c++-skel

Generates a separate file with suffix `_skel.cc` that contains code needed only by servers (i.e., the skeletons). By default, this code is emitted in the standard C++ implementation files. This option requires `-codegen-c++`.

--include-prefix=<path>

If used, included files (via the `#include` directive) are prefixed with `<path>`. This option requires `-codegen-c++`.

--emit-repoids

Causes emission of `#pragma` directives, which associate the repository ID of each IDL construct. This option can only be used in conjunction with the option `-codegen-idl`.

--feed-ir

The CORBA IDL that is specified as a command line option is fed into the interface repository. This option requires the `ird` daemon to be running.

--feed-included-defs

Used only in conjunction with `-feed-ir`. If this option is used, IDL definitions located in included files are fed into the interface repository as well. The default is to feed only the definitions of the main IDL file into the IR.

--repo-id=<id>

The code generation is done from the information contained in the interface repository instead of from a file. This option requires the `ird` daemon to be running. The parameter `id` is a repository identifier and must denote a CORBA module.

--name=<prefix>

Controls the prefix of the file names if a code generation is selected. This option is mandatory if the input is taken from the interface repository. If the input is taken from a file, the prefix is derived from the base name of the file name.

--idl3toidl2

When processing IDL files that contain CORBA component and home definitions, this option performs the "equivalent IDL translation," generating equivalent interfaces for components and homes according to the CCM specification. This option must be used in conjunction with the `-codegen-idl` and `-no-codegen-c++` options, to generate an IDL file containing the equivalent IDL, and the `-name` option to select an output file name that is different from the input file name.

--pseudo

Generates code for "pseudo interfaces." No stubs, skeletons, or code for marshalling data to and from `Any` variables is produced. Only supported for C++ code generation.

--any

Activates support for insertion and extraction operators of user-defined IDL types for `Any`. Can only be used in conjunction with `-codegen-c++`. This option implies `-typecode`.

--typecode

Generates code for typecodes of user-defined IDL types. Can only be used in conjunction with `-codegen-c++`.

--poa-ties

By default MICO's IDL compiler does not generate POA ties. This option has to be used if code for the POA ties are to be generated.

--gen-included-defs

Generates code for IDL statements that were included using the `#include` directive.

--gen-full-dispatcher

Usually, the skeleton class generated for an interface contains only the dispatcher for the operations and attributes defined in this interface. With this option, the dispatcher also includes operations and attributes inherited from all base interfaces.

--codegen-wsdl

This option activates the IDL-to-WSDL mapping as defined by the CORBA specification.

--wsi-wsdl

When translating IDL to WSDL, the IDL compiler will use the SOAP-specific mapping by default. Use option `-wsi-wsdl` if WS-I conformant WSDL is required.

--support-id

This option can only be used in conjunction with `-codegen-wsdl`. If selected, the WSDL generated will make use of `ID` and `IDREF`. These are required for the mapping of value types, but are not supported by many Web Services tools. By default, `ID` and `IDREF` are not used.

--windows-dll-with-export=<dll-prefix>

The IDL compiler has to create different C++ source code when the stubs and skeletons are to be compiled as a Windows DLL (Dynamic Link Library). The necessary declarations that are required to compile the code for a Windows DLL can be activated by defining a special symbol. For example, if `<dll-prefix>` is `MYDLL`, then defining the symbol `BUILD_MYDLL_DLL` using the `-D` or `/D` command line option of the C++ compiler will compile the source code as a Windows DLL.

Examples

Here are some examples of how to use the `idl` tool:

idl account.idl

Translates the IDL specification contained in `account.idl` according to the C++ language mapping. This generates two files in the current directory.

idl --feed-ir account.idl
Same as above but the IDL specification is also fed into the interface repository.

idl --feed-ir -no-codegen-c++ account.idl
Same as above but the generation of C++ stubs and skeletons is omitted.

idl --repo-id=IDL:Account:1.0 -no-codegen-c++
`-codegen-idl -name=out`
Generates IDL code from the information contained in the interface repository. This requires the `ird` daemon to be running. The output is written to a file called `out.idl`.

idl --no-codegen-c++ -codegen-idl
`-name=p account.idl`
Translates the IDL specification contained in `account.idl` into a semantically equivalent IDL specification in file `p.idl`. This could be useful if you want to misuse the IDL compiler as a pretty printer.

B.5 COMPILER AND LINKER WRAPPERS

It can be quite complicated to compile and link MICO applications because you have to specify system-dependent compiler flags, linker flags, and libraries. This is why MICO provides you with four shell scripts:

Wrappers ease the generation of MICO applications

mico-c++
Should be used as the C++ compiler when compiling the C++ source files of a MICO application.

mico-ld
Should be used as the linker when linking together the `.o` files of a MICO application.

mico-shc++
Should be used as the C++ compiler when compiling the C++ source files of a MICO dynamically loadable module. `mico-shc++` will not be available if you specified the `-disable-dynamic` option during configuration.

mico-shld
Should be used as the linker when linking together the `.o` files of a MICO

dynamically loadable module. `mico-shld` will not be available unless you specified the `-enable-dynamic` option during configuration.

The scripts can be used just like the normal compiler/linker, except that for `mico-shld` you do not specify a file name suffix for the output file because `mico-shld` will append a system-dependent shared object suffix (`.so` on most systems) to the specified output file name. These wrapper scripts pass parameters to the respective tools they wrap. For example, you will most likely need to use the `-L` parameter when using `mico-ld` to specify the search path for the MICO library. The `-L` parameter has the same meaning as for the UNIX linker `ld`, which is wrapped with `mico-ld`.

B.5.1 Examples

Let's consider building a simple MICO application that consists of two files: `account.idl` and `main.cc`. Here's how to build account:

```
idl account.idl
mico-c++ -I. -c account.cc -o account.o
mico-c++ -I. -c main.cc -o main.o
mico-ld account.o main.o -o account -lmico<version>
```

As a second example, consider building a dynamically loadable module and a client program that loads the module. We have three source files now, `account.idl`, `client.cc`, and `module.cc`:

```
idl account.idl
mico-shc++ -I. -c account.cc -o account.o
mico-shc++ -I. -c module.cc -o module.o
mico-shld -o module module.o account.o -lmico<version>

mico-c++ -I. -c client.cc -o client.o \
mico-ld account.o client.o -o client -lmico<version>
```

Note the following:

- All files that go into the module must be compiled using the wrapper `mico-shc++` instead of `mico-c++`.
- `module` was specified as the output file, but `mico-shld` will generate `module.so` (the extension depends on your system).

- `account.o` must be linked into both the module and the client but is compiled only once using `mico-shc++`. You would expect that `account.cc` had to be compiled twice: once with `mico-c++` for use in the client and once with `mico-shc++` for use in the module. The rule is that using `mico-shc++` where `mico-c++` should be used does no harm, but not the other way around.

APPENDIX C

MICO IMPLEMENTATION DETAILS

In this appendix we look at certain implementation details of MICO. This appendix is intended for readers who want to understand the inner workings of MICO. Additionally, it should provide a good starting point for system programmers who want to understand, extend, or modify certain parts of MICO.

We begin with a trace of a method invocation through MICO, since that gives a good overview of the interplay of the various components of MICO. We then discuss how to add new invocation adapters, new object adapters, and new transport protocols to MICO. The appendix will be concluded with a section on the structure of the program code generated by the IDL compiler.

C.1 PATH OF AN OPERATION INVOCATION THROUGH AN ORB

This section follows the path an operation invocation takes from the source (client) to the destination (server), using the "Account" client introduced in Section 3.4 that calls a `deposit` operation on the server. As already illustrated in Figure 6.4, the method invocation first passes the SII, the ORB, and the GIOP client in the client process. The GIOP client generates a message that is sent to the server. There, it is received by the GIOP server, passes through the ORB and the object adapter, and finally results in a method invocation on the skeleton of the target object. The results of the method invocation return to the client on the reverse route. The following important classes are involved in the execution of the method invocation in the individual components:

- Static Invocation Interface (SII)
  - — `Account_stub`: The stub generated by the IDL compiler from the IDL interface `Account`.
  - — `Object`: The base class of all CORBA objects, which is inherited by the stub, in files `include/mico/object.h` and `orb/object.cc`.
  - — `StaticRequest`: Represents a method invocation in SII, files `include/mico/static.h`, `orb/static.cc`.

- ORB
  - — `ORB`: Object Request Broker, files `include/mico/orb_mico.h`, `orb/orb.cc`.
  - — `ORBInvokeRec`: Represents a method invocation in ORB, files `include/mico/orb_mico.h`, `orb/orb.cc`.

- GIOP client
  - — `IIOPProxy`: GIOP object adapter, files `include/mico/iop.h`, `orb/iop.cc`.
  - — `IIOPProxyInvokeRec`: Represents a method invocation in the GIOP invocation adapter, files `include/mico/iop.h`, `orb/iop.cc`.
  - — `GIOPCodec`: Generates and decodes GIOP messages, files `include/mico/iop.h`, `orb/iop.cc`.
  - — `GIOPConn`: Represents connection to server, files `include/mico/iop.h`, `orb/iop.cc`.

- GIOP server
  - — `IIOPServer`: GIOP invocation adapter, files `include/mico/iop.h`, `orb/iop.cc`.
  - — `IIOPServerInvokeRec`: Represents a method invocation in the GIOP invocation adapter, files `include/mico/iop.h`, `orb/iop.cc`.
  - — `GIOPCodec`: Generates and decodes GIOP messages, files `include/mico/iop.h`, `orb/iop.cc`.

— `GIOPConn`: Represents a connection into the server, files `include/mico/iop.h`, `orb/iop.cc`.

- Object adapter

  — `POA_impl`: Portable Object Adapter, files `include/mico/poa_impl.h`, `orb/poa_impl.cc`.

  — `StaticServerRequest`: Represents a method invocation in the POA, files `include/mico/static.h`, `orb/static.cc`.

  — `POA_Account`: The skeleton generated by the IDL compiler from the IDL interface `Account`.

The procedures that take place during an operation invocation based on a remote method invocation are shown separately for the client and server processes below. The indentation represents the call chain. A deeper indentation indicates that the method was called by the previously described method.

C.1.1 Client Side

`Account_stub::deposit()`
The initial call made by the client, invoking the `deposit` operation on the stub object.

`StaticRequest::StaticRequest()`
`StaticRequest` constructor, used in the generated stub to create a `StaticRequest` object that represents the method invocation for the object and method name.

`StaticRequest::add_*_arg()`
Inserts parameter values into the `StaticRequest` object. Parameters to these methods are references to `StaticAny` objects containing the values of the parameters.

`StaticRequest::set_result()`
Gives `StaticRequest` a reference to a `StaticAny` object which is to hold the return value of the method invocation.

`StaticRequest::invoke()`

Transfers the method invocation to the ORB, waits for completion of the method invocation, and gets the results from the ORB

`ORB::invoke_async()`

Creates an `ORBInvokeRec` object that represents the method invocation in the ORB; identifies the object adapter to be used and sends it to the method invocation.

`IIOPProxy::invoke()`

Creates an `IIOPProxyInvokeRec` object that represents the method invocation in the `IIOPProxy`; generates a message and sends it to the server.

`IIOPProxy::make_conn()`

Identifies (or creates if it does not yet exist) a `GIOPConn` object that represents the network connection to the server.

`InetAddress::make_transport()`

Creates a new `TCPTransport` object to connect to the server.

`TCPTransport::connect()`

Creates a socket and connects to the server.

`GIOPCodec::put_invoke_request()`

Generates a network message that represents the method invocation.

`GIOPCodec::put_args()`

Processes the input parameters to the operation.

`StaticRequest::get_in_args()`

Marshals the input parameters.

`StaticAny::marshal()`

Marshals one input parameter.

`GIOPConn::output()`

Sends the network message to the server.

`ORB::wait()`

Waits until the method invocation is completed. During this time, incoming network messages are received and processed.

`Dispatcher::run()`

Waits for incoming data on network connections.

`Dispatcher::handle_fevents()`

Detects incoming data on network connections and calls the relevant connection handler.

`GIOPConn::callback()`

The GIOP connection's handler for incoming data.

`GIOPConn::do_read()`

Reads data from network connection.

`GIOPConn::input_ready()`

Is called when a GIOP message is complete.

`GIOPConn::input_ready_callback()`

Is called to notify the IIOP proxy of an incoming message.

`IIOPProxy::input_callback()`

The callback to notify the IIOP proxy of an incoming message.

`IIOPProxy::handle_input()`

Checks the message for its type (i.e., whether it is a reply) and invokes the appropriate method for evaluation of the message.

`IIOPProxy::handle_invoke_reply()`

Decodes the network message and forwards the results.

`GIOPCodec::get_invoke_reply1()`

Decodes the GIOP header.

`GIOPCodec::get_invoke_reply2()`

Processes the invocation's result and other output parameters.

`StaticRequest::set_out_args()`

Marshals the result and output parameters.

`StaticAny::unmarshal()`

Marshals one output parameter.

`IIOPProxy::exec_invoke_reply()`

Sends results to the ORB.

`ORB::answer_invoke()`

Stores the results of a method invocation in the associated `ORBInvokeRec` and designates the method invocation as completed so that `ORB::wait()` returns to its caller.

`ORB::get_invoke_reply()`

Fetches results of method invocation from ORB.

C.1.2 Server Side

`GIOPConn::do_read()`

Reads data from network connection.

`GIOPConn::input_ready()`

Is called when a GIOP message is complete.

`GIOPConn::input_ready_callback()`

Is called to notify the IIOP server of an incoming message.

`IIOPServer::input_callback()`

Callback routine of `IIOPServer` that is invoked when a new message arrives.

`IIOPServer::handle_input()`

Checks the type of message and invokes the corresponding method to evaluate the message.

`IIOPServer::handle_invoke_request()`

Decodes the GIOP message header and forwards parameters.

`GIOPCodec::get_invoke_request()`

Decodes the message, creates a `GIOPRequest` object (equivalent to `Request` object on client side), and creates an `IIOPServer-InvokeRec` object that represents method invocation on server side.

`IIOPServer::exec_invoke_request()`

Passes the invocation request to the ORB.

`ORB::invoke_async()`

Creates an `ORBInvokeRec` object that represents the method invocation in the ORB; establishes the object adapter to be used and passes it the method invocation.

`POA_impl::invoke()`

Checks the object reference of the target object and looks for the POA that manages the target object, and transfers the method invocation to this POA instance.

`POA_impl::local_invoke()`

Executes, delays, or ignores the method invocation depending on the state of the POA manager belonging to the target POA.

`POA_impl::perform_invoke()`

Looks up the servant belonging to the target object, depending on the POA policies. Usually, the servant is found in the active object map. Generates a `StaticServerRequest` object and passes it to the servant's method dispatcher.

`POA_Account::invoke()`

Calls the `dispatch()` methods of the skeleton and its base classes, eventually finding the skeleton that implements the invocation that is being called.

`POA_Account::dispatch()`

Determines the method that is to be invoked, extracts the parameters from the `StaticServerRequest`, calls the method implementation, and stores the results in the `StaticServerRequest`.

`StaticServerRequest::add_*_arg()`

Gives `StaticServerRequest` references to `StaticAny` objects that are to hold the parameter values.

`StaticServerRequest::set_result()`

Gives `StaticServerRequest` references to the `StaticAny` object that is to hold the result value.

`StaticServerRequest::read_args()`

Decodes the input parameters of the method invocation and fills the `StaticAny`s previously registered via `add_*_arg()` with the decoded values.

`GIOPRequest::get_in_args()`

Unmarshals the input parameters.

`StaticAny::demarshal()`

Unmarshals one input parameter.

`POA_Account::deposit()`

Invocation of the target method implemented by the user.

`StaticServerRequest::write_results()`

Encodes the result value and other output parameters by converting the values contained in the `StaticAny` objects that have been previously registered via `add_*_arg()` and `set_result()` into a byte stream.

`GIOPRequest::set_out_args()`

Marshals the result and other output parameters.

`StaticServerRequest::~StaticServerRequest()`

The `StaticServerRequest` destructor informs POA that method invocation is completed.

`POA_impl::answer_invoke()`

The POA informs ORB that the method invocation has completed.

`ORB::answer_invoke()`

Stores the results of a method invocation in associated `ORBInvokeRec`.

`IIOPServer::notify()`

Invokes the correct method for handling a reply message, depending on which kind of request has completed.

`IIOPServer::handle_invoke_reply()`

Retrieves the status of a method invocation from ORB, generates reply message, and sends it to the client.

`ORB::get_invoke_reply()`

Gets the invocation's result from the ORB.

`GIOPCodec::put_invoke_reply()`

Generates a GIOP reply message.

`GIOPConn::output()`

Sends the message to the client.

C.2 INTEGRATION OF A NEW INVOCATION ADAPTER

Operations provided by the ORB

In this section of the appendix we show how to integrate a new invocation adapter into a microkernel ORB. In the following we will describe the methods the ORB supplies for this purpose. The methods are declared in the file `include/mico/orb_mico.h` and implemented in `orb/orb.cc` in the MICO source tree.

```
CORBA::ORBMsgId invoke_async (CORBA::Object_ptr target,
          CORBA::ORBRequest *request,
          CORBA::Principal_ptr principal,
          CORBA::Boolean reply_expected = TRUE,
          CORBA::ORBCallback *callback = 0,
          CORBA::ORBMsgId = 0)
```

This initiates an operation invocation. The parameters given are the target object `target`, the parameter in the form of `request`, as well as the principal `principal`, which contains specific information that can be used to identify the method invoked by the caller. The optional parameters that can be used are the Boolean value `reply_expected`, which indicates whether an operation invocation is *one-way* or *two-way*; the callback object `callback`, the method `ORB Callback::callback()` of which the ORB automatically invokes when a method invocation is completed; and the ID `id` that is to be supplied. The result that is returned is an ID that explicitly identifies the operation invocation and can be used later to wait for the completion of the operation invocation.

```
CORBA::Boolean wait (CORBA::ORBMsgId id,
          CORBA::Long timeout = -1)
```

This waits until either the operation invocation specified by the `id` is completed or the waiting time (in milliseconds) specified by the `timeout` has lapsed. The timeout value `-1` stands for infinite. In the first case, the result `TRUE` is returned, and in the second, the result `FALSE`.

```
CORBA::InvokeStatus get_invoke_reply (CORBA::ORBMsgId id,
          Object_out forwarded_target,
          CORBA::ORBRequest *& request,
          GIOP::AddressingDisposition &ad)
```

This gets the results from the ORB of the completed operation invocation specified by `id`. The result that is supplied is the value of the type `InvokeStatus`, which can assume the values `InvokeOk` (operation completed successfully), `InvokeForward` (object reference of target object has changed), `InvokeSysEx` (a system exception has occurred), `InvokeUsrEx` (a user exception has occurred), or `InvokeAddrDisp` (a different object addressing is requested). In the case of the `InvokeForward` value, `forwarded_target` is set to the new object reference, and the operation invocation has to be repeated. In the case of `InvokeAddrDisp`, the requested addressing type is indicated by `ad`, and the operation invocation has to be repeated. `request` is set to the `ORBRequest` instance specified with `invoke_async`.

```
void cancel (CORBA::ORBMsgId id)
```

This terminates an operation invocation specified by `id`.

```
CORBA::InvokeStatus invoke (CORBA::Object_ptr &target,
  ORBRequest *request, CORBA::Principal_ptr principal,
  CORBA::Boolean reply_expected
```

This is a convenient combination of `invoke_async()`, `wait()`, and `get_invoke_reply()`, which blocks until an operation invocation is completed.

The `ORBRequest` object, which contains the parameters and results of an operation invocation, plays a central role in the development of an operation invocation. This is an abstract class from which a concrete implementation must be derived. This involves the implementation of the methods explained below. The declaration of the class `ORBRequest` can be found in the file `mico/include/mico/orb_fwd.h` in the MICO source tree.

`ORBRequest` represents operation invocation

```
const char *op_name()
```

Supplies the name of the invoked operation.

```
CORBA::Boolean get_in_args (CORBA::NVList_ptr params,
     CORBA::Context_ptr &ctx)
```

Pads `params` with the list of parameters and `ctx` with the optional `Context_` object.

```
CORBA::Boolean get_in_args (
     ORBRequest::StaticAnyList *params,
     Context_ptr &ctx)
```

Pads `params` with the list of parameters and `ctx` with the optional `Context_` object.

```
CORBA::Boolean get_in_args (CORBA::DataEncoder *encoder)
```

Codes the input parameters and the optional `Context_` object (in this sequence) using `encoder`.

```
CORBA::Boolean get_out_args (CORBA::Any *res,
      CORBA::NVList_ptr params, CORBA::Exception *&ex)
```

Pads `res` with the result of the method invocation and `params` with the output parameters or `ex` with the exception in the event that one occurred.

```
CORBA::Boolean get_out_args (CORBA::StaticAny *res,
      StaticAnyList *oparams, CORBA::Exception *&ex)
```

Pads `res` with the result of the method invocation and `params` with the output parameters or `ex` with the exception in the event that one occurred.

```
CORBA::Boolean get_out_args (CORBA::DataEncoder *encoder,
      CORBA::Boolean &is_except)
```

Codes the result and the output parameters of an operation invocation (in this sequence) or an exception that occurred using `encoder` and sets `is_except` to `TRUE` in the event an exception occurred; otherwise it sets it to `FALSE`.

```
CORBA::Boolean set_out_args (CORBA::Any *res,
      CORBA::NVList_ptr params)
```

Sets the result and the output parameters from `this` to the supplied value `res` or `params`.

```
CORBA::Boolean set_out_args (CORBA::StaticAny *res,
      StaticAnyList *params)
```

Sets the result and the output parameters from `this` to the supplied value `res` or `params`.

```
void set_out_args (CORBA::Exception *ex)
```

Stores the exception `ex` as a result of the operation invocation in `this`.

```
CORBA::Boolean set_out_args (CORBA::DataDecoder *decoder,
      CORBA::Boolean is_except)
```

Sets the result and the output parameters of `this` to the coded values in `decoder`. `is_except` indicates whether an exception occurred.

```
CORBA::Boolean copy_out_args (CORBA::ORBRequest *req)
```

Copies the output parameters from `req` to `this`.

```
CORBA::Boolean copy_in_args (CORBA::ORBRequest *req)
```

Copies the input parameters from `req` to `this`.

```
const char *type ()
```

Supplies a string that identifies the type of request object.

C.3 INTEGRATION OF A NEW OBJECT ADAPTER

In addition to having an interface for new invocation adapters, the ORB also has one for the integration of new object adapters. This interface is described below. In addition, each object adapter must provide an object of the type `CORBA::ObjectAdapter` over which the ORB has access to the functionality of the object adapter.

Object adapters inherit from basic class `ObjectAdapter`

`ObjectAdapter` is an abstract basic class from which an object-adapter-specific concrete implementation must be derived. It must provide implementations for the methods explained below. The declaration for the class `ObjectAdapter` can be found in the file `include/mico/orb_mico.h` in the MICO source tree.

```
const char *get_oaid () const
```

Supplies a string that identifies the type of object adapter.

```
CORBA::Boolean has_object (CORBA::Object_ptr obj)
```

Then exactly supplies `TRUE` if the object adapter is responsible for executing an operation invocation on the object `obj`.

```
CORBA::Boolean is_local () const
```

Then exactly supplies `TRUE` if the object adapter is local, that is, if the execution of the operation invocation does not require any interprocess communication.

```
CORBA::Boolean invoke (CORBA::ORBMsgId id,
     CORBA::Object_ptr obj, ORBRequest *req,
     CORBA::Principal_ptr principal,
     CORBA::Boolean response_expected = TRUE)
```

Initiates an operation invocation with ID `id` on the object `obj`, with parameters `req` and `principal`. `response_expected` indicates whether it is a *one-way* or a *two-way* operation invocation. The result returned is `TRUE` if the method invocation could be initiated successfully. Note that this by no means signifies that the operation invocation was completed successfully. The return message indicating whether an operation invocation was completed and what the results were uses the method `ORB::answer_invoke()`.

```
CORBA::Boolean bind (CORBA::ORBMsgId id,
     const char *repoid,
     const ORB::ObjectTag &tag,
     CORBA::Address *addr)
```

The ORB invokes this method to determine whether the object adapter is managing an object with repository ID `repoid` or object ID `tag` under the address `addr`. The address is important if the object adapter is not local, such as a GIOP proxy. The invocation returns `TRUE` if the process was initiated successfully. As with `invoke`, the result is conveyed to the ORB through an invocation of `ORB::answer_bind()`.

```
CORBA::Boolean locate (CORBA::ORBMsgId id,
     CORBA::Object_ptr obj)
```

The ORB invokes this method to determine whether the object reference `obj` has changed in the meantime due to a migration process. Then exactly supplies `TRUE` as the result if the process could be initiated successfully. As with `invoke`, the result is conveyed to the ORB through the invocation of `ORB::answer_locate()`.

```
CORBA::Object_ptr skeleton (CORBA::Object_ptr obj)
```

Invoked by the ORB to query the object adapter for the object reference `obj` about the possible existence of a collocation stub. Delivers the collocation stub as a result or a `NIL` if one is not available.

```
void cancel (CORBA::ORBMsgId id)
```

Terminates the operation invocation with the ID `id`.

```
void shutdown (CORBA::Boolean wait_for_completion)
```

Initiates the termination. As soon as an object adapter has completed its termination, it invokes `ORB::answer_shutdown()` to notify the ORB. If `wait_for_completion` `TRUE` occurs, this invocation cannot take place until all operation invocations currently being executed have been completed.

```
void answer_invoke (CORBA::ORBMsgId id,
      CORBA::Object_ptr obj,
      CORBA::ORBRequest *req,
      CORBA::InvokeStatus status)
```

Invoked by a skeleton interface (SSI or DSI) when an operation invocation is completed in order to inform the object adapter of the results of the invocation. `status` is the status value familiar from Section C.2.

Operations provided by the ORB

The ORB supplies the following methods that are associated with the integration of new object adapters. The methods are declared in the file `include/mico/orb_mico.h` and implemented in the file `orb/orb.cc` in the MICO source tree.

```
void register_oa (CORBA::ObjectAdapter *oa)
```

Registers the object adapter oa at the ORB.

```
void unregister_oa (CORBA::ObjectAdapter *oa)
```

Deregisters the object adapter oa at the ORB.

```
void answer_invoke (CORBA::ORBMsgId id,
      CORBA::InvokeStatus status,
      CORBA::Object_ptr obj,
      CORBA::ORBRequest *req,
      GIOP::AddressingDisposition ad)
```

The object adapter invokes this method to notify the ORB of the completion of the method invocation under ID `id` with status `status` and result `req`. If `status` has the value `InvokeForward`, then `obj` contains the new object reference. If status has the value `InvokeAddrDisp`, then `ad` contains requested addressing type.

```
void answer_bind (CORBA::ORBMsgId id,
      CORBA::LocateStatus status,
      CORBA::Object_ptr obj)
```

The object adapter invokes this method to notify the ORB that the bind process with ID id has been completed. status is an instance of the type LocateStatus that can assume the value LocateUnknown (object being searched does not exist), LocateHere (the object being searched has been found), or LocateForward (object reference of object being searched has changed). The values LocateUnknown and LocateHere are the only values that can occur in connection with answer_bind. In the above case, obj contains the object reference of the found object.

```
void answer_locate (CORBA::ORBMsgId id,
      CORBA::LocateStatus status,
      CORBA::Object_ptr obj,
      GIOP::AddressingDisposition ad)
```

This is invoked by the object adapter to notify the ORB of the completion of the locate process with ID id. If status has the value LocateHere or LocateForward, obj contains the current object reference of the queried object; otherwise it contains NIL. If status has the value LocateAddrDisp, then ad contains requested addressing type.

```
void answer_shutdown (CORBA::ObjectAdapter *oa)
```

The object adapter oa invokes this method to notify the ORB of the completion of the termination.

C.4 INTEGRATION OF A NEW TRANSPORT MECHANISM

New GIOP mapping

In Mico a new transport mechanism can generally be incorporated simply through the implementation of an object adapter and the corresponding invocation adapter on the model of the GIOP client and the GIOP server (see Section 6.3.2). However, this is usually a complicated process. An easier way consists of using the framework described in Chapter 6 to map the GIOP to the transport mechanism being used. This involves implementing the classes listed below for transport mechanism X. These classes are described in the following sections. The paths given below are subdirectories in the Mico source tree.

XAddress:
Address, files include/mico/address.h, include/mico/address_impl.h, orb/address.cc.

XAddressParser:
Decodes addresses from a given string, and the same for files.

XProfile:
IOR profiles, files `include/mico/ior.h`, `include/mico/ior_impl.h`, `orb/ior.cc`.

XProfileDecoder:
Decodes IOR profiles from a given byte stream, and the same for files.

XTransport:
Client-side transport class, files `include/mico/transport.h`, `include/mico/transport_impl.h`, `orb/transport.cc`, `orb/transport/*.cc`.

XTransportServer:
Server-side transport class, and the same for files.

Also see Section 6.3.2 for the inheritance relationships between these classes and the GIOP framework.

C.4.1 XAddress

Specifying the address prefix

First an address type string (similar to "`inet`") that has not yet been used, such as "`x`", has to be specified. This string serves as the prefix for addresses in string form. The prefix is followed by arbitrary address information, such as a globally explicit number in "`x:42`".

A class `XAddress` implementing the following methods is then derived from `CORBA::Address`.

```
string stringify () const
```

Supplies the address in string form, such as "`x:42`".

```
const char *proto () const
```

Supplies the type of this address, such as "`x`".

```
CORBA::Transport *make_transport () const
```

Creates a `Transport` object that matches the type of address.

```
CORBA::TransportServer *make_transport_server () const
```

Creates a `TransportServer` object that matches the type of address.

```
CORBA::IORProfile *make_ior_profile (CORBA::Octet *key,
    CORBA::ULong keylength,
    const CORBA::MultiComponent &components,
    CORBA::UShort version = 0x0100) const
```

Creates an `IORProfile` object that matches the type of address. The parameters provided are the object ID `key`, its length `keylength`, any components `components` that might exist, and the GIOP version `version` (default value 1.0) to be used. The `components` consist of a standardized representation of arbitrary information that could be stored in a profile, which can include the name and the version of the ORB that generated the profile.

```
CORBA::Boolean is_local () const
```

Then exactly supplies `TRUE` if the address refers to the same address space in which it is used.

```
CORBA::Address *clone () const
```

Creates an exact copy of `this`.

```
CORBA::Long compare (const CORBA::Address &addr) const
```

Compares `this` with `addr` and supplies −1 if `this` < `addr`, 0 if `this` = `addr`, or 1 if `this` > `addr`.

```
CORBA::Boolean operator== (
    const CORBA::Address &addr) const
```

Exactly supplies `TRUE` if `this` = `addr`.

```
CORBA::Boolean operator< (
    const CORBA::Address &addr) const
```

Exactly supplies `TRUE` if `this` < `addr`.

C.4.2 XAddressParser

The class `XAddressParser` must be derived from `CORBA::AddressParser` and implement the following methods:

```
CORBA::Address *parse (const char *rest,
    const char *proto) const
```

Converts an address string (for example, `x:42`) into an `Address` object. `proto` contains the address type (for example, `x`), and `rest` contains the rest (for example, `42`) of the string.

```
CORBA::Boolean has_proto (const char *proto) const
```

Supplies exactly `TRUE` if the address parser can parse addresses from the type `proto` (for example, `x`).

C.4.3 XProfile

Specifying the profile ID

In this case too a profile ID that has not yet been used has to be defined (similar to `TAG_INTERNET_IOP`), such as

```
const CORBA::IORProfile::ProfileId TAG_X_IOP = 31415;
```

Then a class `XProfile` is derived from `CORBA::IORProfile` and implements the following methods:

```
void encode (CORBA::DataEncoder &encoder) const
```

Codes `this` using `encoder` in a byte stream.

```
CORBA::Address *addr () const
```

Supplies the address of this profile.

```
ProfileId id () const
```

Supplies the profile ID of this profile.

```
ProfileId encode_id () const
```

Normally supplies the same result of `id()`. `encode_id()` only supplies the profile ID of a basic transport mechanism in special cases (such as the SSL transport mechanism that represents a wrapper for an existing transport mechanism like IIOP).

```
void objectkey (Octet *key, Long keylength)
```

Sets the object ID to the supplied value. `key` contains the new ID and `keylength` its length.

```
const CORBA::Octet *objectkey (
     CORBA::Long &keylength) const
```

Requests the object ID. The result is a reference to the object ID; `keylength` is set to the length of the object ID.

```
CORBA::Boolean reachable ()
```

Return `TRUE` if the address contained in the profile can be reached. For example, the address `local` can only be reached from a process if it was also created in this process. On the other hand, addresses of the type `inet` can always be reached.

```
void print (ostream &outputstream) const
```

Supplies the address in a string form as `outputstream`.

```
CORBA::MultiComponent *components ()
```

Supplies the components contained in the profile.

```
CORBA::IORProfile *clone () const
```

Creates an exact copy of `this`.

```
CORBA::Long compare (
     const CORBA::IORProfile &prof) const
```

Compares `this` with `prof` and supplies −1 if `this` < `prof`, 0 if `this = prof`, and 1 if `this` > `prof`.

```
CORBA::Boolean operator== (
     const CORBA::IORProfile &prof) const
```

Supplies exactly `TRUE` if `this = prof`.

```
CORBA::Boolean operator< (
     const CORBA::IORProfile &prof) const
```

Supplies exactly `TRUE` if `this` < `prof`.

C.4.4 XProfileDecoder

The class `XprofileDecoder` must be derived from `CORBA::ProfileDecoder` and implement the following methods:

```
CORBA::IORProfile *decode (CORBA::DataDecoder &decoder,
     ProfileId id, CORBA::ULong length) const
```

Uses `decoder` to convert a byte stream into an `IORProfile` object. The parameters supplied are the profile ID `id` and the length of the byte stream `length`.

```
CORBA::Boolean has_id (ProfileId id) const
```

Supplies exactly `TRUE` if the profile decoder can decode profiles of the type `id`.

C.4.5 XTransport

The class `XTransport` must be derived from `CORBA::Transport` and implement the following methods:

```
void rselect (CORBA::Dispatcher *disp,
     CORBA::TransportCallback *callback)
```

This method registers a read callback `callback` that is invoked as soon as data can be received and read on a connection or the `Transport` object is destroyed. `disp` is the scheduler used (described in detail in Section C.4.7). Callback objects inherit from the following basic class and implement the method `callback()`. The method `callback()` is invoked with `this` as the first parameter of the `Transport` object and `TransportCallback::Read` (if data can be read) or `TransportCallback::Remove` (if the `Transport` object is being destroyed) as the second parameter.

```
struct TransportCallback {
    enum Event { Read, Write, Remove };
    virtual void callback (Transport *transport,
        Event event) = 0;
    virtual ~TransportCallback ();
};
```

```
void wselect (CORBA::Dispatcher *disp,
     CORBA::TransportCallback *callback)
```

This method registers a write callback that is invoked in a similar way as `reselect()` if data can be written or the `Transport` object is being destroyed.

```
CORBA::Boolean bind (const CORBA::Address *addr)
```

Sets the local address of the transport end point to `addr`.

```
CORBA::Boolean connect (const CORBA::Address *addr)
```

Establishes a connection to a remote address.

```
void close ()
```

Terminates the connection.

```
void block (CORBA::Boolean doblock = TRUE)
```

If `doblock` is `TRUE`, then all subsequent read and write operations block until they have been executed completely. Otherwise read and write operations are only executed to the extent that is possible without blocking and an appropriate result code is returned.

```
CORBA::Boolean isblocking ()
```

Exactly supplies `TRUE` in the event that read and write operations are blocking.

```
CORBA::Boolean isreadable ()
```

Exactly supplies `True` if data is available for reading, thus `read` would not be blocking.

```
CORBA::Long read (void *buffer, CORBA::Long bufferlen)
```

At a maximum reads `bufferlen` bytes from the area referred to by `buffer`. The result supplied is the number of read bytes or −1 in the case of failure (including EOF).

```
CORBA::Long write (const void *buffer,
      CORBA::Long bufferlen)
```

At a maximum writes `bufferlen` bytes from the area referred to by `buffer`. The result supplied is the number of written bytes or −1 in the case of failure.

```
const CORBA::Address *addr ()
```

Supplies local address.

```
const CORBA::Address *peer ()
```

Supplies the remote address of a connection or `NIL` if no connection exists.

```
CORBA::Boolean eof () const
```

Exactly supplies `TRUE` if the connection was terminated and all data was read.

```
CORBA::Boolean bad () const
```

Exactly supplies `TRUE` if an error occurred.

```
string errormsg () const
```

Supplies a textual description of the last error that occurred.

C.4.6 XTransportServer

The class `XTransportServer` must be derived from `CORBA::TransportServer` and implement the following methods:

```
void aselect (CORBA::Dispatcher *disp,
     TransportServerCallback *callback)
```

This method registers an accept callback that, similar to `Transport::rselect()`, is invoked when a connection request arrives or the `TransportServer` object is destroyed. Callback objects inherit from the following basic class and implement the method `callback()`. The method `callback()` is invoked with `this` as the first parameter of the `TransportServer` object and `TransportServerCallback::Accept` (if a connection request exists) or `TransportServerCallback::Remove` (if the `TransportServer` object is being destroyed) as the second parameter.

Callback objects

```
struct TransportServerCallback {
    enum Event { Accept, Remove };
    virtual void callback (TransportServer *server,
        Event event) = 0;
    virtual ~TransportServerCallback ();
};
```

```
CORBA::Boolean bind (const CORBA::Address *addr)
```

Binds the local address of the transport end point to addr.

```
void close ()
```

Terminates the transport end point. No further connections can be accepted.

```
void block (CORBA::Boolean doblock = TRUE)
```

If doblock is TRUE, then all subsequent accept operations block until a connection setup request exists. Otherwise invocations of accept() deliver a NIL if there is no connection setup request.

```
CORBA::Boolean isblocking ()
```

Exactly delivers TRUE in the event accept operations are blocking.

```
CORBA::Transport *accept ()
```

As soon as a connection setup request exists (i.e., if a client has invoked connect() with the address of this TransportServer object), accept() delivers a Transport object that represents the connection to this client.

```
const CORBA::Address *addr ()
```

Supplies the local address.

```
CORBA::Boolean bad () const
```

Exactly supplies TRUE if a failure occurs.

```
string errormsg () const
```

Supplies a textual description of the last failure that occurred.

C.4.7 Dispatcher

The Transport and TransportServer classes work closely together with the scheduler described in Section 5.3.4. Thus the scheduler is usually used to implement the methods Transport::rselect(), Transport::wselect(), and TransportServer::aselect().

All scheduler implementations inherit from the abstract basic class CORBA::Dispatcher. This class provides various methods for the registration of callbacks that can be invoked when certain events occur. The possible events are described by the following enumeration: *Scheduler events*

```
enum Event { Timer, Read, Write, Except, All,
    Remove, Moved }
```

The individual values of this list signify the following:

Timer:
A timeout has run out.

Read:
Data can be read from a channel.

Write:
Data can be written on a channel.

Except:
An exception (for instance, an error) has occurred on a channel.

All:
Concerns all possible events.

Remove:
A callback was removed.

Moved:
A callback was removed from this dispatcher and entered into another one.

The declaration for the class dispatcher can be found in the file include/mico/transport.h and various implementations can be found in the files orb/dispatch.cc, auxdir/x11.cc, auxdir/qtmico.cc, auxdir/tclmico.cc, auxdir/gtkmico.cc, and auxdir/fltkmico.cc in the MICO source tree.

Callback objects inherit from the abstract basic class CORBA::DispatcherCallback and implement the method callback(). The method callback() is invoked by the dispatcher when an event occurs with this as the first parameter and the event that occurred as the second parameter: *Callback objects*

```
struct DispatcherCallback {
```

```
        virtual void callback (CORBA::Dispatcher *disp,
                Dispatcher::Event event) = 0;
        virtual ~DispatcherCallback ();
    };
```

Schedulers inherit from Dispatcher

All implementations of the abstract basic class CORBA::Dispatcher provide the following methods:

```
void rd_event (CORBA::DispatcherCallback *cb,
        CORBA::Long fd)
```

Registers a read callback cb that is invoked when data can be read on the file handle fd.

```
void wr_event (CORBA::DispatcherCallback *cb,
        CORBA::Long fd)
```

Registers a write callback cb that is invoked when data can be written on the file handle fd.

```
void ex_event (CORBA::DispatcherCallback *cb,
        CORBA::Long fd)
```

Registers an exception callback cb that is invoked when an exception occurs on the file handle fd.

```
void tm_event (CORBA::DispatcherCallback *cb,
        CORBA::ULong timeout)
```

Registers a timer callback that is invoked when the time timeout (in milliseconds) has elapsed.

```
void remove (CORBA::DispatcherCallback *cb, Event event)
```

Removes a callback cb previously registered for an event.

```
void run (CORBA::Boolean infinite = TRUE)
```

Waits for the occurrence of the next event and processes it. If infinite = FALSE, it means that exactly one event is being processed. Otherwise an infinite loop is entered.

```
void move (CORBA::Dispatcher *disp)
```

Removes all registered callbacks from `this` and registers them at dispatcher `disp`.

```
CORBA::Boolean idle () const
```

Supplies exactly `TRUE` if there are no pending events for any registered callback at the time of invocation.

C.4.8 Initialization

Registration of `AddressParser` and `ProfileDecoder`

An instance each of `XaddressParser` and `XprofileDecoder` must first be created and registered before a new transport mechanism can be used. The easiest way this can be done is through the implementation of registration or deregistration in the constructor or destructor and the creation of a global instance for both classes. Thus:

```
// XAddressParser

XAddressParser::XAddressParser ()
{
    CORBA::Address::register_parser (this);
}

XAddressParser::~XAddressParser ()
{
    CORBA::Address::unregister_parser (this);
}

// XProfileDecoder

XProfileDecoder::XProfileDecoder ()
{
    CORBA::IORProfile::register_decoder (this);
}

XProfileDecoder::~XProfileDecoder ()
{
    CORBA::IORProfile::unregister_decoder (this);
}
```

Registration with GIOP framework

In addition, the GIOP framework in the client and in the server must be notified of the existence of the new transport mechanism:

```
CORBA::ORB_var orb = ...;
orb->register_profile_id (TAG_X_IOP); // new Profile-ID
```

The new transport mechanism can be used if the server is started with the command line option

```
-ORBIIOPAddr x:42
```

If an object reference is being exported by the server, it will contain an `Xprofile` that triggers the client into using the appropriate transport mechanism when invoking methods on this object.

C.5 THE STRUCTURE OF GENERATED PROGRAM CODE

This section describes the structure of the program code generated by MICO's IDL compiler. The IDL language binding for C++ only stipulates the C++ interface for proxy objects that can be accessed by applications (the basis for portability). However, the CORBA standard does not specify how these interfaces are to be implemented. For example, the MICO-specific Static Invocation Interface (SII) is used for marshaling within MICO. Another possibility would be the Dynamic Invocation Interface (DII) that was actually used with earlier versions of MICO.

Proxies are based on MICO-specific static interface adapters

The IDL specification used earlier in the account application and reproduced in Section D.2 in Appendix D serves as the basis for our discussion. MICO's IDL compiler standardly produces two files during the translation process. We assume that the `–typecode` command line option of the IDL compiler was used during the translation. In our example the IDL specification is contained in the file called `account.idl`:

```
idl –typecode account.idl
```

Two files exist after the translation by the IDL compiler: `account.h` contains all C++ declarations and `account.cc` all the corresponding C++ definitions. Some extracts from the contents of these files are discussed in the following.

Marshaller of an IDL type

The IDL compiler produces a class for each IDL type that is responsible for the marshalling of an instance of that type. The name of the class consists of the prefix `_Marshaller_` followed by the name of the IDL type. The following code fragment shows the marshaller for the IDL type `Account`:

```
 1:  // Code fragment from account.cc
 2:
 3:  class _Marshaller_Account :
 4:    public ::CORBA::StaticTypeInfo {
 5:  public:
 6:    ~_Marshaller_Account();
 7:    StaticValueType create () const;
 8:    void assign (StaticValueType dst,
 9:                 const StaticValueType src) const;
10:    void free (StaticValueType) const;
11:    void release (StaticValueType) const;
12:    ::CORBA::Boolean demarshal (::CORBA::DataDecoder&,
13:                                StaticValueType) const;
14:    void marshal (::CORBA::DataEncoder &,
15:                  StaticValueType) const;
16:  };
17:
18: struct __tc_init_ACCOUNT {
19:   __tc_init_ACCOUNT()
20:   {
21:     _tc_Account =
22:      "010000000e00000024000000010000001000000049444c"
23:      "3a4163636f756e743a312e3000080000004163636f756e"
24:      "7400";
25:     _marshaller_Account = new _Marshaller_Account;
26:   }
27: };
28:
29: static __tc_init_ACCOUNT __init_ACCOUNT;
```

The marshaller is based on the SII and is derived from the class `StaticTypeInfo`. It defines several methods that can be used for marshalling an `Account` instance. An instance of the marshaller class that can be used within the stubs and skeleton is produced in line 25. One feature is the representation of a type code that has to be generated for each IDL type (line 21). For the representation of the type information for `Account`, the CDR representation is produced as a

Representation of a type code

TABLE C.1 Representation of a type code for `AccountType` as a CDR byte sequence

Pos.	Hex	Description
0	01	Little Endian
1	00 00 00	Padding
4	0e 00 00 00	TCKind = tk_objref (14)
8	24 00 00 00	Overall length = 36 octets
12	01	Little Endian
13	00 00 00	Padding
16	10 00 00 00	string length = 16 octets
20	49 44 4c 3a 41 63 63 6f	"IDL:Account:1.0\0"
	75 6e 74 3a 31 2e 30 00	
36	08 00 00 00	string length = 8 octets
40	41 63 63 6f 75 6e 74 00	"Account\0"

character string of hexadecimal values. Since the type code can also appear as the parameter of an operation, the ORB has to be able to interpret this byte sequence anyway. Table C.1 shows the coding of this byte sequence by bytes.

For each interface of the IDL specification, the IDL compiler generates a number of classes for implementing the stubs and skeletons. Following are the declarations for the C++ classes generated for the interface `Account`:

```
// Code fragment from account.h

class Account;
typedef Account *Account_ptr;
typedef Account_ptr AccountRef;
typedef ObjVar< Account > Account_var;
typedef ObjOut< Account > Account_out;

class Account :
  virtual public CORBA::Object
{
public:
  static Account_ptr _narrow( CORBA::Object_ptr obj );
  virtual void deposit( CORBA::Long amount ) = 0;
  virtual void withdraw( CORBA::Long amount ) = 0;
  virtual CORBA::Long balance() = 0;
  // ...
};

class Account_stub:
  virtual public Account
{
```

```
23: public:
24:   void deposit( CORBA::Long amount );
25:   void withdraw( CORBA::Long amount );
26:   CORBA::Long balance();
27:   // ...
28: };
29:
30: class POA_Account :
31:     virtual public PortableServer::StaticImplementation
32: {
33: public:
34:   bool dispatch (CORBA::StaticServerRequest_ptr);
35:   virtual void invoke (CORBA::StaticServerRequest_ptr);
36:   virtual void deposit( CORBA::Long amount ) = 0;
37:   virtual void withdraw( CORBA::Long amount ) = 0;
38:   virtual CORBA::Long balance() = 0;
39:   // ...
40: };
```

C++ templates for tools

The CORBA standard specifies various helper types for each interface with the suffixes `_ptr`, `_var`, and `_out` (lines 3–7). Mico defines several C++ template types for their implementation. The class `Account` (line 9) is derived from `CORBA::Object` and contains the methods required by the CORBA standard (for example, `_narrow` for the type-safe downcast in line 13). All operations that were defined in the interface `Account` are defined as pure virtual methods in the C++ class `Account` (lines 14–16). The class from which the stub objects are instantiated has the (Mico-specific) name `Account_stub` and is derived from the class `Account` (line 20). All pure virtual methods are overloaded here and trigger a remote operation invocation when they are implemented.

The skeleton class based on the POA is called `POA_Account` (line 30) and is derived through an intermediate class of `PortableServer::ServantBase` of the basis class of all servants (see Figure C.1). `POA_Account` is not derived from `CORBA::Object` because a POA makes a distinction between servants and objects. The C++ class `POA_Account` also defines all operations occurring in the interface `Account` as pure virtual methods.

Skeleton has an operation dispatcher

In addition, the class `POA_Account` uses the method `invoke` to define the entry point of incoming operation invocations (line 35). Each skeleton defines a dispatcher that forwards the operations belonging to this interface to the implementation (line 34). The `dispatch` method successively invokes all `dispatch` methods belonging to an interface's direct parents in the interface hierarchy. Figure C.1 shows the inheritance relationships for the C++ class mentioned. Ta-

TABLE C.2 Generated C++ classes for the IDL interface Account

C++ class	Description
Account	Basic class with tools
Account_stub	Stub for remote objects
Account_stub_clp	Stub for collocated objects
POA_Account	POA-based skeleton
POA_Account_tie<T>	Template for tie objects

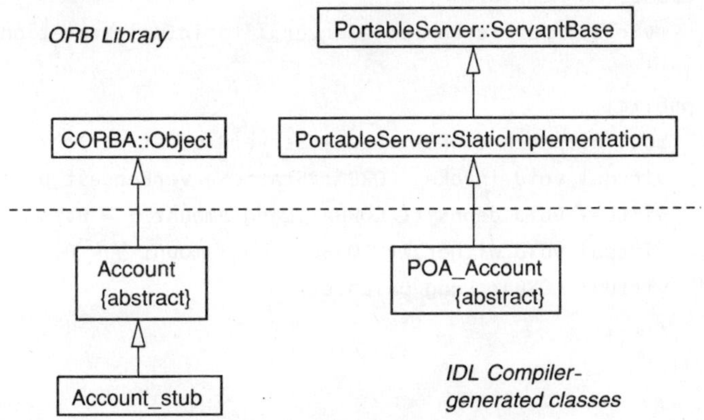

FIGURE C.1 Inheritance relationship between the classes of the generated code and the ORB library.

ble C.2 provides an overview of all C++ classes generated by the IDL compiler through use of the POA. Note that the POA tie template is only generated if the IDL compiler is invoked with the command line option −poa-ties.

We will now take a detailed look at the stub object that triggers a remote operation invocation. First the corresponding code fragment:

```
// Code fragment from account.cc

void Account_stub::deposit( CORBA::Long _par_amount )
{
  CORBA::StaticAny _sa_amount( CORBA::_stc_long, &_par_amount );
  CORBA::StaticRequest __req( this, "deposit" );
  __req.add_in_arg( &_sa_amount );

  __req.invoke();

  // ...
}
```

An instance of the class `StaticAny` encapsulates the actual parameters (line 5) for the input parameter amount. For its representation as a CDR byte sequence, a `StaticAny` requires the right marshaller that has to be passed as an argument to the constructor (e.g., `CORBA::_stc_long` for IDL type `long`). First a `StaticRequest`, which represents the remote operation invocation, is instantiated (line 6). After the actual parameters of the operation have been added (line 7), the operation is sent to the remote server (line 9). If the invocation of this method is returned, it means that the remote operation was carried out and the results were returned automatically through the `StaticAny` instances.

`StaticRequest` instance represents operation invocation

Lastly, we will show the dispatch process in the skeleton on the server side:

```
// Code fragment from account.cc

bool
POA_Account::dispatch (CORBA::StaticServerRequest_ptr __req)
{
  if( strcmp( __req->op_name(), "deposit" ) == 0 ) {
    CORBA::Long _par_amount;
    CORBA::StaticAny _sa_amount( CORBA::_stc_long, &_par_amount );

    __req->add_in_arg( &_sa_amount );

    if( !__req->read_args() )
      return true;

    deposit( _par_amount );
    __req->write_results();
    return true;
  }
  // ...
  return false;
}

void
POA_Account::invoke (CORBA::StaticServerRequest_ptr __req)
{
  if (dispatch (__req)) {
      return;
  }

```

```
30:   // ...
31: }
```

dispatch calls up all dispatchers of an interface's direct parents

The method POA_Account::invoke is invoked during an incoming operation invocation (line 24). The operation forwards the invocation directly to the skeleton dispatch method (line 4), which is responsible for invoking all dispatchers of a interface's direct parents. The StaticServerRequest instance contains all information, such as operation name and actual parameters, related to the operation invocation. Based on the operation name, the dispatcher determines whether this operation invocation belongs to the interface. If the dispatcher is responsible, it takes all actual parameters from the invocation (lines 7–13) and then invokes the pure virtual method of the operation (line 15) that is implemented in a class derived from POA_Account.

APPENDIX D

SAMPLE APPLICATION

Following are the complete source texts for the CORBA application presented in Chapter 3. The line numbers correspond to the extracts shown in Chapters 2 and 3. The design for the application and the UML class diagram can be found in Chapter 2.

D.1 STAND-ALONE APPLICATION IN C++

The stand alone implementation is explained in Section 2.4.2 on page page 28.

```
// File: account.cc

#include <iostream>


using namespace std;

// Implementation for interface Account
class Account_impl
{
private:
  int _balance;

public:
  Account_impl ()
  {
    _balance = 0;
```

```
  }

  void deposit (int amount)
  {
    cout << "Server: deposit " << amount << endl;
    _balance += amount;
  }

  void withdraw (int amount)
  {
    cout << "Server: withdraw " << amount << endl;
    if (_balance >= amount)
      _balance -= amount;
    else
      cout << "Server: withdraw failed" << endl;
  }

  int balance ()
  {
    cout << "Server: balance " << _balance << endl;
    return _balance;
  }
};

int
main (int argc, char *argv[])
{
  int balance;
  Account_impl* account = new Account_impl();
  account->deposit (700);
  balance = account->balance ();
  cout << "Client: balance is " << balance << endl;
  account->withdraw (50);
  balance = account->balance ();
  cout << "Client: balance is " << balance << endl;
  account->withdraw (200);
  balance = account->balance ();
  cout << "Client: balance is " << balance << endl;

  return 0;
}
```

D.2 IDL SPECIFICATION

The IDL specification is explained in Section 3.4.1 on page 42.

```
// File: account.idl

interface Account {
  void deposit (in long amount);
  void withdraw (in long amount);
  long balance ();
};
```

D.3 IMPLEMENTATION OF THE SERVER IN C++

See Section 3.4.3 on page 44 for a description of the implementation of the server.

```
// File: server.cc

#include <iostream>
#include <fstream>
#include "account.h"

using namespace std;

// Implementation for interface Account
class Account_impl : virtual public POA_Account
{
private:
  CORBA::Long _balance;

public:
  Account_impl ()
  {
    _balance = 0;
  }

  void deposit (CORBA::Long amount)
```

```
  {
    cout << "Server: deposit " << amount << endl;
    _balance += amount;
  }

  void withdraw (CORBA::Long amount)
  {
    cout << "Server: withdraw " << amount << endl;
    if (_balance >= amount)
      _balance -= amount;
    else
      cout << "Server: withdraw failed" << endl;
  }

  CORBA::Long balance ()
  {
    cout << "Server: balance " << _balance << endl;
    return _balance;
  }
};

int
main (int argc, char *argv[])
{
  // Initialize the ORB
  CORBA::ORB_var orb = CORBA::ORB_init (argc, argv);

  // Obtain a reference to the RootPOA and its Manager
  CORBA::Object_var poaobj =
          orb->resolve_initial_references ("RootPOA");
  PortableServer::POA_var poa =
          PortableServer::POA::_narrow (poaobj);
  PortableServer::POAManager_var mgr =
          poa->the_POAManager();

  // Create an Account
  PortableServer::Servant account_servant =
          new Account_impl;

  // Activate the Account
  CORBA::Object_var the_account =
```

```
            account_servant->_this();

  // Write the object's IOR to a file
  CORBA::String_var ior =
            orb->object_to_string (the_account);
  ofstream of ("account.ior");
  of << ior;
  of.close ();

  // Activate the POA and start serving requests
  cout << "Running." << endl;
  mgr->activate ();
  orb->run();

  // Shutdown (never reached)
  poa->destroy (TRUE, TRUE);
  delete account_servant;

  return 0;
}
```

D.4 IMPLEMENTATION OF THE CLIENT IN C++

See Section 3.4.4 on page 48 for a description of the implementation of the client.

```
// File: client.cc

#include <iostream>
#include <fstream>
#include "account.h"

using namespace std;

int
main (int argc, char *argv[])
{
  // Initialize the ORB
```

```
    CORBA::ORB_var orb = CORBA::ORB_init (argc, argv);

    // Connect to the Account
    ifstream f ("account.ior");
    string ior;
    f >> ior;
    CORBA::Object_var obj =
             orb->string_to_object (ior.c_str());
    Account_var account = Account::_narrow (obj);

    // Deposit and withdraw some money
    account->deposit (700);
    cout << "Client: balance is "
         << account->balance () << endl;
    account->withdraw (50);
    cout << "Client: balance is "
         << account->balance () << endl;
    account->withdraw (200);
    cout << "Client: balance is "
         << account->balance () << endl;

    return 0;
}
```

D.5 IMPLEMENTATION OF THE SERVER IN JAVA

See Section 3.6.1 on page 53 for a description of the implementation of the server in Java.

```
// File: Server.java

import org.omg.CORBA.*;
import org.omg.PortableServer.*;


// Implementation for interface Account
class AccountImpl extends AccountPOA
{
```

```
  private int _balance;

  public AccountImpl ()
  {
    _balance = 0;
  }
  public void deposit (int amount)
  {
    System.out.println ("Server: deposit " + amount);
    _balance += amount;
  }
  public void withdraw (int amount)
  {
    System.out.println ("Server: withdraw " + amount);
    if (_balance >= amount)
      _balance -= amount;
    else
      System.out.println ("Server: withdraw failed");
  }
  public int balance ()
  {
    System.out.println ("Server: balance " + _balance);
    return _balance;
  }
}


public class Server {

  public static void main (String args[])
  {
    try {
      // Initialize the ORB
      ORB orb = ORB.init (args, null);

      // Obtain a reference to the RootPOA and its Manager
      org.omg.CORBA.Object poaobj =
            orb.resolve_initial_references ("RootPOA");
      POA poa = POAHelper.narrow (poaobj);
      POAManager mgr = poa.the_POAManager();

```

```
      // Create an Account servant
      AccountImpl account_servant = new AccountImpl ();

      // Activate the Account object
      org.omg.CORBA.Object the_account =
                          account_servant._this();

      // Write the object's IOR to a file
      String ior = orb.object_to_string (the_account);
      java.io.FileWriter file =
          new java.io.FileWriter ("account.ior", false);
      file.write (ior + "\n", 0, ior.length() + 1);
      file.flush();
      file.close();

      // Activate the POA and start serving requests
      System.out.println ("Running.");
      mgr.activate();
      orb.run();
    } catch (Exception e) {
      System.err.println ("Exception in Server " +
                           "Startup " + e);
    }
  }
}
```

D.6 IMPLEMENTATION OF THE CLIENT IN JAVA

See Section 3.6.2 on page 56 for a description of the implementation of the client in Java.

```
// File: Client.java

import java.io.*;
import org.omg.CORBA.*;


public class Client {
```

```

  public static void main (String[] args) {
    // Initialize the ORB.
    ORB orb = ORB.init (args, null);

    String ior = null;
    try {
      FileReader file = new FileReader ("account.ior");
      BufferedReader br = new BufferedReader (file);
      ior = br.readLine();
    } catch (IOException e) {
      System.out.println ("Could not open file " +
                          "'account.ior'");
      System.exit (1);
    }

    org.omg.CORBA.Object obj =
            orb.string_to_object (ior);
    Account account = AccountHelper.narrow (obj);

    account.deposit (700);
    System.out.println ("Client: balance is " +
                         account.balance ());
    account.withdraw (50);
    System.out.println ("Client: balance is " +
                         account.balance ());
    account.withdraw (200);
    System.out.println ("Client: balance is " +
                         account.balance());
  }
}
```

LIST OF FIGURES

ACRONYMS

ACE	Adaptive Communications Environment
ANSA	Advanced Network Systems Architecture
ANSI	American National Standards Institute
BOA	Basic Object Adapter
CCM	CORBA Component Model
CDR	Common Data Representation
CORBA	Common Object Request Broker Architecture
CPU	Central Processing Unit
DCE	Distributed Computing Environment
DCE–CIOP	DCE Common Inter–ORB Protocol
DCOM	Distributed Componenent Object Model
DDCF	Distributed Document Component Facility
DII	Dynamic Invocation Interface
DPE	Distributed Processing Environment
DSI	Dynamic Skeleton Interface
DSOM	Distributed System Object Model
ESIOP	Environment–Specific Inter–ORB Protocol
FIFO	First in First out
GIOP	General Inter–ORB Protocol
GNU	GNU's not UNIX

GNU GPL	GNU General Public License
GUID	Globally Unique Identifier
IDL	Interface Definition Language
IIOP	Internet Inter–ORB Protocol
IMR	Implementation Repository
IOR	Interoperable Object Reference
IP	Internet Protocol
IR	Interface Repository
ISO	International Standards Organization
ITU	International Telecommunication Union
LOA	Library Object Adapter
MICO	MICO Is CORBA
NCCE	Native Computing and Communications Environment
OA	Object Adapter
OMA	Object Management Architecture
OMG	Object Management Group
OODB OA	Object–Oriented Database Object Adapter
ORB	Object Request Broker
OSF	Open Software Foundation
OSI	Open Systems Interconnection
POA	Portable Object Adapter
POS	Persistent Object Service
RFP	Request for Proposal
RIOP	Realtime Inter–ORB Protocol
RMI	Remote Method Invocation
RPC	Remote Procedure Call
SII	Static Invocation Interface
SSI	Static Skeleton Interface
SSL	Secure Sockets Layer
TAO	The ACE ORB
TCP	Transmission Control Protocol

TINA	Telecommunications Information Networking Architecture
UML	Uniform Modelling Language
URL	Uniform Resource Locator
WWW	World Wide Web
YACC	Yet Another Compiler Compiler

GLOSSARY

BOA (Basic Object Adapter) One instance of an object adapter (OA). Serves on the server side as a mediator between the ORB and the object implementation. As its name implies, the BOA offers only primitive services. The BOA's specifications were insufficiently precise and led to a lack of portability in view of vendors' augmentation of the standard. In CORBA version 2.1 the BOA was replaced by the POA.

CCM (CORBA Component Model) An extension of the CORBA object model. Components run in a container, which provides their runtime environment, and express their features and requirements in terms of provided and required interfaces (ports). Applications can then be assembled from components by connecting their ports.

CG (Conceptual Graph) A knowledge representation technique based on a bipartite graph consisting of concepts and relations. Conceptual graphs allow the representation of arbitrary information in a formalized way. Conceptual graphs are used in MICO for a generic user interface to the DII that allows the invocation of user-definable operations at runtime.

CGI (Common Gateway Interface) A specification for transferring information between a WWW server and a CGI program. A CGI program is any program designed to accept and return data that conforms to the CGI specification. The program could be written in any programming language, including C, Perl, Java, or Visual Basic.

CORBA (Common Object Request Broker Architecture) An architecture that enables objects to communicate with one another regardless of what programming language they were written in or what operating system they are running on. CORBA was developed by an industry consortium known as the Object Management Group (OMG).

COSS (Common Object Services Specification) Defines context-independent services that are often required in applications. Services are single-minded modules that bring much of the functionality needed for a truly distributed systems framework. Examples of such services are the naming, event, or security service. MICO offers a variety of services.

DII (Dynamic Invocation Interface) Part of the ORB API on the client side. The client can use it to construct and invoke an operation at runtime. The DII is dynamic in the sense that the operation signature (i.e., its input/output argument types) need not be known at compile time. This is the main difference with IDL stubs, where the interface type is known at compile time.

DSI (Dynamic Skeleton Interface) Part of the ORB API on the server side. The DSI mirrors the DII functionality on the server side. It is used to deliver an operation invocation to an implementation. As with the DII, the DSI is dynamic in the sense that the operation signature need not be known at compile time.

GIOP (General Inter-ORB Protocol) Defines message formats used for communication between ORBs. GIOP is responsible for establishing communication between ORBs. GIOP is part of the interoperability framework whereby applications running on different CORBA implementations are interoperable. GIOP is abstract in the sense that it does not make reference to a specific transport layer.

GNU (Gnu's Not UNIX) A UNIX-compatible software system developed by the Free Software Foundation (FSF). The philosophy behind GNU is to produce software that is nonproprietary. Anyone can download, modify, and redistribute GNU software. The only restriction is that they cannot limit further redistribution. The GNU project was started in 1983 by Richard Stallman at the Massachusetts Institute of Technology.

IDL (Interface Definition Language). The notation used by CORBA to describe object interfaces. This particular notation has distinguished features as it supports subtyping, exception handling, and so on. The IDL syntax resembles Java interface and C++ abstract classes declarations. The CORBA standard defines language mappings, which define rules on how to map an IDL specification to a specific programming language.

IIOP (Internet Inter-ORB Protocol) The instantiation of GIOP using TCP as a transport layer. With respect to GIOP, IIOP only adds transport-layer-specific details.

IMR (Implementation Repository) A database that contains information on object implementations. This information is typically used by an object adapter during the activation of object implementations.

IOR (Interoperable Object Reference) Contains all the information necessary for a client to connect to an object implementation. Among others, the IOR contains a transport layer address as well as an object key of the implementation. The CORBA standard defines a stringified version of an IOR that can be passed to clients by other means (such as email, fax, etc.).

IP (Internet Protocol) Specifies the format of packets, also called datagrams, and the addressing scheme. Most networks combine IP with a higher-level protocol called Transport Control Protocol (TCP), which establishes a virtual connection between a destination and a source.

IR (Interface Repository) A database that maintains IDL specifications of every object interface managed by the ORB. The IR provides an API that allows you to query and modify the interface it manages. The IR provides for the self-describing nature of CORBA objects.

MICO (MICO Is CORBA) An Open Source implementation of the CORBA standard. The complete source code is placed under the GNU General Public License. MICO pays special attention to CORBA compliance.

OA (Object Adapter) CORBA's server side relies on OAs to perform object activation, deactivation, and so on. CORBA allows different OAs for different contexts. In some situations special purpose OAs may be used to simplify the processes involved, for example, when communicating with an OODBMS. The POA is the only OA defined by CORBA.

OMG (Object Management Group) A consortium with a membership of more than 850 companies. The organization's goal is to provide a common framework for developing applications using object-oriented programming techniques. OMG is responsible for the CORBA specification.

ORB (Object Request Broker) The central piece of the CORBA platform. It serves as an "object bus" connecting different objects. Its main task is the forwarding of operation invocations from client to server objects. The ORB transparently handles networking, name resolution, marshalling, type checking, object activation (see **OA**), and such.

OSS (Open Source Software) Promotes software reliability and quality by supporting independent peer review and rapid evolution of source code. Among the many Open Source projects are Linux, Apache, KDE, and, of course, MICO.

POA (Portable Object Adapter) An instance of an object adapter. Configurable via policies, it offers a wide range of adaptation options in support of life state management and scalability.

RM-ODP (Reference Model for Open Distributed Processing) A joint standard of the International Organization for Standardization (ISO) and the International Telecommunication Union, Telecommunication Standardization Sector (ITU-T). It provides a framework for standardization efforts in the domain of Open Distributed Processing (ODP). The reference model describes an architecture to support distribution, interoperability, and portability.

TCP (Transmission Control Protocol) One of the main protocols in TCP/IP networks. Whereas the IP protocol deals only with packets, TCP enables two hosts to establish a connection and exchange streams of data. TCP guarantees delivery of data and also guarantees that packets will be delivered in the same order in which they were sent.

WWW (World Wide Web) A system of Internet servers that support specially formatted documents. The documents are formatted in a language called HTML (HyperText Markup Language) that supports links to other documents, as well as graphics, audio, and video files. This means you can jump from one document to another simply by clicking on hot spots. Not all Internet servers are part of the WWW.

BIBLIOGRAPHY

[1] H. Abelson, G. J. Sussman, and J. Sussman. *Structure and Interpretation of Computer Programs.* MIT Press, 1985.

[2] The Advanced Network Systems Architecture (ANSA), 1989.

[3] S. Bapat. *Object-Oriented Networks, Models for Architecture, Operations, and Management.* Prentice-Hall International, 1994.

[4] Berkeley Motes. *www.xbow.com/Products/Wireless_Sensor_Networks.htm.*

[5] T. Berners-Lee, L. Masinter, and M. McCahill. *RFC 1738: Uniform Resource Locators (URL)*, December 1994.

[6] J. Bohn, V. Coroama, M. Langheinrich, F. Mattern, and M. Rohs. Disappearing computers everywhere—living in a world of smart everyday objects. In *Proceedings of New Media, Technology and Everyday Life in Europe Conference*, London, April 2003.

[7] P. Bonnet, J. E. Gehrke, and P. Seshadri. Querying the physical world. *IEEE Personal Communications*, 7 (5): 10–15, 2000.

[8] G. Booch. *Object Oriented Design with Applications.* Benjamin Cummings Publishing Company, 1991.

[9] A. Boulis, C. C. Han, and M. B. Srivastava. Design and implementation of a framework for programmable and efficient sensor networks. In *Proceedings MobiSys 2003*, San Franscisco, May 2003.

[10] G. Coulouris, J. Dollimore, and T. Kindberg. *Distributed Systems: Concepts and Design*, 3rd edition. Addison-Wesley Publishing Company, 2000.

[11] B. S. Davie, L. L. Peterson, and D. Clark. *Computer Networks: A Systems Approach*, 2nd edition. Morgan Kaufmann Publishers, 1999.

[12] M. E. Fayad and D. C. Schmidt. Object-oriented application frameworks. *Communications of the Association for Computing Machinery*, October 1997.

[13] E. Gamma, R. Helm, R. Johnson, and J. Vlissides. *Design Patterns: Elements of Reusable Object-Oriented Software*. Addison-Wesley Publishing Company, 1995.

[14] M. Henning and S. Vinoski. *Advanced CORBA Programming with C++*. Addison-Wesley Publishing Company, 1999.

[15] J. Hill, R. Szewczyk, A. Woo, S. Hollar, D. Culler, and K. Pister. System architecture directions for networked sensors. In *Proceedings ASPLOS 2000*, Cambridge, MA, November 2000.

[16] The IEEE International Conference on Pervasive Computing and Communication. *www.percom.org*.

[17] The International Conference on Pervasive Computing. *www.pervasive2004.org*.

[18] The International Conference on Ubiquitous Computing. *www.ubicomp.org*.

[19] Jini Architecture Specification. *www.sun.com/jini/specs/*.

[20] U. Kubach and K. Rothermel. Exploiting location information for infostation-based hoarding. In *Proceedings ACM MobiCom 2001*, Rome, July 2001.

[21] P. Landin. A correspondence between Algol 60 and Church's lambda notation: part I. *Communications of the Association for Computing Machinery*, 1965.

[22] U. Lang and R. Schreiner. *Developing Secure Distributed Systems with CORBA*. Artech House Books, 2002.

[23] S. Li, S. H. Son, and J. A. Stankovic. Event detection services using data service middleware in distributed sensor networks. In *Proceedings of IPSN 2003*, Palo Alto, CA, April 2003.

[24] S. R. Madden, M. J. Franklin, J. M. Hellerstein, and W. Hong. TAG: A tiny aggregation service for ad-hoc sensor networks. In *Proceedings OSDI 2002*, Boston, December 2002.

[25] S. Maffeis. Adding group communication and fault-tolerance to CORBA. In *Proceedings of the USENIX Conference on Object-Oriented Technologies*, June 1995.

[26] S. Mullender. *Distributed Systems*, 2nd edition. Addison-Wesley Publishing Company, 1993.

[27] J. Nehmer und P. Sturm. *Systemsoftware: Grundlagen moderner Betriebssysteme*. dpunkt-Verlag, 1998.

[28] Object Management Group (OMG). *The Common Object Request Broker: Architecure and Specification, Revision 3.0*, March 2004.

[29] J. Ousterhout. *Tcl and Tk toolkit*. Addison-Wesley Publishing Company, 1994.

[30] J. Rumbaugh. *Object-Oriented Modeling and Design*. Prentice-Hall International, 1991.

[31] D. C. Schmidt. ACE: An object-oriented framework for developing distributed applications. In *Proceedings of the USENIX Conference on Object-Oriented Technologies*. USENIX Association, April 1994.

[32] D. C. Schmidt, D. L. Levine, and S. Mungee. The design of the TAO real-time object request broker. *Computer Communications Journal*, 1997.

[33] C. C. Shen, C. Srisathapornphat, and C. Jaikaeo. Sensor information networking architecture and applications. *IEEE Personal Communications*, 8 (4): 52–59, 2001.

[34] A. S. Tanenbaum. *Computer Networks*, 3rd edition. Prentice-Hall International, 1989.

[35] A. S. Tanenbaum. *Operating Systems—Design and Implementation*. Prentice-Hall International, 1987.

[36] F. D. Tran and J. B. Stefani. Towards an extensible and modular ORB framework. In *CORBA: Implementation, Use and Evaluation, ECOOP*, Jyväskylä, Finland, June 1997.

[37] B. Warneke, M. Last, B. Leibowitz, and K. S. J. Pister. Smart dust: Communicating with a cubic-millimeter computer. *IEEE Computer Magazine*, 34 (1): 44–51, January 2001.

[38] M. D. Weiser. The computer for the 21st century. *Scientific American*, 265 (3): 94–104, September 1991.

INDEX